THE PRICE OF FREEDOM

Of course it would be folly to argue that the people cannot make political mistakes. They can and do make grave mistakes. They know it, they pay the penalty, but compared with the mistakes which have been made by every kind of autocracy they are unimportant. Oftentimes the inconvenience and loss fall on the innocent. This is all a part of the price of freedom. *Unless the people struggle to help themselves, no one else will or can help them. It is out of such struggle that there comes the strongest evidence of their true independence and nobility, and there is struck off a rough and incomplete economic justice, and there develops a strong and rugged national character. It represents a spirit for which there could be no substitute. It justifies the claim that they are worthy to be free.*

CALVIN COOLIDGE,
at Evanston, Illinois, January 21, 1923.

THE PRICE OF FREEDOM

SPEECHES AND ADDRESSES

BY

CALVIN COOLIDGE

Fredonia Books
Amsterdam, The Netherlands

The Price of Freedom:
Speeches and Addresses

by
Calvin Coolidge

ISBN: 1-58963-538-8

Copyright © 2001 by Fredonia Books

Reprinted from the 1924 edition

Fredonia Books
Amsterdam, The Netherlands
http://www.fredoniabooks.com

In order to make original editions of historical works
available to scholars at an economical price, this
facsimile of the original edition of 1924 is
reproduced from the best available copy and has
been digitally enhanced to improve legibility, but the
text remains unaltered to retain historical
authenticity.

CONTENTS

CHAPTER   PAGE

   I. THE SUPPORTS OF CIVILIZATION 3

  II. THE PILGRIMS 13

 III. THEODORE ROOSEVELT 17

 IV. LAW AND ORDER 29

  V. INAUGURAL ADDRESS AS VICE-PRESIDENT . . 33

 VI. ANDREW CARNEGIE: ORGANIZER FOR SERVICE . 37

VII. THE BANKS AND THE PEOPLE 49

VIII. THOUGHT, THE MASTER OF THINGS 57

 IX. THE POWER OF THE MORAL LAW 71

  X. THE TITLE OF AMERICAN 85

 XI. OUR HERITAGE FROM HAMILTON 101

XII. THE PLACE OF LINCOLN 119

XIII. THE PURPOSE OF AMERICA 135

XIV. ULYSSES S. GRANT 151

 XV. THE INSTRUMENTS OF PROGRESS 163

XVI. GREAT VIRGINIANS 173

vi CONTENTS

CHAPTER   **PAGE**

XVII. THE MEANING OF DEMOCRACY 185

XVIII. THE LIMITATIONS OF THE LAW 195

XIX. THE NEEDS OF EDUCATION 211

XX. THE PRICE OF FREEDOM 229

XXI. MASSACHUSETTS AND THE NATION . . . 247

XXII. PROGRESS TOWARD FREEDOM 269

XXIII. THE FOUNDATION OF OUR INSTITUTIONS . 283

XXIV. WILLIAM MCKINLEY 299

XXV. THE OLD NORTH CHURCH 315

XXVI. THE DESTINY OF AMERICA 331

XXVII. THE GREEN MOUNTAINS 357

XXVIII. THE THINGS THAT ARE UNSEEN 379

XXIX. A PRIZE ESSAY 395

XXX. A MESSAGE TO THE LEGISLATURE OF MASSA-
    CHUSETTS ACCOMPANYING THE GOVERNOR'S
    VETO 405

INDEX 409

THE PRICE OF FREEDOM

I

The process of civilization consists of the discovery by men of the laws of the universe, and of living in harmony with those laws.

THE SUPPORTS OF CIVILIZATION

THE process of civilization consists of the discovery by men of the laws of the universe, and of living in harmony with those laws. The most important of them to men are the laws of their own nature.

This is education, the method whereby man is revealed to himself. It is the instruction of his understanding, the training of his sentiments, the direction of his action. It discloses the physical and the spiritual, the unseen and the seen. It includes every human relationship and shows forth every duty. It is alike the source of the intellectual and moral force of all mankind.

I shall assume that civilization is desirable. I do not think that is questioned in any respectable quarter, though I recall that a wise old Massachusetts magistrate once observed to me that perhaps we should all be better off if our entire efforts were directed to a hoe and a potato. There is honest difference of opinion whether the results of civilization are equitably distributed. That I shall not now discuss. It seems obvious that the present population of the globe could not subsist by that ancient method of the tillage of the soil represented by the hoe-and-potato era. But, even if it could, it is enough to say that existence in such a state is totally inadequate to em-

At the Amherst College Alumni Dinner, New York City, November 27, 1920.

ploy all the powers of man, and it cannot be, either, that man ought to be satisfied to be anything but his best, or that being his best can be inconsistent with the highest welfare of society. The question I propose to consider is what it is necessary to do to sustain modern civilization and provide for its advancement and further development.

It is not necessary to suppose that our civilization is perfect. We Amherst men have heard that "there is first the blade, then the ear, after that the full corn in the ear," and we have further heard that "it doth not yet appear what *man* shall be." It is necessary to be assured that civilization is on a sound foundation, that it is in such a state that it can grow and develop for the general welfare.

Both the answer to this main question and this necessary assurance are found in part in history. Great light is always shed on the question of what ought to be done by finding out what has been done. Progress has lain in the cultivation and maintenance of a state of mind. It has been in general a strong adherence to ideals. The ideal around which the ancient tribes of Israel developed was monotheism. The ideal of Greece was beauty. That of Rome was glory. The strength of the British Empire has been in a sense of obligation. Well might Admiral Nelson appeal to that sense by flying at his masthead as he swung his fleet into battle: "England expects every man to do his duty." To the French it has been a personification of their country. To one of her generals, on trial for surrendering his army, who plead that with many of her cities in the hands of the enemy, with her forces disintegrated, her government in flight, there was no

longer anything for him to fight for, went the reply:
"There is always France." The strongest sentiment of
America has been for that independence which is the basis
of self-government. These are but main features. There
clustered about them many other ideals which in all instances lent strength to the character of the people of
each nation. It was only when the people fell away from
their adherence to their ideals that the disintegration began which ended in the final downfall of the nations of
antiquity. It has but lately been demonstrated to the
fullest extent that the self-governing peoples of the modern world are strong and vigorous, still true to their traditions, still loyal to their ideals. Such a condition has
always indicated a sound foundation in the past, and must
be the best index of it in the present.

Our modern life is very complex. Its conduct is dependent on technical skill. Strike out what is known of
physics and substantially every mechanical device, all
transportation by power-driven motors, all manufacturing, heating, and lighting plants, water-supply, and drain-
age would fail to operate; strike out chemistry and pestilence would overwhelm the earth in a few days. These
are results which affect the entire human race. There is
nothing of such broad application as the practical results
of learning. There is no force so democratic as the force
of an ideal.

But it is not only by technical skill that modern civilization is sustained. It depends to a large degree on accumulated and invested capital, and for its advance will
depend more and more on accumulation and investment
of capital. Civilization and profits go hand in hand. It

is out of the surplus of our efforts that progress is made.
It is only necessary to remember the method of conducting all industry, transportation, banking, mining, and
commerce and to observe that they not only need constant renewal but ever-increasing facilities with which to
meet enlarged demands, to determine that what we call
capital is the chief material minister to the general welfare of all mankind.

Invested capital is the result of brains. All the elements that are assembled in a Corliss engine, a modern
printing-press, or an aeroplane have lain in the earth
throughout all the ages. For countless generations there
has been sufficient human labor to assemble them, yet
they did not appear. They came into being only when
called by the skill and brains of men. The same is true of
the plant whereby is carried on all modern business. It is
also by organizations, by management, that labor is so
directed as to produce a surplus for present and future
investment. Truly capital, surplus, profits, and progress
are the result of brains. In fact, that which we call labor
is intelligent effort directed toward some desired end.
Otherwise such result could well be secured from a machine. In its last analysis, what the workman sells is his
intelligence. But it is still true that the management and
direction, of which surplus and profits are born, is a rarer
skill, a yet more acute intelligence, which we in general
designate as brains. It is on the continued existence of
this power in man, which is the result of effort and training, that not only the advance but the maintenance of our
present standards depends.

But there is need not only of patriotic ideals and a

trained intelligence in our economic life, there is need of a deep understanding of man and his relationship to the physical universe and to his fellow man. There has always been evil in the world. John Fiske has demonstrated very clearly that of necessity evil and good are coexistent possibilities. What virtue would there be in choosing the good unless thereby the evil was rejected? There are evil forces at work now. They are apparently organized and seek the disintegration of society. They can always be recognized by a direct appeal to selfishness and nothing else. They deny that the present relationship of men to each other, which exists by reason of organized society, has any sound basis for its existence. They point out to men with untrained minds that it takes effort to maintain themselves and support government, and claim that they ought to exist without effort on the accumulation of others, and they deny that men have any obligations toward each other.

The answer to this lies in a knowledge of past human experience and a realization of what man is. These claims are very old. They have had trial times without number, and always with disastrous results. Men are not so constituted that selfishness satisfies them, and the only result of attempting to evade their obligations to others has been to destroy themselves. Man has been so created, his environment is such, his nature is such, that he cannot succeed in that way.

Surely the wonderful experience of man shows he is a being that can only be satisfied with higher things than these. After contemplating his advance from the beginnings of evolution up to the scientist and the philosopher, of him well might the ancient prophet Isaiah have inquired: "Who hath measured the waters in the hollow of his hand, and meted out Heaven with the span, and comprehended the dust of the earth in a measure, and weighed the mountains in scales, and the hills in a balance?"

"Who hath directed the spirit of *man* or being his counsellor hath taught him?"

"With whom took he counsel, and who instructed him, and taught him in the path of judgment, and taught him knowledge, and showed to him the way of understanding?"

They little understand what men have done, or what they are, who expect they can long be content with the husks of existence. Surely men will not long follow false prophets or long serve their betrayers.

What are the sources, then, of that state of mind which supports civilization? There are but two sources, education and religion. From them are derived the teachings of science necessary to give the requisite technical skill and moral ideals sufficient to support and advance civilization. But when we ask what education, the answer must be the higher education; for in the first place primary schools have been a development of higher education and would not long survive without it, and in the second place we have seen that modern society cannot exist save by the ministrations of the highest scientific skill. We could not survive, then, with only primary education. But what about religion? In so far as that is dependent upon the teachings of the clergy, we come at once to the inquiry, who teach the clergy? and we learn that the higher education was anciently instituted solely for their instruction. Not only the higher sciences, but philosophy, morals, and religion all centre in our colleges and universities. It is not too much to say that in them is the foundation of all civilization, and that their influence is all-embracing.

That is not saying that everybody ought to have a university education. It is saying that in these days everybody must and does come under the influence of a university education. Neither Washington nor Lincoln had the advantage of a college education, but had it not been for colleges neither Washington nor Lincoln would ever have been heard of.

Is not the conclusion of all this perfectly plain? We hold by the modern standards of society. We believe in maintaining modern civilization for the protection and support of free governments, and the development of our economic welfare. We claim they are sound and minister in the best way to human welfare. The great test of an institution is its ability to perpetuate itself. It seems fairly plain that whether or not these institutions can survive with the aid of higher education, without it they have not the slightest chance. We justify the greater and greater accumulations of capital because we believe that therefrom flows the support of all science, art, learning, and the charities which minister to the humanities of life, all carrying their beneficent effects to the people as a whole. Unless this is measurably true our system of civilization ought to stand condemned. It is to be condemned, anyway, unless it possesses the ability to perpetuate itself. This can only be true by supporting higher education to such a degree that its good influence may

more than match the rising tide of the influence of evil.
Those who want a continuation of stability and confidence must seek it by supporting the efforts of our colleges and universities. It is not too much to say that all that we mean when we say America is dependent on the adequacy of this support.

This appeal has not failed. From earliest times Americans have lavished the most solicitous care on advanced education. As our settlements have swept westward they have set up the most efficient State universities. There is no contemporary effort of greater promise or more propitious than the increasing endowment that has been sought and secured by our institutions of higher learning. It shows a recognition of the need both by those intrusted with their management and by those who have the means to respond.

There is satisfaction too in the greatly increased college attendance. With these manifestations all about, what wonder that while the rest of the world is in a turmoil America is serene. This glory we owe in no small part to the all-embracing influence of our colleges and universities. They have wrought mightily in the making of America. While they can command adequate support America cannot fail. They stand like mighty fortresses within whose protection the truth is secure. Against them no enemy shall prevail.

II

Plymouth Rock does not mark a beginning or an end. It marks a revelation of that which is without beginning and without end—a purpose, shining through eternity with a resplendent light, undimmed even by the imperfections of men; and a response, an answering purpose, from those who, oblivious, disdainful of all else, sailed hither seeking only for an avenue for the immortal soul.

THE PILGRIMS

THREE centuries ago to-day the Pilgrims of the *May-flower* made final landing at Plymouth Rock. They came not merely from the shores of the Old World. It will be in vain to search among recorded maps and history for their origin. They sailed up out of the infinite.

There was among them small trace of the vanities of life. They came undecked with orders of nobility. They were not children of fortune but of tribulation. Persecution, not preference, brought them hither; but it was a persecution in which they found a stern satisfaction. They cared little for titles; still less for the goods of this earth; but for an idea they would die. Measured by the standards of men of their time, they were the humble of the earth. Measured by later accomplishments, they were the mighty. In appearance weak and persecuted they came—rejected, despised—an insignificant band; in reality strong and independent, a mighty host of whom the world was not worthy, destined to free mankind. No captain ever led his forces to such a conquest. Oblivious to rank, yet men trace to them their lineage as to a royal house.

Forces not ruled by man had laid their unwilling course. As they landed, a sentinel of Providence, humbler, nearer to nature than themselves, welcomed them in their own tongue. They came seeking only an abiding-place on

At the exercises on the Three Hundredth Anniversary of the Landing of the Pilgrims, at Plymouth, Massachusetts, December 21, 1920.

13

earth, "but lifted up their eyes to heaven, their dearest country," says Governor Bradford, "where God hath prepared for them a city." On that abiding faith has been reared an empire, magnificent beyond their dreams of Paradise.

Amid the solitude they set up hearthstone and altar; the home and the church. With arms in their hands they wrung from the soil their bread. With arms they gathered in the congregation to worship Almighty God. But they were armed, that in peace they might seek divine guidance in righteousness; not that they might prevail by force, but that they might do right though they perished.

What an increase, material and spiritual, three hundred years has brought that little company is known to all the earth. No like body ever cast so great an influence on human history. Civilization has made of their landing-place a shrine. Unto the Commonwealth of Massachusetts has been intrusted the keeping of that shrine. To her has come the precious heritage. It will be kept as it was created, or it will perish, not with an earthly pride but with a heavenly vision.

Plymouth Rock does not mark a beginning or an end. It marks a revelation of that which is without beginning and without end—a purpose, shining through eternity with a resplendent light, undimmed even by the imperfections of men; and a response, an answering purpose, from those who, oblivious, disdainful of all else, sailed hither seeking only for an avenue for the immortal soul.

III

No man was ever meanly born. About his cradle is the wondrous miracle of life. He may descend into the depths, he may live in infamy and perish miserably, but he is born great. Men build monuments above the graves of their heroes to mark the end of a great life, but women seek out the birthplace and build their shrine, not where a great life had its ending but where it had its beginning, seeking with a truer instinct the common source of things not in that which is gone forever but in that which they know will again be manifest. Life may depart, but the source of life is constant.

THEODORE ROOSEVELT

GREAT men are the ambassadors of Providence sent to reveal to their fellow men their unknown selves. To them is granted the power to call forth the best there is in those who come under their influence. Sometimes they have come as great captains, commanders of men, who have hewed out empires, sometimes as statesmen, ministering to the well-being of their country, sometimes as painters and poets, showing new realms of beauty, sometimes as philosophers and preachers, revealing to the race "the way, the truth, and the life," but always as inspirers of noble action, translating high ideals into the practical affairs of life. There is something about them better than anything they do or say. If measured at all, they are to be measured in the responsive action of what others do or say. They come and go, in part a mystery, in part the simplest of all experience, the compelling influence of the truth. They leave no successor. The heritage of greatness descends to the people.

No man was ever meanly born. About his cradle is the wondrous miracle of life. He may descend into the depths, he may live in infamy and perish miserably, but he is born great. Men build monuments above the graves of their heroes to mark the end of a great life, but women seek out the birthplace and build their shrine, not where

Address before the Women's Roosevelt Memorial Association, New York City, January 23, 1921.

a great life had its ending but where it had its beginning, seeking with a truer instinct the common source of things not in that which is gone forever but in that which they know will again be manifest. Life may depart, but the source of life is constant.

For the purpose of ministering and giving expression to this sentiment, your association has been formed, formed in the memory of one of America's great men, yet not solely for perpetuating the memory, but for extending the services to the people he loved, of Theodore Roosevelt.

If that ministration is to represent truly, and adequately represent, the spirit of that great man, it will be through and through patriotic. In all the criticisms that his zeal for the right, whatever the consequences, brought him, no one ever questioned his patriotism, no one ever doubted his love for his country. Standing once in the presence of death, which had overtaken his companion and narrowly missed him, when asked if he did not fear violence against himself, he replied: "Not half so much as I fear that I may make some mistake which will work injury to my country." That country he loved above all else, and on her altar he laid not merely his own life but the greater sacrifice of those whose lives were dearer to him than his own. Yet it was not in the time of military peril but in the time of civil peril that he performed his most valuable services for America.

The greatest peril to our institutions does not lie in a direct assault upon them, nor will it come from those who, with evil intent, strive for their destruction. Disaster will come from those who probably with good in-

tentions seek the private control of public action. It is
an old story known to all, but in the exercise of that
eternal vigilance which they tell us is the price of liberty
it requires constant reiteration, and no estimate of the
services and character of Theodore Roosevelt can be
made without the retelling of it.

The underlying theory of the American form of government is the rule of the people through their representatives, thus creating a republic. There were those who
distrusted popular sovereignty, still more who distrusted
all forms of monarchy; out of their deliberations came not
any form of monarchy nor a pure democracy, but a republic, in which all functions of government are to be
executed by chosen representatives, acting under constitutional restraints dictated by reason alone, but in all
things and at all times recognizing and declaring the sovereignty of the people and the supremacy of their will
expressed in accordance with prevailing law.

The great contests in our government have partaken
of the character of an effort to substitute for this public
will some form of private will, for the public welfare some
private interest. In its very broad aspects the American
Revolution was a contest over this principle, the British
contending for the rule of the commercial interests of the
empire, the colonists defending their right to govern themselves in accordance with the public welfare. This principle had to be determined anew in the war between the
States, when the issue was very squarely drawn between
the execution of the public will, lawfully determined, and
the supremacy of the private interests represented in human slavery. For half a century that interest had domi-

nated the South, and it was claimed it had dominated the National Government. At last the people asserted their right to control the government, and the irrepressible conflict began which ended in the reassertion of the sovereignty of the people and a rededication of our nation to the cause of freedom. The great menace that had threatened our government from its very beginnings, weak and unheeded once, then powerful and dominant, was forever removed. But the old tendency remained, to break out in a new conflict between private interest and public welfare.

When the country recovered from the devastation of the war it entered an era of great industrial expansion. Many thousands of miles of railroads were laid, minerals were mined in great profusion, manufacturing plants increased enormously; there was a great influx of population causing the building of teeming cities, all of which led to a fabulous increase of wealth. It was distinctly a commercial age marked by a consuming desire for financial success. Along with this, however, went that spread of culture which wealth brings. Colleges were endowed, public libraries were built, hospitals were provided, science and the arts were supported and advanced. All this was done by the power of wealth as a result of business success.

It was no wonder that men were dazzled by its magnificence, and, seeing the good it had accomplished, sought to increase the means for the production of wealth by great combinations which in some instances partook of monopoly. Owning the business of the country, through it there was growing up the attempt to exercise an improper control over the affairs of government. "Surely," men said, "business is supreme, see what great good it has accomplished. How better can the government be conducted than in the interests of business?" This certainly was well intended and believed to be patriotic on the part of its proposers. This condition culminated about twenty years ago. It had gone on unformulated in men's minds, unconsciously tending to monopoly in business, and by that means private control of government, substituting the age-old formula of private interest for the public welfare. Logically developed it would have meant stagnation in business through the loss of all initiative, and bureaucracy in government through the loss of a true representation of the public will. The man who finally brought the business men of the nation to see that their course was economically unsound, and therefore to be abandoned, and who roused the American people to the assertion again of their right to control their government for the public welfare, was Theodore Roosevelt. No man had done so much to destroy an unsound economic theory, and to restore his country to its true form of representative government since the days of Abraham Lincoln. And as with Lincoln, no one, whether formerly victor or vanquished, would return to the old order. He broke the menace of monopoly. He made the sovereignty of the people again supreme.

In all this he stood for a great principle impartially applied. He declared and enforced the supremacy of the public law alike against those who opposed it in the name of capital or in the name of labor. In that he was the true friend of both, the benefactor of employer and employee and the defender of the republic of the United States. He found it menaced and he left it free.

In a struggle of that nature not all good men or all patriots are on one side. Had it been so there would be no struggle. Nor is it alone the guilty who suffer. There were many Americans who, conscious of their own rectitude, assumed the rectitude of others and therefore disapproved of the Roosevelt policies. They were using their power unselfishly for the public welfare. But there were others who were not. Men said in derision that Roosevelt had discovered the Ten Commandments. What they said derisively let us state seriously. He had discovered the Ten Commandments, and he applied their doctrine with great vigor in places that had assumed they had the power to discard the Ten Commandments.

We have seen that the reaction of public opinion went too far. It created a condition in which men of large interests, no matter how innocent of any offense, have since felt they would be misjudged and their motives misconstrued if they took part in public affairs. That sentiment is wrong and, being wrong, works a grave public injury. The public business has come to be the largest single business that there is. Unless it can have the benefit of the training and ability that is developed in great private enterprises it cannot be conducted successfully, and if not successful the people suffer. Innocence is not enough in government administration, as Theodore Roosevelt well knew. There must be added that character and ability that come only from grappling with the great problems of life, most usually gained by Americans in great business and administrative activities. He did not fail to surround himself with advisers of that kind. He had them in his Cabinet. He sought their counsel from the Senate and from private life. The war helped to dissipate this unwholesome state of public opinion by reason of the universally patriotic and active assistance rendered by the business interests to the government. The American people are entitled by right to have their public business administered by a training and intelligence, a capacity and character, the equal of that which any private enterprise can command. It is the duty of men in business life to provide such service at some inconvenience to themselves, some risk of being misunderstood, and some likelihood of being publicly abused.

There was another reaction against the management of business which greatly strengthened organizations of employees in the estimation of public opinion. That increased until such organizations undertook to dictate to the government, sometimes successfully. That menace, again, of private will against the public will has been met and defeated not only without but within their own ranks. It did not have the support of the rank and file of employees, who have been at all times patriotic, law-abiding, and God-fearing men and women. If there be any class who should seek the public welfare, they are that class, for, more nearly than any other body of our citizens, the wage-earners are the public. The counsel and assistance of their representatives, their true representatives, should be sought, will be sought in State and nation, as it was sought and followed by Roosevelt. No government can be successful which outlaws any good influence, wherever its source, whatever its calling. The sovereignty of the people means the sovereignty not of a self-selected few. It means the supremacy of the matured convictions of all the people. Our franchise is not granted to class or caste. It is the acquired right of all Americans.

There was another service which he rendered not merely to his fellow countrymen this time but to the world. There is a tendency on the part of men and people to lapse into a contented ease, to regard the difficulties of others and the perils of our neighbors as none of our particular business. Theodore Roosevelt never lapsed. He was against what he believed to be wrong everywhere. He was against it in his speech, he was for taking effective action against it; for he was no carpet-knight—his headquarters through his life were always in the field. When the Great War broke out he refused to be neutral. He had no hesitation in declaring he was an American, and he immediately proclaimed that the war was an American war, and that he was on the side of America.

Our country has known little of foreign affairs. It has desired to know little of them. It has been our tradition that what went on in Europe could have little effect here. But we have declared and maintained the Monroe Doctrine of no interference here by Europe. The closing of our exchange, the denial of our access to the sea, the death of our nationals when peacefully engaged, did not seem to wake us from our delusion. We wanted peace, and rightfully; but it was the voice of Roosevelt that roused the nation to the meaning and the menace of the war to America. In this he was never so disinterested, so patriotic, so eager for the right for its own sake. He

appealed from the things that seemed to be to the soul
of the things that are.

This was his last great service. He roused the national
conscience into righteous action. He spoke to the soul
of his country and he saw her response. He saw her rise,
triumphant again above every sordid motive, resurgent
to the everlasting realities. He saw his fellow countrymen make their sacrifices and he made his. He knew
their suffering, but he knew their courage.

He saw their final victory. He saw the beginning of
the return of those never-conquered banners as they came
streaming home. In that triumphant sound of drum-
beat and bugle he too was summoned home, under the
brighter banners of truth and righteousness which in him
never suffered defeat.

His work goes on. His battle line strengthens. His
principles have more defenders, his actions more admirers.

His devoted followers are building a shrine at his birthplace to increase the influence of his life. The people
whom he loved and trusted and served are the contribu-
tors. Here men may come and remember that he re-
established a representative government of all the people, reopened the closing doors of opportunity, reawakened the soul of his country, and reinforced the moral
fibre of America. Let the people make pilgrimages to
this shrine where his great life began, where Theodore
Roosevelt learned to kneel in prayer, let them contemplate his works and recall his sacrifices, and out of their
pilgrimage, their contemplation, and their recollection
will be born the unyielding conviction, "Greater love
hath no man than this."

IV

*It is no accident that the people of the Common-
wealth of Massachusetts believe in law and order.
It is their heritage.*

LAW AND ORDER

IT is a very great honor that you have bestowed upon me by awarding me this medal. I shall hold it in part as a trustee. If it had not been for the clear insight and the determination of Edwin U. Curtis, a former mayor and then police commissioner of the city of Boston, the question that came to me would never have come. It was because he decided that question right in the first instance that I had the opportunity of supporting him in the second instance. And it was due not only to Commissioner Curtis, but it was due to the united efforts of the people of the Commonwealth of Massachusetts. It was due to her public press, to her patriotic citizens, who at once raised a half million dollars, and to her citizenship all up and down the Commonwealth that united, without party distinction, in making that victory supreme at the polls.

It is no accident that the people of the Commonwealth of Massachusetts believe in law and order. It is their heritage. When the Pilgrim Fathers landed there in 1620 they brought ashore with them the *Mayflower* compact which they had drawn up in the cabin of that little bark under the witness of the Almighty, in which they pledged themselves, one to another, to make just and equitable

In accepting the gold medal awarded by the National Institute of Social Sciences for his action in connection with the police strike in Boston, New York, January 23, 1921.

laws, and not only to make them, but, when they were made, to abide by them.

So that, for three hundred years, that has been the policy and the principle of that Commonwealth. And I shall hold this medal as a testimony to the service that was begun three hundred years ago and has continued through these generations; and in the hope that its example may still continue as a beacon light to all civilization.

V

The great object for us to seek here, for the Constitution identifies the vice-presidency with the Senate, is to continue to make this chamber, as it was intended by the fathers, the citadel of liberty.

INAUGURAL ADDRESS AS VICE-PRESIDENT

FIVE generations ago there was revealed to the people of this nation a new relationship between man and man, which they declared and proclaimed in the American Constitution. Therein they recognized a legislature empowered to express the will of the people in law, a judiciary required to determine and state such law, and an executive charged with securing obedience to the law, all holding their office, not by reason of some superior force, but through the duly determined conscience of their countrymen.

To the House, close to the heart of the nation, renewing its whole membership by frequent elections, representing directly the people, reflecting their common purpose, has been granted a full measure of the power of legislation and exclusive authority to originate taxation. To the Senate, renewing its membership by degrees, representing in part the sovereign States, has been granted not only a full measure of the power of legislation, but, if possible, far more important functions.

To it is intrusted the duty of review, that to negotiations there may be added ratification, and to appointment approval. But its greatest function of all, too little mentioned and too little understood, whether exercised in legislating or reviewing, is the preservation of liberty. Not merely the rights of the majority, they little need protection, but the rights of the minority, from whatever source they may be assailed. The great object for us to seek here, for the Constitution identifies the vice-presidency with the Senate, is to continue to make this chamber, as it was intended by the fathers, the citadel of liberty. An enormous power is here conferred, capable of much good or ill, open, it may be, to abuse, but necessary, wholly and absolutely necessary, to secure the required result.

Whatever its faults, whatever its human imperfections, there is no legislative body in all history that has used its powers with more wisdom and discretion, more uniformly for the execution of the public will, or more in harmony with the spirit of the authority of the people which has created it, than the United States Senate. I take up the duties the people have assigned me under the Constitution, which we can neither enlarge nor diminish, of presiding over this Senate, agreeably to its rules and regulations, deeply conscious that it will continue to function in harmony with its high traditions as a great deliberative body, without passion and without fear, unmoved by clamor, but most sensitive to the right, the stronghold of government according to law, that the vision of past generations may be more and more the reality of generations yet to come.

VI

If ever the citizen comes to feel that our government does not protect him in the free and equal assertion of his rights at home and abroad, he will withdraw his allegiance from that government, as he ought to, and bestow it on some more worthy object. It is idle to assume that the privilege of the strong has been destroyed unless the rights of the weak are preserved. The American theory of government means that back of the humblest citizen, supporting him in all his rights, organized for his protection, stands the whole force of the nation. That is the warrant and the sole warrant of his freedom. He can assert it in the face of all the world. The individual has rights, but only the citizen has the power to protect rights. And the protection of rights is righteous.

ANDREW CARNEGIE: ORGANIZER FOR SERVICE

THERE is a greatness that is distinctly American, a true greatness which enlarges man's dominion. It is an achievement which comes from obedience to that admonition given on creation morn to subdue the earth. It has meant the bringing of the forces of nature under control, loosing their gigantic powers and setting them to do the work of the world. Obedience to that Word, spoken at the beginning, is still showing forth to man, from revelation to revelation, his power, his dignity, and his ever-increasing mastery. Those who have been inspired by this motive, those finishers of creation, represent a type of greatness which is peculiarly American.

This is still a new and young country. The frontier still lingers. The hardy pioneer still defends the outworks of civilization. The tide of immigration still sets toward our shores. America is still the land of opportunity. But strong as are these characteristics, powerful as are these influences, in the first half of the nineteenth century they were yet stronger and more powerful. This city of Pittsburgh, so rich in an abundant colonial history, was then a frontier town. It was just touching its metal development, but the vast resources that lay at its feet were unrecognized and undeveloped. Around it, beneath it, clustered stores of coal, of ore, of

At the Founders' Day Celebration of Carnegie Institute, Pittsburgh, Pennsylvania, April 28, 1921.

oil, of gas waiting for the touch of genius, for obedience
to the Word, to marshal them into new forms and send
them forth toiling in the cause of civilization, the responsive and more responsive servants of mankind.

Into these surroundings, in 1848, came the twelve-year-
old Andrew Carnegie and his family, weavers of cloth by
trade, handicraftsmen who had found themselves displaced by the power of machinery. This was the undoing of the crafts, it meant want and distress, or re-
adjustment. It was the steam-engine that drove this
family out of Scotland to America. Thereby was to be
more cloth for their homeland, and a yet untold addition
to the prosperity, convenience, and welfare of the human
race, flowing out from the land of their adoption. A remarkable achievement for a steam-engine. So great is
the power of an idea let loose upon the world. Men can
reject it and perish, or obey it and prosper.

Two continents know well the success of the founder
of this institute. There is scarce a youth in either land
who would not wish a career ending where his ended.
That may be a vain wish, but it may have some measure
of accomplishment, if youth would but begin where he
began. His family came here with scanty earthly possessions but well endowed with character. His father was
a man of broad but deep piety, who believed in the gospel
of hard work. His mother was a woman of marked nobility of purpose, with a great pride in well-doing, brave,
loyal, who reared her sons to a high sense of honor. A
great man comes from the devotion of a great mother.
About that household were cherished those virtues,
homely yet supreme, described by Robert Burns in "The

Cotter's Saturday Night." They hated privilege and loved liberty. From amid such circumstances come those marked by destiny for the high places of the earth, prepared for great services to mankind.

Everybody knows that Andrew Carnegie began life at very humble toil for very meagre pay. But it is a recollection that may well be refreshed by frequent contemplation. Many others have had that experience. But by application, by attention to his own work, by learning the work of his superiors, he rose to messenger-boy, to telegraph operator, to superintendent of the Pittsburgh division of the Pennsylvania Railroad at the age of twenty-five, and soon after made his first venture in the iron trade. At the end of forty years he sold out the steel business and retired from accumulation to take up the task of distribution, the distribution of more than three hundred million dollars in public benefactions. In this effort of bestowal he was not without success.

Such were the attainments of this Scotch boy, nurtured on the doctrine of equal rights, who hallowed the memory of Bruce, not because he was a king but because he was a patriot, but who held to Wallace as his ideal, because he was a patriot without the taint of privilege; this boy who had seen his father beg for work amid conditions of distress, who had seen his mother toiling for a pittance to maintain their home, and yet was reared to hold that not want but idleness was a disgrace; this boy who despised rank and cherished liberty, who wanted a republic and found himself in a kingdom, yet withheld nothing in affectionate loyalty and devotion, throughout all his years, to the land of his birth and to its duly constituted

authority; this boy who glorified in being born and bred
a Scotchman, and remained a Scotchman all his life, and
yet, pre-eminently cherishing and exemplifying our ideals,
is entitled to be called a great American.

There was no secret about his success, he was an ideal-
ist.   He had the genius of hard work and careful saving.
But his chief aim in life was not acquisition but bestowal.
When he was earning his first modest wages he was telling his mother that she should yet ride in her carriage.
He amassed one of the stupendous fortunes of all history, yet it is not as a merely rich man that he is so
grandly placed in history, but as the benefactor of his
fellow men in the New World and the Old.

The means by which he wrought his magic lay for the
most part in organization.   As an organizer of men, as
a judge of human nature, as a leader, he has had few
equals.   He boasted that he did not know the mechanics of his business, but that he did know men.   No wonder he was called the iron master.   That mastery came
from the ability to organize.

There has been great hesitation in our country to accept
fully and work out to its logical conclusion the principle
of organization.   We have adopted it as the foundation
of our government after a great struggle and continued
opposition to nationalism.   But it is naturally irksome.
It is forever under assault from all radical sources as a
limitation of our liberty.   As a matter of fact, under government it enlarges and supports liberty, and under industry enlarges and supports production.

We Americans have been individualists.   We are individualists still.   That sturdy spirit which makes the pi-

oneer is self-reliance. Without it no people ever achieved
liberty. With it no people can be held in subjection.
In the protection of the rights of the individual our Constitution and our laws set up a new standard, guaranteeing their maintenance against all the forces of society,
or even of government itself. Nothing must be permitted
to encroach upon those rights. They are the foundation
upon which stands the whole edifice of our institutions.
If ever the citizen comes to feel that our government
does not protect him in the free and equal assertion of his
rights at home and abroad, he will withdraw his allegiance
from that government, as he ought to, and bestow it on
some more worthy object. It is idle to assume that the
privilege of the strong has been destroyed unless the
rights of the weak are preserved. The American theory
of government means that back of the humblest citizen,
supporting him in all his rights; organized for his protection, stands the whole force of the nation. That is the
warrant and the sole warrant of his freedom. He can
assert it in the face of all the world. The individual has
rights, but only the citizen has the power to protect
rights. And the protection of rights is righteous.

Likewise in industry to secure the maximum results of
effort there must be an organization, there must be co-
operation. There are those who have resisted this tendency, but it has gone steadily on. They have resisted
it when it related to ownership, they have resisted it
when it related to employment. There have been many
errors and many bad motives manifested in each, and
actions which it has been well to check with the stern
hand of the law, but the desirability of organization, the

natural and inevitable development of the unification of effort, remains.

But society must and will judge the purpose, the intent, and must and will finally conclude, that organization for service is right, but that organization for oppression is wrong. Organization for oppression carries within itself the seeds of its own destruction. It cannot succeed. Organization for service works with an inspired purpose. It cannot fail. Some time this rule will be applied, alike to capital and labor, to employer and employed. It will hasten the adjustment of many difficulties when each recognizes his duty to act under it.

The organization which Andrew Carnegie perfected was for service. How great that service was, its far-reaching effects, its relation to the every-day life of the men and women of the nation, can scarcely be comprehended. The development of the steel industry is in itself an epic. This city knows it too well to need more than a reminder of it. But it is an epic in which the whole nation is glorified. The contribution which it has made to the cause of civilization in the past sixty years surpasses that of any other industry. It has crossed rivers and levelled mountains. It has broken the barrier between the Atlantic and the Pacific. It has descended into the depths and brought up precious metals. It has wrought new and wonderful forms of architecture. It has been man's chief instrument in subduing the earth. As a benefactor of the race it were fame enough for any man to have been the foremost in developing that industry in America. More than that fame belongs to Andrew Carnegie.

As a part of his organization he did not neglect science. When his competitors thought they could not afford a chemist he thought he could not afford to be without one. He knew the power of knowledge. Cut off with little schooling in his early life, he was yet a student all his days. No one knew better than he that the achievements of our modern days were the results of exact science, that all progress lies in a directing intelligence. It is not the mere force of work, not the power alone of labor, but the vitalizing force of trained minds that maintains and advances civilization. Without that he knew that all effort had been and would be in vain. The greatest benefit that can be bestowed upon those who toil is skilled and wise management. That has always meant and always will mean an opportunity to help themselves. There can never be any success in any plan of economic and industrial relationship which leaves out the element of brains.

It was the clear perception of these fundamental principles that caused the great benefactor to endow his fellow men not with the things that perish, but with the things that abide. He was always seeking out the realities. He offered opportunity. He knew it was all his beneficiaries could profitably receive. If they were to have life more abundantly he knew it could come only through their own effort. He could not give the means by which others could provide these for themselves. He did not pauperize. He ennobled. He did not undertake to support persons, but to endow a cause. Governments everywhere, in State and nation, may profitably study his example. His benefactions were real. They will be written into the soul of all who come in contact with them. There they will last through eternity.

There is little wonder that he turned his thoughts toward education. The great need of it must have appealed to him both as one who loved his fellow man and one who loved his country. How great that need is has recently been disclosed by the records of the draft army. They represented the best type of the youth of the nation, yet nearly one-fourth of them are said to have been unable to read and write in any language. This was not confined to any locality, it was fairly general. The reason was twofold, bad school laws and immigration.

There is no more pressing need than popular education. There is no greater blessing that can be bestowed upon the youth of the land. As a call of humanity it strikes a sympathetic chord in every heart. But the other side is also of great importance. The very foundation of the republic breaks down unless it is supported by an intelligent and informed electorate. Whatever may have been the case in past generations, with the present resources of society there must be found means to meet this call of humanity and supply this defense for our republic.

But, great as have been the benefactions of Andrew Carnegie in the development of the material and the intellectual welfare of his fellow men, it is not by these that he makes his greatest appeal for a place in history. His greatest achievement lies in the addition he made to the moral force of his fellow men. This came by precept and by example.

The question of human welfare is not an economic question. It is a moral question. There is no difficulty with the present advance of scientific knowledge in providing for the welfare of the race. The ability is not lacking even if no further advance were made in discovery and invention. The material and intellectual force are sufficient. They could be much greater—must be made much greater, but the present deficiency is not there. It is the disposition—the moral force that is lacking. Men are not doing as well as they can with what they have. Our civilization perishes unless the great powers it has developed are directed by a greater moral force.

It was on this force that he depended. To it he made his appeal. By it he guided his action. He sometimes told his men that he would not fight them but he would sit down. He appealed to their sense of justice and held their deep affection. His shops had differences with their workmen; one was serious, but temporary. It can be said that he never developed a labor problem. He put his trust not in force but in reason. It was that which gave him a vision of world peace, it was that which gave him the power to believe in its ultimate accomplishment under some form.

Here was a man who represents American ideals. The whole nation—yes, the whole world—following out his plan can advance the cause of civilization. Under it the conditions of life have steadily grown better, there has been a wider and wider distribution of property, a higher and higher standard of education, a deeper and deeper appreciation of the obligation of self-sacrificing service. Of all these results Andrew Carnegie is a prominent example.

There are those who would discard this plan and substitute they know not what. They would turn from a certainty, tested by time, approved by experience, to some vague experiment. They point out imperfections, for even Americans have not fully realized their ideals. There are imperfections. But the ideal is right. It is everlastingly right. What our country needs is the moral power to hold to it.

There are readjustments to be accomplished. There are sacrifices to be made. They cannot be evaded. They cannot be made vicariously. They must be made by all the people. It is no time for bickerings. We must go back to work, in accordance with the best standard that the public can maintain, but we must go back to work. That done, the rest will take care of itself. Beneath the wrangling, beneath the tumult, is the sturdy, hard-working, home-loving American. He decided things in this country and his decision stands. He has decided to cast his lot where Andrew Carnegie cast his. In that decision, made in his spirit, calm, courageous, final, lies the greatest hope of a stricken world.

VII

There can be no permanent prosperity of any class or part. Such a condition can only be secured through a general and public prosperity. This means that to secure this end there must be a general distribution of the rewards of industry. Wherever this condition is maintained there you have the foundation for an increasing production and a sound financial and economic condition.

THE BANKS AND THE PEOPLE

NEW ENGLAND has represented a great deal in American history. It is not merely that there are located the home of the Pilgrim and Puritan, the tall monument on Bunker Hill and the bridge at Concord, or the old road to Ticonderoga, or the famous Charter Oak, or the home of Stark and of Pepperill, or the land of Roger Williams. Nor does New England hold merely by its great educational institutions, its manufacturing, its arts, and its commerce. The position of New England is determined more by what her people have done for the nation and for the world than by what they have done within the confines of their own six States.

This service has been both financial and personal. When the untamed regions of the nation were opened up for settlement, some of the best blood of New England streamed westward, and has made its mark broad and deep on the history of all the Western States, so that many of their representative men trace some connection to the northeast corner of the nation. The enterprise and business ability which here originated has played a leading part in the building of railroads which span the continent, the opening up of the mineral resources of the nation, the development of public utilities, and, in short, the making of our Western empire. All this has been a prodigious service, nobly performed, worthy of the sons

At a dinner attended by New England Bankers, New York City, June 27, 1921.

of the Pilgrims and the Puritans. It has lent an untold strength to the guarantees of civilization.

This great service is still going on, and it is this which gives New England a right to demand the means by which this work can be continued. You are without many of the great natural resources which have endowed other parts of the nation. There is little production here of the raw materials which go into manufacturing, and while this country has always been the abode of the thrifty farmer, it is unblessed by those great agricultural resources which are the heritage of other parts of the nation. There are here, however, vast plants of intricate machinery, men and women of great skill, and large capital resources which make the foundation for industrial and commercial prosperity. In these there is independence, but they can only be utilized through the transportation of raw materials in and the transportation of the finished product out, so that the entire future of this section of the nation depends, primarily, on transportation. It is the combination of these circumstances which gives to New England the right to require, in order that it may serve the nation, reasonable and adequate transportation. The furnishing of this is a duty which reaches to the managers and operators of your own transportation systems, and to the managers and operators of those other transportation systems which ship in and out of your territory.

I speak of this as one of the fundamental requirements which, while bounded by a small locality, is nation-wide in its effect; while it relates to the operations of a comparative few, yet will make by its success or failure the prosperity or the destitution of millions of Americans.

This is a very pertinent example of the interrelationship of our modern economical life. There can be no permanent prosperity of any class or part. Such a condition can only be secured through a general and public prosperity. This means that to secure this end there must be a general distribution of the rewards of industry. Wherever this condition is maintained there you have the foundation for an increasing production and a sound financial and economic situation.

One of the strongest reasons for supporting American institutions is that under them this condition is more nearly attained than under any other form of government that has ever met with any permanent success.

You are assembled here representing banking institutions. Too often the uninformed think of a bank as the possession of a few rich people, and as the creditor of the people at large. You who have had any experience with banking know that it is the opposite of this which is true. The resources of banks are not the resources of a few rich, but the resources of the people themselves, small perhaps in any individual instance, but, in the aggregate, very large. Nor are banks exclusively a creditor class. It is usually true that they owe to their depositors more than their borrowers owe to them. Every banker knows that to depend on the business and patronage of the rich would be in vain, that if any success attends his efforts it must be by serving and doing the business of the people. The stock is generally owned by the people, the deposits are always made by the people. This is the reason that banks partake of the nature of a public institution and perform real public service. They are the

sole means by which modern commercial activities can
be carried on. They afford the method by which the
people combine their individual resources, providing a
collection of capital sufficient to extend the mecessary
credit for financing the whole people of the natiom. They
hold great power and are under the very gravest responsibilities. A bank is not a private institution, reæponsible
to itself alone, or to a few. It is a public institution, under a moral obligation to be administered for tlhe public
welfare. In so far as this standard is accepted and followed, it is my belief that a bank will be prosperous; in
so far as 'it is disregarded, it will be a failure. Any power
which is not used for the general welfare will im the end
destroy itself.

There is need of a more sympathetic attitudee and co-
operation between the banks and the people. Ewery such
institution ought to realize the necessity of serving the
public to the extent of its ability. A financial imstitution
which takes advantage of no man's necessity, which as-
sumes no unreasonable risks for the sake of umreasona-
ble gains, which is able to know the personality of its
customers as well as the value of its collateral, becomes
an instrument of great value, and a contribuitor to a
marked degree of economic contentment. Such an institution is doing the work of the people.

This condition has not yet been universally established,
but it is being established. Nothing can tend more to
promote it than to have the man in the shop realize that
transportation and financial activities are being carried on
for his benefit; that the railroad brings raw material so
that he may earn a livelihood by making them into fin-

ished products; that the bank exists in order to furnish credit from which he receives a weekly wage, while those products are being sent far away and sold to the people. While the man in the bank needs to realize that his success lies in the freight-yard, in the manufacturing plant, on the farm, and in the mine as well as at the discount window.   If all this were to be translated into one word, I should say it was the need of vision, need of a recognition of our interdependence, need of less destructive criticism and more constructive action, need of that spirit which has given character, fame, and fortune to New England, whether it has guided the plough or inspired the pulpit.

VIII

The age of science and commercialism is here. There is no sound reason for wishing it otherwise. The wise desire is not to destroy it, but to use it and direct it rather than to be used and directed by it, that it may be, as it should be, not the master but the servant, that the physical forces may not prevail over the moral forces, and that the rule of life may not be expediency but righteousness.

THOUGHT, THE MASTER OF THINGS

WE come here to-day in defense of some of the great realities of life. We come to continue the guarantee of progress in the future by continuing a knowledge of progress in the past. We come to proclaim our allegiance to those ideals which have made the predominant civilization of the earth. We come because we believe that thought is the master of things. We come because we realize that the only road to freedom lies through a knowledge of the truth.

Mankind have always had classics. They always will. That is only another way of saying they have always set up ideals and always will. Always the question has been, always the question will be, what are those ideals to be, what are to be the classics? For many centuries, in education, the classics have meant Greek and Latin literature. It does not need much argument to demonstrate that in the Western world society can have little liberal culture which is not based on these. Without them there could be no interpretation of language and literature, no adequate comprehension of history, no understanding of the foundations of philosophy and law. In fact, the natural sciences are so much the product of those trained in the classics that, without such training, their very terminology cannot be fully understood.

At the Annual Meeting of the American Classical League, the University of Pennsylvania, July 7, 1921.

Education is undertaken to give a larger comprehension of life. In the last fifty years its scope has been very much broadened. It is scarcely possible to consider it in the light of the individual. It is easy to see that it must be discussed in the light of society. The question for consideration is not what shall be taught to a few individuals. Nor can it be determined by the example of the accomplishments of a few individuals. There have been great men with little of what we call education. There have been small men with a great deal of learning. There has never been a great people who did not possess great learning. The whole question at issue is, what does the public welfare require for the purpose of education? What are the fundamental things that young Americans should be taught? What is necessary for society to come to a larger comprehension of life?

The present age has been marked by science and commercialism. In its primary purpose it reveals mankind undertaking to overcome their physical limitations. This is being accomplished by wonderful discoveries which have given the race dominion over new powers. The chief demand of all the world has seemed to be for new increases in these directions. There has been a great impatience with everything which did not appear to minister to this requirement.

This has resulted in the establishment of technical schools and in general provisions for vocational education. There has been a theory that all learning ought to be at once translated into scientific and commercial activities. Of course the world to-day is absolutely dependent on science and on commerce. Without them great areas would be depopulated by famine and pestilence almost in a day. With them there is a general diffusion of comfort and prosperity, not only unexcelled, but continually increasing. These advantages, these very necessities, are not only not to be denied, but acknowledged and given the highest commendation. All this is not absolute but relative. It is neither self-sufficient nor self-existing. It represents the physical side of life. It is the product of centuries of an earlier culture, a culture which was none the less real because it supposed the earth was flat, a culture which was pre-eminent in the development of the moral and spiritual forces of life.

The age of science and commercialism is here. There is no sound reason for wishing it otherwise. The wise desire is not to destroy it, but to use it and direct it rather than to be used and directed by it, that it may be, as it should be, not the master but the servant, that the physical forces may not prevail over the moral forces, and that the rule of life may not be expediency but righteousness.

No question can be adequately comprehended without knowing its historical background. Modern civilization dates from Greece and Rome. The world was not new in their day. They were the inheritors of a civilization which had gone before, but what they had inherited they recast, enlarged, and intensified and made their own, so that their culture took on a distinctive form, embracing all that the past held best in the Roman world of the Cæsars. That great empire fell a prey, first to itself and then to the barbarians. After this seeming catastrophe scholarship and culture almost disappeared for nearly a thousand years, finally to emerge again in the revival of learning.

This came almost entirely out of the influence of the Christian Church. The revival of learning was the revival of the learning of Greece and Rome plus the teachings of revealed religion. Out of that revival has grown the culture of Western Europe and America. It is important to keep foundations clearly in mind. The superstructure is entirely dependent upon them for support whatever may be its excellence. However worthy a place it may fill, it cannot stand except on a sound foundation. In the revival of learning the philosophy of Greece played an important part. It was under its stimulus that the two methods of induction and deduction, experiment and reason, by which the human mind gains knowledge, were firmly established. This swept away the vain imaginings of the schoolmen, gave a new freedom to thought, and laid the beginnings of modern scientific research. It has brought about the modern era of learning which is reflected in every avenue of human life. It is in business. It is in education. It is in religion. No one questions its power. No one questions its desirability, but it is not all-sufficient.

It is impossible for society to break with its past. It is the product of all which has gone before. We could not cut ourselves off from all influence which existed prior to the Declaration of Independence and expect any success by undertaking to ignore all that happened before that date. The development of society is a gradual accomplishment. Culture is the product of a continuing effort. The education of the race is never accomplished. It must be gone over with each individual and it must continue from the beginning to the ending of life. Society

cannot say it has attained culture and can therefore rest
from its labors.   All that it can say is that it has learned
the method and process by which culture is secured, and
go on applying such method and process.

Biology teaches us that the individual goes through the
various stages of evolution which have brought him to his
present state of perfection.   All theories of education
teach us that the mind develops in the same way, rising
through the various stages that have marked the ascent
of mankind from the lowest savagery to the highest civilization.   This principle is a compelling reason for the
continuance of the classics as the foundation of our educational system.   It was by the use of this method that
we reached our present state of development.

This does not mean that every person must be a classical scholar.   It is not necessary for every one who crosses
the ocean to be an experienced mariner, nor for every one
who works on a building to be a learned architect, but if
the foreign shore is to be reached in safety, if the building
is to take on a form of utility and beauty, it will be because
of direction and instruction given according to established principles and ideals.   The principles and ideals
on which we must depend not only for a continuance of
modern culture but, I believe, for a continuance of the
development of science itself, come to us from the classics.
All this is the reason that the sciences and the professions
reach their highest development as the supplement of a
classical education.

Perhaps the chief criticism of education and its resulting effect upon the community to-day is superficiality.
A generation ago the business man who had made a suc-

cess without the advantages of a liberal education, sent his son to the university, where he took a course in Greek and Latin. On his return home, because he could not immediately take his father's place in the conduct of business, the conclusion was drawn that his education had been a failure. In order to judge the correctness of this conclusion it would be necessary to know whether the young man had really been educated or whether he had gone through certain prescribed courses, in the first place, and, in the second place, whether he finally developed executive ability. It cannot be denied that a superficial knowledge of the classics is only a superficial knowledge. There cannot be expected to be derived from it the ability to think correctly, which is the characteristic of a disciplined mind. Without doubt a superficial study of the classics is of less value than a superficial acquaintance with some of the sciences or a superficial business course. One of the advantages of the classics as a course of training is that in modern institutions there is little chance of going through them in a superficial way. Another of their advantages is that the master of them lives in something more than the present and thinks of something more than the external problems of the hour, and after all it was the study of the classics that produced the glories of the Elizabethan age with its poets, its philosophers, its artists, its explorers, its soldiers, its statesmen, and its churchmen.

Education is primarily a means of establishing ideals. Its first great duty is the formation of character, which is the result of heredity and training. This by no means excludes the desirability of an education in the utilities, but is a statement of what education must include if it meet with any success. It is not only because the classical method has been followed in our evolution of culture, but because the study of Greek and Latin is unsurpassed as a method of discipline. Their mastery requires an effort and an application which must be both intense and prolonged. They bring into action all the faculties of observation, understanding, and reason. To become proficient in them is to become possessed of self-control and of intelligence, which are the foundations of all character.

We often hear Greek and Latin referred to as dead languages. There are some languages which may have entirely expired, but I do not think any such have yet been discovered. There are words and forms in all languages which are dead because no longer used. There are many such in our own language. But Greek and Latin are not dead. The Romance languages are a modified Latin, and our own language is filled with words derived from Greek and Latin which have every living attribute. This is so true that to a certain extent there can be no adequate comprehension of the meaning of a large part of the language employed in every-day use, and the language of science and scholarship almost in their entirety, without a knowledge of Greek and Latin. Our literature is so filled with classical allusions that an understanding of its beauties can scarcely be secured by any other means.

The most pressing requirement of the present hour is not how we are to solve our economic problems, but: Where are we to find the sustaining influences for the realities of life? How are we to justify the existing form of government in our republic? Where shall we resort for teachings in patriotism? On what can we rely for a continuation of that service of sacrifice which has made modern civilization possible? The progress of the present era gives no new answers to these problems. There are no examples of heroism which outrival Leonidas at Thermopylæ, or Horatius at the bridge. The literature of Greece and Rome is through and through an inspiring plea for patriotism—from the meditations of their philosophers to the orations of their statesmen and the despatches of their soldiers.

The world has recently awakened to the value and the righteousness of democracy. This ideal is not new. It has been the vision which the people of many nations have followed through centuries. Because men knew that that ideal had been partially realized in Greece and Rome, they have had faith that it would be fully realized in Europe and America. The beginnings of modern democracy were in Athens and Sparta. That form of human relationship can neither be explained nor defended, except by reference to these examples, and a restatement of the principles on which their government rested. Both of these nations speak to us eloquently of the progress they made so long as their citizens held to these ideals, and they admonish us with an eloquence even more convincing of the decay and ruin which comes to any people when it falls away from these ideals. There is no surer road to destruction than prosperity without character.

There is little need to mention the debt which modern literature owes to the great examples of Greece and Rome. Even the New Testament was written in Greek. It is unthinkable that any institution founded for the purpose of teaching literature should neglect the classics. Nowhere have the niceties of thought been better expressed than in their prose. Nowhere have music and reason been more harmoniously combined than in their poetry, and nowhere is there greater eloquence than in their orations. We look to them not merely as the writers and speakers of great thoughts, but as the doers of greater deeds. There is a glory in the achievements of the Greeks under Themistocles, there is an admiration for the heroics of Salamis, there is even a pride in the successful retreat of the Ten Thousand which the humiliating days of Philip and Alexander cannot take away.

But when we turn to Rome we are overwhelmed by its greatness. When we recall the difficulties of the transportation of that day, which made the defense easy and attack difficult, her achievement not only in conquering all that there was of the then civilized Western world, but of holding it in subjection with a reign of law so absolute that the world has never known a peace so secure as that of the Pax Romana, strikes us with wonder. They gave to the world the first great example of order and a tolerable state of liberty under the law. As we study their history there is revealed to us one of the greatest peoples, under the guidance of great leaders, exhausting themselves in their efforts that the civilized world might be unified and the stage set for the entrance of Christianity. In their conquests we see one of the most stupendous services, and in their disintegration one of the most gigantic tragedies which ever befell a great people.

Every one knows that the culture of Greece and Rome is gone. It could not be restored; it could not be successfully imitated. What those who advocate their

continued study desire to bring about is the endurance of
that modern culture which has been the result of a famili-
arity with the classics of these two great peoples. We do
not wish to be Greek, we do not wish to be Roman. We
have a great desire to be supremely American. That
purpose we know we can accomplish by continuing the
process which has made us Americans. We must search
out and think the thoughts of those who established our
institutions. The education which made them must not
be divorced from the education which is to make us. In
our efforts to minister to man's material welfare we must
not forget to minister to his spiritual welfare. It is not
enough to teach men science; the great thing is to teach
them how to use science.

We believe in our republic. We believe in the principles of democracy. We believe in liberty. We believe in order under the established provisions of law.
We believe in the promotion of literature and the arts.
We believe in the righteous authority of organized government. We believe in patriotism. These beliefs must
be supported and strengthened. They are not to be inquired of for gain or profit, though without them all gain
and all profit would pass away. They will not be found
in the teachings devoted exclusively to commercialism,
though without them commerce would not exist. These
are the higher things of life. Their teaching has come to
us from the classics. If they are to be maintained they
will find their support in the institutions of the liberal
arts. When we are drawing away from them, we are
drawing away from the path of security and progress. It
is not yet possible that instruction in the classics could be

the portion of every American. That opportunity ought to be not diminished but increased. But while every American has not had and may not have the privilege, America has had it. Our leadership has been directed in accordance with these ideals. Our faith is in them still.

We have seen many periods which tried the soul of our republic. We shall see many more. There will be times when efforts will be great and profits will vanish. There have been and will be times when the people will be called upon to make great sacrifices for their country. Unless Americans shall continue to live in something more than the present, to be moved by something more than material gains, they will not be able to respond to these requirements and they will go down as other peoples have gone down before some nation possessed of a greater moral force. The will to endure is not the creation of the moment; it is the result of long training. That will has been our possession up to the present hour. By its exercise we have prospered and brought forth many wonderful works. The object of our education is to continue us in this great power. That power depends upon our ideals. The great and unfailing source of that power and these ideals has been the influence of the classics of Greece and Rome. Those who believe in America, in her language, her arts, her literature, and in her science, will seek to perpetuate them by perpetuating the education which has produced them.

IX

The trial which the civilization of America is to meet does not lie in adversity. It lies in prosperity. It will not be in a lack of power, but in the purpose directing the use of great power. There is new danger in our very greatness.

THE POWER OF THE MORAL LAW

CIVILIZATION is always on trial. Sometimes it seems to succeed. Sometimes it seems to fail. There are those who see in the unfolding of human history the carrying out of a divine plan—the march of an inspired progress. There are others who doubt if there be any law of progress, who, matching the present genius of man with that exhibited in the earliest dawn of discovered existence, see nothing but a rise and fall of empires, an alternate broadening and narrowing of culture which leaves man unchanged.

If by this it is meant that man does not change in kind, it is undoubtedly true. Who can say that there is any keener intellect now than that which made the civilization at the confluence of the Tigris and Euphrates, with its transportation, banking, commerce, and public laws five thousand years ago, or raised the pyramids, or wrote the Iliad, or wrought the wondrous forms of beauty in art and literature that have come down from ancient times? So near as we can read it, the history of the world has been alternate light and shadow, in which dark ages have followed golden ages. There have been eras which shine forth with great brilliancy through multitudinous records, and other eras notorious by the absence of recorded achievements. The old saying that there are but

Address at the Community-Chest Dinner, Springfield, Massachusetts, October 11, 1921.

71

three generations from shirt-sleeves to shirt-sleeves, has had its counterpart in the history of nations. A people gather, grow strong under adversity, weaken under prosperity, and fall, first victims of weakness within and then victims of strength without. No one can deny this. Nor need it unduly alarm us.

The American theory of society is founded in part on this condition. It asserts the equality of men. That means equality of kind. All are endowed with the same kind of mind, for it is mind alone that makes man, the capacity to know the truth. That capacity, once it comes into being, does not change. It is the same now as at the dawn of its creation, however it was created. The quality of man with all his glories is a constant factor, but the quantity seems to vary with each individual. To some is given one talent and to some many talents, but each is equal in the fact that he has talent. Some know one truth, others know many truths, but all know the truth. We need not be disturbed then because the possession of intellect has remained constant so far as we can trace man. We need not feel that therefore there has been and will be no progress. If there be a law of progress it will be found in some other direction.

It is not to the advance of knowledge or the development of science that I refer. A stupendous advance has been made even in the last six hundred years, since the time when civilization was confined to a small part of a single hemisphere, supposed the earth was flat, and that it was the centre of the universe. A yet more powerful development of science has been witnessed in the last century, which has gone from steam to radium. In physics

and chemistry, in surgery and medicine, the distance between to-day and the seventeenth century is almost
infinite. Yet the intellectual quality of Shakespeare and
Milton has not been surpassed. The resources of men, the
mechanical power of the world, the influence that comes
in all ways from the possession of wealth, all these are
greater in the present time than in any previous period of
history, notwithstanding the losses of war; but this great
increment does not of itself insure progress. In fact, it
may all be devoted to destruction, was devoted to destruction for more than four years, in which it wrought
more destruction of life and of property than had been
wrought before in all the wars of which there is any au-
thentic record. The increase of knowledge, the development of science, have only given society new weapons with
which it is possible for civilization to commit suicide. So
far as we can see that happened time and again in the
ancient world; they obliterated Carthage with an appalling
completeness, overcame Greece in spite of the brilliancy
of its letters and its arts and the pleading of Demosthenes,
most eloquent of men; they destroyed Rome by the very
weight of the imperialism of her far-flung empire; they
have cast down gigantic Russia to where, apparently, if
she is rescued at all, she must be rescued from without.
By how slight a margin other nations escaped perhaps we
shall never know. Lands under the oppression of despotism crumbled, even if their allies won. Lands under the
inspiration of freedom remained firm, enduring to the end.
Neither shall we know by how wide a margin the cause
of that civilization we represent, under the most tremendous shock that ever shook the world, yet survived. The

great fact is that so far it has survived.   It is ours to say whether it shall survive.

No one can compare society of the twentieth century with that which has gone before without comprehending at once the tremendous differences.   It is true that there have been for many centuries men of as acute intellectual ability, men moved by as high a moral purpose, as any that make up the present world.   There is a significance in their being regarded among primitive peoples as supernatural.   They were thought to be something more than human, or they acted under direct command of the Almighty.   They did not correspond with ordinary experience.   These figures stand out in Old Testament history and the early legends of Greece and Rome.   There are others that stand out in well-authenticated record, leaders and lawgivers like Hammurabi and Moses. There are great captains like Alexander and Cæsar. There are philosophers and thinkers like Aristotle and Lucretius.   There are men of supreme moral quality, outside the Christian faith, like Socrates and Marcus Aurelius.   It is possible to bring a like record almost down to modern times.   But with the exception of a limited few in Athens, in the day of her glory, and still fewer at Rome, in the day of her early power, these men represent no condition of the people.   There is an early ardor of patriotism, a great beauty of literature and art, deep thought and high ideals which will be classic forevermore.   But this does not represent the condition of the people any more than the piety of the Bible represents the condition of the people when it was written.   Their rulers sought instructions from the Oracle of Delphi, or followed the omens they thought were disclosed in the appearance of animals they sacrificed. There was an early freedom, and a type of democracy, later superimposed on a great mass of slaves and dwindling. The individual was without consideration, but the Roman citizen had rights. Finally, authority came to rest not with the people but with the legions. The power of the rich remained, not the just power of service, but the naked power of possessions, while all about was superstition, fear, and slavery of body and of mind. The moral force was gone; with it went intellectual force, and finally the empire itself. Might ruled, and ruled alone.

Then set in those centuries of migration, conquest, and pillage known as the Dark Ages, creating a condition where finally men bartered their liberty for the privilege of existence and security under the system of feudalism. This created a reign of order which is the beginning of progress. Under it men turned their thought to the humanities. For centuries the church frowned on slavery, though the government legalized it. William the Conqueror drove it out of England; but it was not until 1833 that Parliament outlawed it in the colonies. Through this lapse of time men had turned their thoughts both inward and outward. They discovered themselves, and they discovered humanity. What they discovered, the printing-press not only recorded in permanent form but diffused among the people. The Revival of Learning, the Reformation, the victory of Oliver Cromwell and the Glorious Revolution, the establishment of American Independence, the French Revolution, and the Reform Bill of 1832, were great movements by the people themselves. At the least they represented a new assertion of moral power, if not a new moral power itself. Henceforth humanity was pitched in a higher register. If the world had produced no greater intellect it had produced far greater intelligence; if it brought no new moral quality, it brought far greater morality. For the first time the mass of the people, in high places and in low, realized that the moral law was not a mere theory but a practical rule of action. For the first time the people began to live by it, and to require the sanction of its authority.

It is this quality which separates present civilization from all that has gone before. The power of the people, under the modern forms of self-government, increasingly to conform to the sanctions of the moral law, is the direction in which must be found the law of human progress, if it be found at all. It takes little study to be persuaded that this is what has been going on throughout history, with an increasing momentum during the last century. Whether it shall continue, and by what means it shall continue, are the questions eternally before the people.

No American can contemplate his own country without mingled emotions of satisfaction and responsibility. He can see it discovered, just as the Old World was taking on a new life, just as new forces were stirring among men, fitting them to take up the settlement of new lands, which were to be dedicated to a new era. He can see the line of their settlements along the Atlantic coast, long and thin and disconnected. But it was a line of pioneers, not only of discovery and of settlement but pioneers of thought. In the new birth of Europe these men had taken the lead. They never faltered and they never turned back. They sought the New World that they might be free from the customs and traditions which hampered the progress of the Old. To them, for a time, was to be intrusted the preservation of the liberties of the world by the preservation of the moral power of the people. In this great service, performed alike for the salvation of America and of Europe, New England took a most prominent part. The English historian, John Richard Green, declares that: "In education and political activity New England stood far ahead of its fellow colonies, for the settlement of the Puritans had been followed at once by the establishment of a system of local schools, which is still the glory of America. 'Every township' it was enacted, 'after the Lord has increased them to the number of fifty householders, shall appoint one to teach all children to write and read; and when any town shall increase to the number of one hundred families, they shall set up a grammar-school.'" This clearly states both a fact and a reason. They led in the determination to live by the moral law. That meant freedom. That meant education. For those were the just portion due to that all-important being, man, rediscovered in the new birth of Europe.

This was the prologue of that strongest and most permanent of all assertions of the right of men to be free, the Constitution of the United States of America, supported by the determined loyalty of the American people.

Under this that thin and disconnected line along the eastern coast has crossed the continent. The few weak settlers, the struggling colonies have become a great nation. It saved freedom from the hand of impending des-

potism in 1776 and in 1917. Had the first been lost, where
would have been the power of sacrifice by which the last
was won?

Dedicated to this high purpose, America has marched
on. There is her glorious history. There is her progress.
There is her prosperity. There is the wonderful organization of her government, perfected in its ultimate decisions to reflect the will of the people. There is her system of education, developed in accordance with the public
schools established in Massachusetts in 1647. There is
her transportation, superior to that of any other country.
There is her banking organization, richer than any other
on earth. There is her commerce, which flows to the
world markets. There is her industrial plant, superior to
that of any place or time. There is her agriculture, vast
beyond the imagination to comprehend. At the end of
the most exhausting of wars, which left the great nations
of the earth prostrate, our country finds itself burdened,
but still erect, still able from current resources to meet
current expense. All these are but the reflection of the
genius, not of a select few but of a wonderful people,
great in intelligence, great in moral power, great in character.

The trial which the civilization of America is to meet
does not lie in adversity. It lies in prosperity. It will
not be in a lack of power, but in the purpose directing the
use of great power. There is new danger in our very
greatness. There are all the old dangers in our incompleteness. It is impossible to overlook our imperfections.
The war has greatly diminished the substance of some
and greatly increased the substance of many. It has al-

ready given a new tongue to envy. Without doubt it will give a new grasp to greed.

In a land of schools there is a vast amount of illiteracy. Surrounded by luxury there is a wide fringe of degradation and poverty. In spite of surpassing agricultural production, there are those who lack food, and amid a flood of commerce there are those who lack clothing and shelter. Notwithstanding the wide range of industry there are those who lack employment. With all the light that comes from learning and religion, with all the deterrent power of organized society, there is still an appalling amount of vice and crime. There is no lack of those who, seeing but this side of the picture, say civilization has already failed. It has not failed, as any one can see who looks at history. It must be supported and continued. It cannot be preserved without effort, and it is not yet done. The work must go on. As society grows more complicated, as civilization advances, the burden of its support is not less; it is more. It was never so great as now. Society in America is in a healthy state of progress, but it cannot go alone; it must be supported.

There is always a tendency to point to the great business of the country, its wealth and intelligence, and say that economic laws will run their course and provide a final adjustment. They would, but these are not enough, never have been enough, and would not give the result we require. The foundations of civilization do not rest alone on economic laws. Human progress must be paid for, but it cannot be bought. The patricians of declining Rome thought they could protect themselves from uprisings at home and invasions from abroad with legions filled with Gauls and Numidians, and other barbarian tribesmen. They found protection could not be purchased, and, beset within and without, the civilization they represented perished. Last month, in a case which almost escaped notice, the Supreme Judicial Court of Massachusetts announced a principle of great importance. "Mere intellectual power," the decision runs, "and scientific achievement, without uprightness of character, may be more harmful than ignorance. Highly trained intelligence combined with disregard of the fundamental virtues is a menace." America has not sought to purchase protection with mercenaries. When the call came Americans went themselves. They did not send. But there is in our land to-day a great mass yet to be won to the American ways of thought. Uprightness of character and the fundamental virtues prevail, but the very ease of existence leads many to disregard their laws. Nor is the application of blind justice enough.

"Use every man after his desert, and who should 'scape whipping?"

There is another element on which progress depends and without which it cannot go on. We need wealth and science and justice in human relationship, but redemption comes only through sacrifice. There is no other process that can sustain civilization; no other law of progress. If we make any headway against the perils of society it will be by that process, and that process alone. Let justice and the economic laws be applied to the strong; but for the weak there must be mercy and charity; not the gratuity which pauperizes, but the assistance which restores. That, too, is justice.

The ideals which are derived from the higher education come from college and university. They were founded by charity. The beliefs for which men have been willing to suffer martyrdom come from religion, the greatest charity of all. Ideals and beliefs determine the whole course of society.

When there has been failure it has meant that there was no longer sacrifice made to secure success. Selfishness defeated itself. That has been the malady of every empire that has fallen, from Babylon to Russia. Where there has been success it has meant that there sacrifice has prevailed. That has been the salvation of every people, from early civilization to the present day. America was laid in the sacrifices of Pilgrim and Puritan and the colonists of that day. It was defended by the sacrifices of the Revolutionary period. It was made all free by the sacrifices of those who followed Lincoln, and insured by all who accept him. It was saved by the sacrifices of the World War.

These are the great charities of man on which civilization has rested. They cannot be administered by government. They come from the heart of the people or they do not come at all. They are for the redemption of man. There is no other. Civilization is always on trial, testing out, not the power of material resources, but whether there be, in the heart of the people, that virtue and character which come from charity sufficient to maintain progress. When that charity fails, civilization, though it "speak with the tongues of men and of angels," is "become as sounding brass or a tinkling cymbal." Its glory has departed. Its spirit has gone out. Its life is done.

X

Titles to nobility cannot be granted or seized. They can only be achieved. They come through service, as yours came, or they do not come at all. If men in civil life, in these days of peace, would put their thought and effort into the success of the people of the whole country, as in military life you put your thought and effort, in time of war, into the success of the whole army, the victories of peace would follow as surely as did the victories of war.

THE TITLE OF AMERICAN

THE Legion holds, by righteous conquest, the title of American. There was never reposed in any other military force the proud distinction of so completely representing the whole nation. It is notorious that the people of the colonies were divided. Many of their number, of most respectable attainments and most unquestioned character, doubted the wisdom of the patriot cause. When the Revolution became victorious they left by scores of thousands, or remained silent but unconvinced. In the War of 1812, with its strange commingling of the most ignominious defeats with the most brilliant victories, both by land and sea, there was grave lack of popular approval, which in some sections bordered on open resistance. The war with Mexico was widely criticised. Abraham Lincoln, while withholding no note of support for the army in the field, violently denounced the motives which brought on the conflict. The war between the States needs but to be named to show the complete division of two sections of our people, which even the war with Spain did not completely reunite. The opportunity to make this nation one, the sacrifice which made this nation one, was of your day alone. All the streams of that great spirit are gathered up in you. You represent a new national consciousness. You represent the consummation of those great forces, coming into action in the early days

At the Convention of the American Legion, Kansas City, Missouri, October 31, 1921.

of this century, which not only made America more American, but made humanity more humane. The hope of this nation, which more than ever before corresponds with the hope of the world, lies in your power to minister to that spirit, to preserve that consciousness, and to increase those forces.

You saw the mighty urge of all these causes which began on July 28, 1914, and culminated on November 11, 1918. When the Great War broke on an unsuspecting world, few people in Europe, and fewer still on this side of the Atlantic, understood it. Stunned by its reported atrocities, we were principally interested in keeping out of what we believed was no concern of ours. There were those who recognized that it was an attack on all that was represented by our civilization, who declared from the outset that it was an American war, and urged an immediate preparation for a victorious defense. Denounced in official quarters, looked on as jeopardizers of peace, they went, for the most part, unheeded. But there came a day when the violation of our rights, the loss of our property, the destruction of the lives of our citizens, and the assertion that these were to continue left no choice but to declare that all this constituted the making of war upon our country, and that force must be resisted with force.

To meet the requirements of that situation it is scarcely too much to say that the American people presented themselves at the altar of their country with the offering of their every dollar and their every life. The flame of patriotism swept over the whole land, consuming away the dross of all past differences, and fusing the entire people into one common national unity. The army and navy, forever unmatched among men, born of this new spirit; the money with which it filled the treasury; the gigantic charities which it supported; the stupendous and unending flood of all kinds of supplies that it created; the victory that it made possible—these are now known to all the world.   All this gave a new meaning to the life of our country, a new meaning which found its finest expression in a new nationalism, deeper and more fervid than ever before, summed up in one word, American. As the months have passed, as public opinion has found expression, it is more and more evident that the people fought in self-defense; they fought to preserve America, and in that sacrifice found a new life.

The tremendous contribution which our military forces made to this new national spirit can never be overestimated.   There were those who saw our country enter the war with great regret.   They were willing to sacrifice the undoubted rights of our citizens to the maintenance of peace.   There were those who opposed sending an army overseas.   They were critical of the purpose of the government.   But when once our navy reached the scene of conflict, when once our soldiers and marines were in France, all regret and all criticism ceased in the most loyal support ever given by a people to their forces in the field. Devotion to you and your comrades removed all discord, and out of the intensity of that same devotion was created a new conception of the responsibility and dignity of citizenship and a new national spirit.   When the results of winning the war are considered, this stands out most prominently, and for it, as for victory, the chief credit must go to those who bore arms.

This may not be the ultimate result, but it is the
result up to this time, and if it become fixed in the
life of the nation it is worth all it cost.   There may be
other steps to take, but this one had to be taken first,
for without that unity of purpose that comes from an intense national spirit there can be no permanent progress,
no promotion of our domestic welfare, no service to the
world.

It is because the American Legion stands in a position,
by its broad and representative membership, by its common experience and common sacrifice, which no other organization can occupy that it holds the greatest hope for
the maintenance of a true national spirit.

When we consider the service that you and your comrades performed, the stupendous scale of the operations,
the wide-reaching results, the courage and devotion constantly displayed, that you saved America and doing it
saved the world, we realize something of the gratitude
that is your due, something of the glory that you have
won.   Your countrymen will ever hold these among their
choicest treasures.

There are some things that can wait.   Others perish in
the waiting.   The most commanding duty that resulted
from the war was the proper relief of all incapacitated
veterans.   This the last administration attempted to do.
The task was large and new.   It required law and organization.   A generous beginning was made, but the work
lagged.   There is nothing closer to the heart of President
Harding than making this relief absolutely complete.   No
man not in the service has a deeper appreciation of what
that service meant, of the sacrifice made by the veterans,

of the obligations incurred by the country; and no man will go farther to minister to the true welfare of those who have been in the service, and their dependents, than the President of the United States. He will never sacrifice you for his own welfare. He will sacrifice himself for your welfare. He will do all that can be done to prevent the need of your again sacrificing yourselves for your country's welfare.

I know that you are well aware that your glory lies in what you have given, and may give, to your country, not in what your country has or may give to you. But a country which is worth defending takes care of its defenders. You have a right to a report of what your country is doing for your comrades. All relief has been reorganized and consolidated in one department, under a new law passed on the recommendation of the Legion. The Veterans' Bureau and the agencies now included in it, up to October 1 have paid $71,000,000 for medical and hospital services, $267,000,000 for compensation, $254,000,000 for insurance awards, $582,000,000 for allotments and allowances, $171,000,000 for vocational education. The amount disbursed by this Bureau in September was $34,237,000. This reaches a total of $1,345,000,000, about one-third of all pensions paid by the government from its beginning up to our entry into the World War.

The yearly expenditures of the Veterans' Bureau are running at the rate of about $411,000,000, which is more than one-half the entire expense of the government before this war.

Every effort is being made to avoid delay in passing on

claims. There have been established 14 district offices, and 140 suboffices, for the presentation and determination of compensation and insurance awards. Late in April there were 200,000 claims pending before the War Risk Insurance Bureau. About 150,000 of these have been adjudicated. Except in cases of dispute, each application secures immediate determination. Out of about 975,000 requested medical examinations there are less than 30,000 claims now awaiting review by the medical department. This includes claims which are up on appeal and which were reopened by the generous provisions of the new law. Seven thousand new hospital beds have been supplied, bringing the total up to 26,750. There is money available and construction is under way which will provide 6,000 additional beds, all under government operation. There are at the present time about 6,000 vacant beds in government-controlled institutions. One of the most promising efforts of rehabilitation has been the establishment of a university at Camp Sherman, Ohio, which will provide an academic, commercial, industrial, and agricultural course. Some idea of the tremendous activities of the Veterans' Bureau can be gained when it is remembered that there are now:

29,000 men in hospitals,
207,000 monthly awards of compensation are being paid,
140,000 monthly awards of insurance are being paid,
636,000 men are carrying insurance,
$4,000,000,000 of insurance is in force,
1,200 insurance claims are received per month,

17,000 compensation claims are received per month,
93,000 men are receiving vocational training.

It is the most cherished ambition of President Harding
that there may be no veteran or dependent anywhere
within our country entitled by law to relief who shall
not be able, promptly and adequately, to secure it.   This
is not done with any purpose of undertaking to pay for
that which is priceless, but of undertaking to discharge
the most solemn obligation which comes to any government.

You represent every part of this nation, every activity
of its citizens.   It was under your inspiring example that
the two greatest obstacles to our full national life were
destroyed—sectionalism and class consciousness.   The
war was won because each section of our nation, and each
class of our citizens contributed its full strength to a
common cause.   The nearly five millions distributed over
the entire country, representing in so great a degree the
entire people and their entire interests, cannot be divorced
from the public welfare.   Whatever works injury to any
of the great activities of the land works injury to them;
whatever contributes to the general prosperity contributes
to their prosperity.   They are, at once, the man-power
and the material power of the nation.   They not only
take the field but supply the public treasury.

The prosperity and welfare—yes, more than that, the
righteousness—of our country lies in the service which one
section can render to another.   The East found success
in building railroads, opening mines, and developing the
resources of the West; the West found success in feeding

the people and supplying the raw products for the factories of the East; the North finds success in the sale of its manufactures in the South; the South finds success in supplying the North with the production of her plantations. This is not competition but co-operation. Fundamentally this process is right. It is the law of service. Practically it should continue because it is the only means to success and prosperity. There is no path to permanent prosperity and success which narrowly excludes any section.

It is always easier to think of the part than of the whole. It is easier for men to remember that they work at the plough, the forge, the drill, the spindle, the bench, the desk, or that they follow transportation, the law, medicine, banking, or the ministry than it is to remember that into the life of every man there goes a part of all these activities, and many more, and that whatever his occupation, each is a part of the whole nation, and that the permanent prosperity of each will stand or fall with the permanent prosperity of the whole. No man is wise enough, no combination is strong enough, to transgress this law and long escape its penalties. All artificial privilege always has and always will destroy itself. The law of service is a law of action. No artifice can long circumvent it; no fraud can long cheat it. The United States Constitution is right. Titles to nobility cannot be granted or seized. They can only be achieved. They come through service, as yours came, or they do not come at all. If men in civil life, in these days of peace, would put their thought and effort into the success of the people of the whole country, as in military life you put your thought and effort, in time of war, into the success of the whole army, the victories of peace would follow as surely as did the victories of war. Government and industry, locality and society, all need the national outlook you so proudly achieved. It is time in every activity in our land, for men in every relationship, to stop trying to get the better of each other and begin trying to serve each other.

Under these circumstances, considering the great sacrifice you represent, and the great stake you have in the country, it is small wonder that you not only exemplify patriotism in your own actions, but insist, as you have a right to insist, on patriotic action in others. You have great patience with ignorance and weakness, but no patience at all with any informed and powerful attempt to make a mockery of our institutions, defy the execution of our laws, and violate the rights of our citizens. But in resisting all attacks upon our liberty, you will always remember that the sole guarantee of liberty is obedience to law under the forms of ordered government. The observance of the law is the function of every private citizen, but the execution of the law is the function only of duly constituted public authorities.

The last act has been closed in that war which, with the help of your efforts, was brought to a complete victory. A treaty of peace between the United States and the German Empire, made for the purpose "of restoring the friendly relations" formerly existing between the two nations, negotiated late in August, 1920, ratified by both countries, now awaits only the proclamation of the President of the United States. This treaty expressly reserves to the United States both the rights acquired under the Armistice, signed on that historic date of November 11, 1918, and those rights provided by the Treaty of Versailles. Generally speaking, it grants to the United States all of the privileges which it would have gained had it ratified the former treaty, and imposes none of the obligations, exclusive of all consideration of the rights and duties proposed by the Covenant of the League of Nations. This has brought to a formal close the greatest of all human conflicts. Having accepted it, it becomes our duty to observe not only its letter but its spirit. The position which our country holds in its relationship abroad is shown by the experience of our army on the Rhine. There is every indication that it desires to remain there; it is reported that England and France wish for its continuance, and that most of all Germany is earnestly solicitous that it shall not be withdrawn. The occupation of this army appears to be complete.

But, though the war be done, its results, for good and for all, remain. Its exactions have not yet all been met, nor have its benefits yet all been realized.

There has been appropriated for the support of the National Government for the current political year, approximately, four billions of dollars. Of this amount one and a third billion is on account of the war debt; more than a quarter of a billion goes to pay pensions of previous wars; three-quarters of a billion is required to maintain our present military establishment for our protection on land and on sea. The relief work administered by the Veterans' Bureau reaches nearly one-half billion more. This means that the current cost of previous and prospective wars is two and five-sixths billions, while the cost of the nation's peace activities is one and one-sixth billions. There are considerable expected savings on these amounts, but the proportion will not be greatly changed. This is a burden nearly six times as great as that which was necessary for the nation to bear prior to the war. It exacts a tribute, directly or indirectly, of about forty dollars from every inhabitant of our country, or about two hundred dollars from the average family. This enormous expenditure the public cannot evade, and cannot shift. It must be met. No one who has observed the diminishing returns from taxation, the acute depression which overtook all business and which has become prominently acute in agriculture, can fail to realize that every possible relief must be sought and applied.

All this is a mighty obligation even for a great people of great wealth. There is no present service that can be performed for those who have so unselfishly and so gloriously sacrificed themselves in the service, or for their dependents, or for the country at large, which in a peculiar and a sacred sense is their country, so important, so considerate of their welfare, so calculated to discharge a part of the great debt which is their due, as to reduce these obligations, reduce the great drain upon the resources of the people which will restore the nation to a state of prosperity, not for an hour or a day, but a lasting and a permanent prosperity for all. This means that economy that comes from a consciousness of peace.

Our own national existence presupposes the national existence of others. Were there no other countries there would be no choice between countries, and therefore no loyalty to one to the exclusion of others, no patriotism. That virtue we claim for ourselves we must recognize in others. If it be well for America to have a strong national spirit, it must be well for others to cherish the same sentiment. The war did not break this spirit; in any free country it strengthened it, strengthened it for the glory of all. America first is not selfishness; it is the righteous demand for strength to serve. And America has been dedicated to an unselfish service. I weigh my words when I say that both in Europe and in the Orient that service for humanity has not been exceeded by any other nation. It will not be, then, in diminishing but in enlarging the national spirit that true progress for the race will be found. There can be no society without a home, no civilization without citizenship.

But, as a true national spirit calls for a harmonious adjustment of the relationship between all the sections and all the people in the nation, so it calls for a harmonious relationship between the different nations. This is the spiritual lesson of the war.

The work of Washington was not finished at Yorktown, the work of Lincoln was not completed at Appomattox; they live in our institutions, one in the Constitution which his efforts caused to be adopted, the other in the amendments which his sacrifice caused to be ratified. Your work was not all done on the sea or on the fields of France.

In recognition of the solemn obligation to you and to your countrymen of economy and peace, a conference of certain Great Powers, called on the initiative of the President of the United States, is about to assemble at

Washington. It proposes to search for a solution of problems arising from the convergence of many different nations in the Pacific and to provide, by mutual agreement, for a limitation of armaments. I do not understand that this means that any nation is to divest itself of the power to resist domestic violence or suffer any diminution of independence, but out of mutual understandings the great burden, and it may be the menace, of competitive armaments may be removed. That is a new expression of a great hope, all the greater because it seeks the practical. It proposes something that America can do at home. It surrenders no right, it imposes no burden, it promises relief at home and a better understanding abroad. If it be accomplished its blessings will be reflected at every fireside in the land. The economic pressure of government will be lifted, the hope of a righteous and abiding peace will be exalted.

The hour is still with the veterans of the war. The power, but also the responsibility, not only of citizenship, but of inspiring leadership is theirs. Their work goes on. In its process there is no room for discouragement. Steadily, silently, but irresistibly the great principles for which their imperishable sacrifices were made are prevailing over the face of the earth. They have not only overcome the sword of resistance, they have convinced the mind. If anywhere opposing views are held, it is in sullen silence; they dare not be openly declared by any government. They have at once proclaimed a new America, and thereby a new world, to be made secure in mutual understanding and in righteous conduct.

XI

All the elaborate functions of the government will be of no avail, unless there abide in the people the simple, homely virtues of industry and thrift, honesty and charity. Without these characteristics there can be no advance in the general effectiveness of the government or the general welfare of the people. All of our natural resources, all of our attempted industrial organization, all of our guarantees of freedom will avail nothing without the support of character. There can be no national greatness which does not rest upon the personal integrity of the people.

OUR HERITAGE FROM HAMILTON

WE may not know the source of greatness. We do not need to know. But when once it is revealed, we disregard it at our peril. To the uncivilized all things are common. The measure of the strength and the enlightenment of a people is the measure of their appreciation of their great men, their devotion to their memory and the defense of the institutions which they have established. When the reverence of this nation for its great men dies, the glory of the nation will die with it. While that reverence lives, the glory of the nation will live.

It was in that spirit that this club was formed, by men conscious of the obligation due to the memory of a great man, and thereby the obligation due to themselves and to their country. Civilization and progress depend upon the genius of the people themselves, but that genius depends to a large extent upon the ability to perceive and accept leadership. The great man is he who can express the unuttered opinions of his time, direct energy along profitable channels, divine the spirit of the people, and unify action under just and stable institutions of government. Such a man was Alexander Hamilton. When America ceases to remember his greatness, America will be no longer great.

He lived in the age which not only established the in-

Address on the anniversary of the birthday of Alexander Hamilton, before the Hamilton Club, at Chicago, January 11, 1922.

dependence of our country, one of the most remarkable
of achievements, but also saw the adoption of the Federal
Constitution and provided an economic system. These
gave this nation liberty, order, and prosperity. His fame
rests on the deep influence which he had in producing
these results.

The place of Washington in history is secure. He
stands as a world figure. He ranks as a great captain, a
foremost statesman, and the supreme patriot. Without
him it is difficult to comprehend how independence could
have been won. Holding at all times the complete affection of all his soldiers and the highest confidence of his
fellow countrymen, his approval aided greatly in the
adoption of the Constitution, his honesty opposed any
repudiation of the debts of his country, and his character
gave to the office of the presidency a position and influence which contributed greatly to stability in the formative period of our government. But along with Washington goes Hamilton, neither none the less great because
their talents mutually increased the success and greatness of each other.

That service together, which has set its mark upon the
world, began in the summer of 1776, when the young captain of artillery was presented to the commander-in-
chief of the Continental Army. Becoming soon after
his aide and military secretary, he contributed to the remarkable quality of the despatches and letters of his chief.
This intimacy, thus begun in the field, continued almost
without interruption until broken by death. Some of
the most important accomplishments of constructive
statesmanship made for the welfare of his country, Ham-

ilton made in his different posts as secretary under Washington.

He stayed in the army from that day in 1776 until after he had captured the first redoubt in the charge at Yorktown. But it was as an administrator and statesman rather than as a soldier that he was destined to render his most distinguished services to the cause of civil liberty.

The most conspicuous talent of this great man lay in his ability to put principles into practical effect. He carried in his mind the vision of a powerful nation. Patrick Henry had declared, years before, that he was no longer a Virginian but an American. But when the time came to realize that vision to the full, Henry let it fade away while Hamilton transformed it into the enduring form of our Federal Union.

If there be one principle for which he contended with more vigor than another it is the principle of integrity in governmental affairs. He saw not only the great practical value but the supreme moral requirement of meeting obligations.

Terms of peace were concluded after the war, which provided for a just treatment of those who had adhered to the British cause. There soon arose criminations and recriminations in relation to the observance of this treaty. Notwithstanding its provisions Tories were badly used, practically denied the administration of justice, and visited with the confiscation of their property. This went on until Hamilton, not only in his capacity as a lawyer but in recognition of his own and the public obligation to abide by the solemn covenants of a treaty, accepted the cause of one of the Loyalists and successfully enforced his rights in court. Laws and treaties meant to him not only a declaration engrossed on parchment but a rule of action which required performance. Later he carried this principle over into his dealings with the debt of his country.

In common with his countrymen he saw the confusion and disorder which followed the war. He saw the disposition for repudiation of both private contracts and public debt. He saw the disorder of such an uprising as Shays's Rebellion in Massachusetts, the economic disaster which followed the issue of great amounts of paper money through State agencies, the paralysis alike of credit and trade, and the entire impotence of the central government.

He recognized that the one remedy for disaster at home and humiliation abroad lay in a central government intrusted with sovereign powers. Whether or not he was the first to suggest a convention to propose a form for such a government, he was one of the most instrumental in bringing it about. In that convention he took a conspicuous part. He had a great love for liberty, and desired that it might be perpetuated as the heritage of his countrymen. He had a faith in the people which carried him beyond their expression of the mere passion and fancy of the hour, giving him the insight and courage to appeal to their calmer selves and to depend upon their deep and abiding convictions. He believed in a representative government, Republican in form, provided with checks and balances. "Give all power to the many, and they will oppress the few," he said. "Give all power to the few and they will oppress the many. Both, therefore, are to have the power that each may defend itself against the other."

No concourse of men assembled to promote the art of government ever attained a position which this convention is entitled to hold in the estimation of the American people. Justly, since that day they have been termed the Fathers. The result was our Federal Constitution, since aptly described as the most remarkable document ever struck off by the hand of man at a given time.

When the Constitution was submitted to the States for ratification, to defend its provisions, expound its meaning, and urge its ratification, Hamilton prepared the large part of those masterly essays on government which, when collected, became known as "The Federalist." Great as was this accomplishment, it was surpassed by his achievement in the New York convention. At its inception it was more than two to one against the Constitution. Yet by his persuasive and enlightened arguments, Hamilton secured the ratification of the Constitution. There is no more remarkable victory in parliamentary history. The ratification of the Constitution by a sufficient number of States soon followed. There was at last in existence a Federal Government which was founded on national integrity.

In the affairs of a nation, especially of a free people, no one man is ever entitled to all the credit of a great accomplishment. But when it is recalled that it was the genius of Hamilton that conceived of a national government, that he played a leading part in the framing of the Constitution which established that government, that he was the chief author of the arguments by which it was commended to the several States for ratification, it appears probable that without him the American nation would not have come into being. This were distinction enough to give any man an important place in history. But there lay before him services which it is hard to say were not of equal importance.

When Washington was chosen President he made Hamilton the first secretary of the treasury. His tremendous task was to provide for funding the national debt, establish the public credit, and provide for the government revenue. He insisted upon the assumption alike of the debts of the old Confederacy and of the several States which had been contracted in the prosecution of the war, both foreign and domestic. Nine years before he had sent two memorandums to Robert Morris, concerning the establishment of a national bank. As an incident to the collection of the nation's revenue and the carrying out of its fiscal policy, he finally secured the establishment of such a bank. Although not specifically provided for in the Constitution, he justified it on a theory of implied powers which he developed, arguing that what the Constitution had provided should be done, necessarily warranted the inference that the Federal Government had power to create all instruments necessary and desirable for doing it. This was a wise and profound theory of the Constitution, which transformed it from a dead parchment into a vital fabric. In addition to these purely fiscal operations of the government, Hamilton made a great contribution to political economy in his "Report on Manufactures." He considered the establish-

ment of these first of all a national policy through which
his country might secure economic integrity. It was in
this document that he developed his theory of protection.
While statesmen have recognized perhaps more and more
the difficulty of putting this theory into practice, yet, on
the other hand, experience has more and more demonstrated the soundness of the principles.

He believed in protection in the first place as a means
of national defense. He desired his country to be self-
sustaining and self-sufficient. He wished to encourage
manufactures in order that no hostile force should ever
be able to deprive the country of "the means of subsis-
tence, habitation, clothing and defense." After national
defense he advocated protection as the method by which
the nation would increase its power to produce wealth.
In a diversification of industry he saw an enlarged productive power. But beyond these material benefits of
protection he sought to confer upon his countrymen the
spiritual benefits which he believed would accrue. He
knew that diversification would call forth more energy,
more effort, and more of the spirit of enterprise. No one
would deny that there have been instances where rates
have been excessive and the policy of protection has been
abused, where selfish interests have unduly profited and
where provincial minds have seen in the tariff only a local
issue; but this is neither the principle nor the application
of the protective theory of Hamilton, which stands to-day
almost as the accepted doctrine of the world.

He had no delusions, however, about the fact that commerce consists of a mutual exchange of merchandise. He
saw the folly of attempting, as he expressed it, to "sacri-

fice the interests of a mutually beneficial intercourse to the vain project of selling everything and buying nothing."

The prevailing activity of his day was agricultural. Though he was reporting on manufactures, he had that interest steadily in mind. His vision always comprehended the whole situation. "It is evident," he said, "that the exertions of the husbandman will be steady or fluctuating, vigorous or feeble, in proportion to the steadiness or fluctuation, adequateness, or inadequateness of the markets on which he must depend for the vent of the surplus which may be produced by his labor. . . . To secure such a market there is no other expedient than to promote manufacturing establishments." And he added another great truth: "The aggregate prosperity of manufactures and the aggregate prosperity of agriculture are intimately connected."

This is the great heritage which Hamilton bequeathed to his countrymen. It is a legacy in which every American has a share. He did not make his appeal to the more ordinary and common motives of human action, which characterized the appeal of Jefferson. He did not trust so implicitly in the popular side of our institutions. He did not realize so thoroughly that whatever forms of government have been provided, whatever economic system has been adopted, that however great and necessary these contributions may have been, the liberty, good order, prosperity, and the moral and spiritual condition of the people depend upon themselves. His great contribution was in providing the means by which these results might be secured. The disposition to ignore or to adopt these means can only be determined by the people themselves.

He had faith that they would make the right choice. That faith has been justified. When great tests have come, when supreme choices have been made, the American people have always stood with Washington, with Hamilton, and with Marshall.

The party now in power in this country, through its present declaration of principles, through the traditions which it inherited from its predecessors, the Federalists and the Whigs, through their achievements and through its own, is representative of those policies which were adopted under the lead of Alexander Hamilton. They are the parties which have kept steadily in view the Union, and the whole Union. They cherished it through the necessary compromises of Henry Clay. They supported it through the wise and patient statesmanship of Abraham Lincoln. Without their vision the Union would never have been formed. Without their sacrifice it would not have been preserved.

No one speaks of dissolving the Union now. Its necessary advantages, supplemented by that true spirit of loyalty, make such an appeal impossible. Yet such proposals have their counterpart in those who, while remaining in the Union, selfishly undertake to escape bearing their share of its burdens and rendering due allegiance to its laws. This sometimes appears in the form of sectionalism, sometimes in an attempted class distinction. I do not object to sectionalism because through its action there might be worked an injury to that part of the country in which I live; I do not object to alleged class distinctions because thereby that class to which I should be presumed to belong might suffer harm; I object to them because,

by whatever section or class they may be exhibited, they
are an injury and a menace to my country; they are narrowing and withering, undertaking to substitute a temporary advantage for the permanent welfare. They are
bound to end in destruction. When a people begin to
cherish plans for anything save the common welfare, the
decay of that country has begun. No party can survive
which does not minister to national integrity.

As the inheritors of those principles which saved the
young republic from repudiation in its weakness and infancy, we saved it again in its strength and maturity from
the attempt at repudiation through the issues of green-
backs in the 1870's, and from the delusions of free silver in
the 1890's. Our country at the present time is going
through a period of deflation, apparently completed, and
through a period of retrenchment in public expenditures,
both against the opposition of those who were under the
misapprehension that they could reap profit out of an
unsound condition, and that the country could continue
to afford to do through the public treasury what it could
not afford to do through private enterprise. While no
one at the moment is advocating unsound money, there
has been no lack of advocates of unsound credit and unsound prices. Inflation is repudiation. Deflation is assumption. The one undertakes to suspend economic law,
and the other undertakes to support it. Either the nation had to bring down the burden, or the burden would
bring down the nation. It is the policy of the Republican
party, in so far as it can influence conditions, to re-establish financial stability. Like everything which is of value
it could not have been had unless we were willing to pay

the price. On that firm foundation, which it was absolutely necessary should be built, and which has been built with the least possible inconvenience and loss, there is every reason to expect that the country will go forward into an era of prosperity, tempered, of course, by war conditions, like that which followed the liquidation of the early 1890's. The only hope of such a prosperity lies in the establishment of economic integrity.

Commensurate with the work of building up was the work of regulation. There came a time at the beginning of this century when economic freedom was threatened, when great combinations were gaining the power to control the business life of the nation and extending an undue influence over the affairs of the government itself. The open door of opportunity, which had always been the American ideal, was in danger of being closed. Through the enactment of new laws, but more especially through the administration and enforcement of old laws, that danger and that threat were averted. Government control and regulation are still new. They have at times been mistakenly applied. They will need the modification which experience shall demonstrate both of withdrawal and advance; but they have kept open the door, they have re-established freedom. This was again the application of the theory of Hamilton to present conditions, that the government have and use the power necessary for the economic welfare of the country. This doctrine our party still supports and still applies to the business regulations of this republic, not that business may be hampered but that it may be free, not that it may be restricted but that it may expand.

There are those who give great expression to their solicitude for the welfare of the people. Their expressions are, no doubt, sincere, and they may entertain a candid desire to accomplish such a purpose; but the great power of production which diversification of industry has brought about has created a condition of interdependence. There is no such thing as the general welfare of the people in a period of business depression. If those policies are adopted which do all that can be done to produce a business prosperity which follows, there is no power which can prevent such prosperity from being diffused among the people. It is the doctrine of the Republican party to encourage business, not merely for its own sake but because that is the surest method of administering to the general welfare. Those who criticise will be justified in their criticism when they can point out a better way.

Amid the changing conditions of the present day, hampered by the uncertain fluctuations in foreign exchange, confused by those costs of production abroad, which cannot be estimated, nevertheless the party is undertaking to re-establish the ancient and always beneficial policy of protection. It is seeking to give it the quality of elasticity that it may be administered in accordance with duly ascertained facts. It will undertake to be a national tariff under which different groups will profit in accordance with duly ascertained facts. It will undertake to be a national tariff under which different groups will profit in accordance with what such action will contribute to the national welfare. It will undertake to be a tariff under which the individual will benefit whenever such benefit would accrue to the common good. While the manufacturer might appear to benefit most in the first instance because he comes into direct competition with foreign production, if the theory of Hamilton be sound the indirect benefit to agriculture will be as large, if not larger. The products of agriculture are consumed by the industrial population. They are the customers of the farmer. If they be prosperous, his markets will grow. On the other hand, the great outlet for manufactured products is on the farm. A prosperous state of agriculture is the foundation of all national prosperity. The manufacturer must look to the farmer not only for his supply of food but for the sale of his commodities. Not in trying to overreach each other, but in putting forth their effort to assist each other, each will find a common salvation.

The ancient power of leadership has not left the republic, the wisdom and statesmanship of those who contributed to its beginnings and supported its continuation are with us yet. The old American spirit lives again in President Harding. Conscious of the burdens which are borne by his countrymen, solicitous for their prompt and effective relief, meeting new occasions with new remedies, rising to new heights as he advances, he is administering the affairs of our country with courage, with resource, with decision, and with a patriotic devotion that is fine and true. The nation looks to him with affection and follows him with admiration.

Hamilton was a soldier not by profession but to accomplish a specific purpose. He was ever a firm advocate of national defense. He laid down the theory of neutrality, not the neutrality of a nation suffering impositions through its weakness, but the neutrality of a nation commanding respect through its strength. He never sought military glory for himself or for his country. His fame does not rest on plans for military conquest. It rests on a firm, secure, and permanent foundation of sound government and economic development. No one can doubt that he desired pre-eminence for his country, but it was the pre-eminence which was to be won not through military aggrandizement but through the example of economic service and enlightened liberty.

The nation has attained that diversification of industry which was the vision of Hamilton. How wisely he built it, how successful were his plans is demonstrated by the gigantic resources of our country. In many important products and fabrics our output exceeds that of all the rest of the earth combined. We have attained a world pre-eminence, an unsurpassed agricultural, industrial, and economic strength. It was not merely the courage of the soldiers or the military skill of their commanders, but the enormous unit production of our manufacturing establishments, which won the war. That fervid enterprise, that intellectual ardor, that comprehensive grasp, which Hamilton so successfully sought to call into being, is known the world over as the American spirit.

But it is not merely through economic grandeur that the Republican party desires to see this nation serve itself and serve mankind. Unsupported by a moral grandeur all this glory fades away. Unless these resources can be so administered that they increase the material and spiritual welfare of the people, their accumulation has been in vain. All the elaborate functions of the government will be of no avail, unless there abide in the people the simple, homely virtues of industry and thrift, honesty and charity. Without these characteristics there can be no advance in the general effectiveness of the government or the general welfare of the people. All of our natural resources, all of our attempted industrial organization, all of our guarantees of freedom will avail nothing without the support of character. There can be no national greatness which does not rest upon the personal integrity of the people.

Great powers bring great responsibilities. We are no longer, as in the days of the fathers, suppliants, depending for our national existence in part upon the jealous rivalries of others. We stand forth independent of all except ourselves. We are advancing toward a new leadership among the peoples of the earth, which must be promoted not by our power to take but by our power to bestow. That same moral grandeur which has been the national ideal in our domestic relations is being made the ideal of our foreign relations. We are the first great nation which ever submitted an authoritative and responsible proposal for the voluntary reduction and limitation of the armed power to coerce. We are the first to secure the consent of the representatives of the great nations to such limitations. It is the record of history that nations follow their interests. We shall follow ours. But the highest interests of our nation lie not in promoting a desire for war but in promoting the arts of peace. Conscious of her strength, serene in her security, rejoicing in her duty, rising to the inspiring vision of Hamilton, America is coming to the position of a nation which:

"Doth not behave itself unseemly, seeketh not her own, is not easily provoked, thinketh no evil;

"Rejoiceth not in iniquity, but rejoiceth in the truth;

"Beareth all things, believeth all things, hopeth all things, endureth all things," and "never faileth."

XII

Whenever men look upon his life, they are filled with a new wonder. About him there was never any needless thing. No useless burdens held him back. No wilderness of tangled ideas bewildered his vision. For him the outward show of the world was cast aside that he might be a larger partaker of reality. His cradle was bare, but above it was the precious canopy of the love of a gentle mother. When she was borne away in his early boyhood, he had learned the great lesson that all this world is mortal. From his youth he knew that anguish is the common lot of mankind. In his rearing there was no false art. Like the strengthening of his body, the strengthening of his mind came from great Nature.

THE PLACE OF LINCOLN

WE see in great men a brighter gleam of the Infinite. Unto them is given the power to show forth to their fellow man not only what he longs to be but what he is. They are the means by which the people raise themselves to a new and higher order of nobility. They see. They do. They inspire. In the greatness of Lincoln the people of this nation are lifted up to their own greatness. As they looked on him they beheld their better selves. They felt with him the bond of a common spirit. He was Father Abraham. They loved him. They followed him. They knew that through his life they came unto a larger knowledge of the truth.

Men long have hallowed this day. It brought into the world the miracle of a new life. But it was far more than his nativity. Held within the many great meanings it would come to have was the answer to the prayer which his life made, "that this nation under God may have a new birth of freedom." On this day was born a man that a nation might be reborn.

To some men there are given a few great moments in life, while all the rest is commonplace. Lincoln had his great moments, for "he grew in stature and in wisdom," but he was never commonplace. He was marked by a solemn grandeur from the rude and lonely hut on the

At the Observance of the Birthday of Abraham Lincoln, Springfield, Illinois, February 12, 1922.

frontier until a nation stood beside his tomb. There was about him a dignity which no uncouthness of surroundings could blot out. He had a mind which no lack of letters could leave undeveloped. He had a faith which could move mountains. Two generations have sought out whatever could be associated with him, have read the record of his every word with the greatest eagerness, and held his memory as a precious heritage. Where he trod is holy ground. Yet never was a man more simply human.

Wherever men look upon his life, they are filled with a new wonder. About him there was never any needless thing. No useless burdens held him back. No wilderness of tangled ideas bewildered his vision. For him the outward show of the world was cast aside that he might be a larger partaker of reality. His cradle was bare, but above it was the precious canopy of the love of a gentle mother. When she was borne away in his early boyhood, he had learned the great lesson that all this world is mortal. From his youth he knew that anguish is the common lot of mankind. In his rearing there was no false art. Like the strengthening of his body, the strengthening of his mind came from great Nature.

In the common meaning of the term, he had no chance for learning. For him there was to be no university. Even the way to a log schoolhouse was almost closed; but he had that which overcomes all these. He had that which broke through the bonds of an almost letterless and bookless frontier. He had a deep yearning to learn. Out of the power of that wish, which, never ceasing, went with him through life, alone, self-taught (so far as any one can be self-taught), he gained great learning.   He ran for office among a people where personality and character meant more than the utterance of high-sounding partisan claims.   He was the choice of such a people.   In the strict sense of the old phrase, he read law.   For some time he held office where the holding of office called for a steady and unselfish effort to serve the public welfare. For many years he was pleading law in a country where statutes were still so few, and precedents were so much in the making, that pleading law meant very largely being able to find out the truth and carry it to the minds of a jury.   It was in this work that he grew.   Mingling with the crowds that the court brought together, hearing the full story of their quarrels, learning their high sense of right and wrong, seeing their ever-ready wish for justice, he came to know not only the weakness but the great strength of the people.   He learned how to make facts clear and a principle of the law plain.   Seeing his great ability, knowing his self-sacrificing honesty, the people came to have a great faith in him as he had a great faith in them.

In the course of events he was sent to Congress.   In time he would have been a leader anywhere, but it is doubtful if he would ever really have liked the way the work of the Congress was done; still his putting in of what were known as the Spot Resolutions, dealing with the quarrel with Mexico, showed that the trial of jury cases had taught him how to ask questions of a political party as well as of a witness which it was hard for the opposition to answer without telling the truth.   Nothing ever seemed to stand in the way of his being able to see the

simple truth, and nothing ever seemed to move him
from his wish to see the truth win. He had no will to
fight for what was wrong. He might stay his hand for a
while, but in the end, knowing the right, he held to it
with a power which finally could not be overcome.

Coming home at the end of his term, he took up again
the work of the law, but soon he had other work to do.
There was never any question about what he thought of
slavery. He hated it with the whole force of his whole
being; but he believed not only in freedom, he believed
in the Constitution of his country. He said that slavery
was legal; that a Fugitive Slave Act would be valid. He
had a great faith in the law. He knew that without it
there would be no freedom. While he would stretch out
no lawless hand against slavery, while he would observe
the finding of the court in its favor, he was against its
extension through the passage of any new law or the unwarranted interpretation of any old law. He was not a
radical, but a conservative. He never sought to waste,
but always to save. He had a love for his country so
great, a faith in its people so deep, that he believed if the
Union could stand according to the Constitution and the
law the evil of slavery would finally fall of its own weight.
He was against its legal growth. He knew it was a great
moral question.

This was his state of mind when he began the great
debate with Douglas. The main question of that debate
was whether there was any plan or any power to extend
slavery over all the nation. Douglas denied that there
was any such plan, but always said that the Constitution
made slavery legal, that whatever the law provided about

it the whole nation must observe. He put out his claim
that each State should decide for itself and said that he
did not care whether slavery was voted up or voted down.
Lincoln never denied the binding force of the Constitution. As he had done in Congress, he now asked a question. Under the construction which Douglas put on the
Constitution, was there any legal way by which the people of a Territory could keep slavery out against the
wish of one man who wanted to bring it in? Douglas
had to answer, legally, no; practically, yes, by not making local laws to protect slavery. This answer pleased
the North; it did not please the South. Douglas won the
senatorial election then. In two years Lincoln had won
the debate and won the Presidential election. He never
failed to say that slavery was wrong. He knew that in
the end no law which man might make could stand against
the moral law.

The story of this man spread. He was called to the
Eastern States. He made a speech at Cooper Union in
which he showed, by a plain statement of facts made
from much searching, a clear argument, and the even
greater force of his own honest mind and high character,
that those who had made America a nation were against
slavery. It would be hard to point out where a greater
speech was ever made.

When the men of the new Republican Party met, many
leaders had many different plans, but in the end the urge
of the will of the people chose Lincoln. He was elected.
He took office amid great stress and strain. Many States
had already fallen away. Others wavered. Yet he told
them that we were not enemies, but friends; that it was

not their duty to destroy the government, but his sworn duty to preserve it. Clearly, steadily, drawing those who loved their country more than all else around him, he kept one end alone in view, the saving of the Union. He did not ask a question now; he made a question. The armed forces of the government rightfully, legally, constitutionally held Fort Sumter in the harbor of Charleston. He would not take them away. On the 12th of April, 1861, the first gun was fired on our flag over that fort. The answer had been given. He knew then that the people of the nation must know that there were those who were willing to break up the Union by force. He knew more than any one else that against force used for that end there would be no lack of a will on the part of his countrymen to fight. Others doubted, but he had faith; he knew.

Amid many and conflicting forces he held to this one issue in spite of evil counsels throughout the North, in spite of staggering losses in the field. He walked alone. Loving peace, hating war, tender of heart, full of mercy, he was forced to see his countrymen slay each other. He carried a new burden on that soul which was always touched with anguish. How he poured out the agony of his soul on the field of Gettysburg and in his second inaugural address!

He saw the failure of his armies through nearly two campaigns; then came Antietam. Knowing that the time for which he long had waited had come, he issued the Emancipation Proclamation. He believed at last that it was possible, by breaking slavery, to keep the Union whole. Henceforth the war was not only to save the nation but to make it free. Slowly but steadily, with Farragut, with Sheridan, with Sherman, with Grant, it was brought to a close. The great evil which had lain on the soul of the whole nation had been purged away by the awful scourge of war. The flag of our country had come to have the meaning which Webster said it should have. At last Liberty and Union were one and inseparable. In this hour, which was to him not one of triumph but of duty done, the spirit of Lincoln, released from a life of anguish, returned to God who gave it.

So there came to an end this life in which the meaning of human existence reached its flood. It had within its scope every range of experience between the most humble and lonely beginning and the highest and most famous place that man could hold in all the world. Who can look upon it and feel that stern circumstances have denied to any one a chance? Who could know Lincoln and not have hope and faith? He showed that the only bounds set to the height to which a man shall rise are those which he sets himself. In the practice of law he never relied on deceit. In seeking office he used no pretense. The end he sought in life was truth through honesty. He wished to have what that could bring; no more. He did not ask that others should take his burden from him; he asked to take their burdens from them, humbly seeking the guidance of man and of God as to how it might be done. He worked with the Unseen.

What an answer he is to all those who would tear down. All of his work was to save and to build up. He wished to make himself better; he wished for gain; he wished for place. He did not try to get these by casting aside the

only sure means by which they could be had. He did
not seek them without humility, without industry, without honesty, without forbearance, and without faith. He
spoke against the seizing and pulling down of the house
of another, and in favor of building up and making safe
the house of oneself. He knew that those who made the
best of what they had were the only ones who were sure
to have more.

Lincoln made the same appeal to his countrymen which
all great men have made. There was in it nothing small
or mean. No man ever had a greater love of humanity.
But it came not from his belief in their weakness but in
their strength. His faith was not in the things of the
flesh. He held out no promise of ease. He knew there
could be no growth without toil, no character without
effort. His faith was in the things of the spirit. He believed all men were great enough to be free. He besought
them to strive mightily that they might come unto their
true estate. He knew that freedom was not easy, that
its burden was not light; that it could be only for those
who dwelt in the high places; that to have it and keep it
was a great task. But he did not hesitate to call the
people up into the high places; he did not cease to urge
that with increased devotion they should highly resolve
to be dedicated to the great task. They heard and they
obeyed.

The place which Lincoln holds in the history of the
nation is that of the man who finished what others had
begun. What they had dared to dream of, he dared to
do. He does not lessen the glory of what they did, rather
he adds to it. They built a base that was sound and solid.

They left plans by which it was to be finished. The base which they made was the Union. The plans which they drew, and stated time and time again, were for a free people. But Lincoln rises above them all in one thing. He never halted; he never turned aside. He was no opportunist. He had no lack of tact. He had a mighty sense of what was timely. He was wise as a serpent. But he did not stop part way; he followed the truth through to the end. In this peculiar power it is not too much to say that he excels all other statesmen.

He closed forever the great contest which had been waged for three-quarters of a century between the power of the States and the power of the nation. He answered for all time the question of whether the selfish interests of a part, or the greater interest of the whole should be supreme. This contest had been confined to no one locality and to no one issue. New England had turned to it when she thought it would make for her welfare. The South clung to it when she believed it was for her advantage. The National Union which Washington and Hamilton had formed, which Marshall had declared, which Webster and Jackson and Clay had defended, Abraham Lincoln saved, and, saving, made it free. He stands with those who believed in the righteous power and the just authority of a free government. He saw clearly that no free government could derive its just powers from anything less than a free people. What he saw, what he believed, when the time came he was ready to do. In all things he followed the truth to the end.

The influence of Lincoln did not abide in America alone. The great cause which he led to victory went forth into the world. Instead of leaving several States weak in their material resources, and weaker still in their moral power, he held together a great people in one strong nation, mighty in the strength of its arms, unequalled in the righteousness of its purpose. He took away whatever wicked hope those who hated freedom had that this republic might fall. When his action had established his claim that right makes might, he raised the hope of freedom everywhere. He did not change; he continued the course of history. He did not discover freedom; he showed that it had a power of its own. He was not the first who had faith in the people; he was the first who dared to put that faith to the test of every truth. His life was a force great enough to reach to the heart of every man through all eternity. He broke down all the bounds which ages of fear and tyranny had set to the hope of the world.

He opened up to the vision of mankind a new heaven and a new earth. That vision has not yet been fully realized, but people see it more and more clearly; they strive for it with greater and greater success. How greatly the past ten years have justified his faith!

It is with deep humility that any one would speak of Abraham Lincoln here. This is sacred ground. These streets of Springfield he had often trod. Here stand the walls of buildings which have echoed his voice. Over these fields and along these streams he walked alone and thought. When his eyes closed for the last time on this world, at Washington, Secretary Stanton said: "Now he belongs to the ages." That is true. He belongs to every age in which men shall struggle for an ideal. He belongs to every place where men fight for human rights; but in a peculiar, more intimate way, he belongs to you.

He had served your city well before it became his home. With his help, while a member of the legislature, Springfield had been made the capital of this State. Here in an office he began the regular study of the law. From this city your fathers sent him to Congress. He came back to his home at the end of his term and let it be known that his political career was done—from that time forward he would give himself wholly to the law.

So men work and plan and tell their plans, but the issue lies in another Hand. In May, 1854, the Missouri Compromise was repealed. In October, at your State Fair Grounds, Abraham Lincoln spoke. He was beginning to make that fight against evil for which he had been raised up. Even those of your fathers who knew him best heard him with wonder. "He felt upon his soul the truths burn which he uttered," a local paper said, "and all present felt that he was true to his own soul. His feelings once or twice swelled within and came near stifling utterance. He quivered with emotion. The whole house was still as death."

Here, in a letter to a friend, he wrote: "Can we, as a nation, continue permanently—forever—half slave and half free? The problem is too mighty for me—may God in His mercy superintend the solution." In and out of your homes he moved restlessly during the week of the Chicago convention. Here in the doorway of a store he heard the shout: "Mr. Lincoln, Mr. Lincoln, you are nominated!" The crowd thronged across the street from the telegraph office. He raised his hat. "My friends,

I am glad to receive your congratulations," he said; "and as there is a little woman down on 8th Street who will be glad to hear the news, you must excuse me until I inform her."

Here was that upper room, above a store, across the street from the State House, to which he went some months later, where, with no books but a copy of the Constitution, the Speech of 1850 of Henry Clay, the Proclamation against Nullification of Andrew Jackson, and the reply to Hayne of Daniel Webster, he prepared his first inaugural address. At your railroad station he made his tender, heartfelt little speech of farewell as he went to the task which he said was "more difficult than that of Washington had been."

He never forgot Springfield. Always, a visitor from here might be sure of a warm welcome at the White House. In the last year of his first term, when it seemed likely that he might fail of re-election, he spoke often of his coming plans to his family and friends. All of these plans were centred here. Perhaps a little house on the street, perhaps a farm on the outskirts—but somewhere, somehow, he would find a place in Springfield which would keep him for the rest of his years in the town and among the people he loved.

It is not to the city of Washington that men must turn if they would understand Abraham Lincoln. The beginning and the end of his nature is here. Here was the life which he carried with him. The frank and open ways of the neighbor were his. The indulgent patience of the friend who knows how hard and difficult is the path of the common man. Too often the world turns its eyes to the high places, thinking that from them will come its revelations and its great events, forgetful that a greater wisdom is in those who "mind not high things, but condescend to men of low estate." The greatest epoch in all human history began in a manger. This great American, the foremost world figure of the nineteenth century, came out of a frontier clearing and spent his early manhood in a village of a few hundred souls.

In the memory of these facts there lies a solid basis for our faith. There is in the people themselves the power to put forth great men. There is in the soul of the nation a reserve for responding to the call to high ideals, to nobility of action, which has never yet been put forth. There is no problem so great but that somewhere a man is being raised up to meet it. There is no moral standard so high that the people cannot be raised up to it. God rules, and from the Bethlehems and the Springfields He sends them forth, His own, to do His work. In them we catch a larger gleam of the Infinite.

XIII

Nations do not come into existence without a purpose. The world soon casts aside organizations which do not minister to its welfare. . . . In the fulness of time America was called into being under the most favoring circumstances, to work out the problem of a more perfect relationship among mankind that government and society might be brought into harmony with reason and with conscience.

THE PURPOSE OF AMERICA

THIS is a day which Destiny has dedicated to a larger freedom. It takes us back to the early eighteenth century. That period was marked as one of preparation rather than attainment. Both before it and after it the manifest course of history touched a higher crest. Marlborough, the victor of Blenheim, had just departed from the scene. George II, who with his grandson George III was destined to reign over the British Empire for almost one hundred years, had just come to the throne. Men were still living whose fathers might have known Shakespeare and Milton, might have followed Cromwell at Marston Moor and Dunbar, or might have seen the *Mayflower* as she carried her passengers forth upon a journey which they have not yet completed, and men were living whose sons were to stand at Concord bridge; were to write the Declaration of Independence and adopt the American Constitution; were to take part in the French Revolution and behold the triumphs of Napoleon end at Waterloo; and finally were to see that century which this day began in 1732 close in 1832 with the Parliamentary Reform Bill. It was to be a century of most remarkable achievements, and if its beginning was not heralded by brilliant events, it held one significant fact. Robert Walpole was prime minister. George II might reign, but he ruled. He was the first of the great commoners, a fore-

At Johns Hopkins University, Baltimore, Maryland, February 22, 1922.

runner of Pitts and Gladstones in the Old World, and in the New of plain men who would rise to even greater eminence. In the colonies legislative assemblies chosen by popular vote were slowly gaining in their claim of independence. While the people had not yet come to the full exercise of their liberties, they had reached the power to administer, and would soon be seeking the power to control their governments.

It was during this century that the true purpose of America began to be revealed. As we behold it our patience ought to be increased, our faith strengthened, and our belief in human progress reaffirmed. Whatever this might require is more than supplied as we contemplate the birth of George Washington, with all that it has come to mean.

Nations do not come into existence without a purpose. The world soon casts aside organizations which do not minister to its welfare. As we examine the course of known history, as we trace the progress of the race, as we see the problems of existence which had been met and solved by past civilization, and then as we learn of the discovery of a new continent and come to know the cause of its early settlement and mark the spirit of its institutions, there is disclosed to us the meaning and the purpose of our nation. In the fulness of time America was called into being under the most favoring circumstances, to work out the problem of a more perfect relationship among mankind that government and society might be brought into harmony with reason and with conscience. The great events and the great men of our country are those that have made the largest contribution to this purpose. The method by which men have always advanced this cause, the only method by which they ever can advance it, is through service and sacrifice. There can be no great people who are not willing to dedicate themselves to this high purpose.

It was this spirit in the Pilgrim and the Puritan which has drawn to them the admiration of three centuries. For all of them the comfort of the most highly civilized society at home was open; for many of them the enjoyment of wealth and place, reaching up to the splendor of the court; all these were cast aside that they might leave tyranny behind and found a free state amid the hardships of the wilderness, where that which they believed and which they held sacred might have broader scope. Nor was it of themselves even then that they thought most. Believing in piety they formed their church. Believing in freedom and equality they did not scruple to pay the price for their maintenance. "Every township," their early law decreed, "after the Lord hath increased them to the number of fifty householders, shall appoint one to teach all children to write and read; and when any town shall increase to the number of a hundred families, they shall set up a grammar-school." To such a people liberty was a birthright and independence could not long be denied.

But there was that in the experience of colonial life which brought those who crossed the sea from a somewhat different motive to the same conclusion when they considered their rights were in danger. There had been bred in the English through the centuries which disappear from view in their old German home, a genius for local self-government and an intolerance of foreign interference. If the Pilgrims had landed with a miniature, but none the less complete, charter of democracy in the *Mayflower* Compact, the early settlers of Virginia, landing with a royal charter, were none the less determined to maintain their rights. They early established a free government under an assembly, now one of the oldest legislative bodies in the world which has been in continual session.

It is not my purpose to trace in detail the well-known course which led up to the American Revolution. A misguided ministry, under a despotic King, secured from a servile Parliament the passage of laws regulating and imposing stamp taxes on the commerce of the colonies. There was never any objection to granting such supplies as were requested, however large, but there was every objection to the imposition of any unlawful tax, however small. But a government which openly flouted public opinion at home was likely to pay even less attention to public opinion in the colonies. These acts were recognized, however, as a direct challenge to the rights of the subjects of the realm everywhere. The Assembly of Virginia led in declaring such taxes unconstitutional, and Massachusetts followed. The great Pitt supported their opposition in Parliament. "Sir, I rejoice," he said, "that America has resisted. Three millions of people, so dead to all the feelings of liberty as voluntarily to submit to be slaves, would have been fit instruments to make slaves of the rest." He saw that it was not merely the freedom of the colonies but the freedom of all the realm which was in danger.

Although these taxes were modified under the stress of fear and open rebellion, the right to their imposition was declared and reasserted in a vexatious tax on tea. When this was resisted, a fatuous and tyrannical King resorted to repression by force. "The colonists must either triumph or submit," he declared. They did not submit. They answered force with force. They would live free or, in resisting usurpation, they would die.

What began in the assertion of constitutional rights ended in the assertion of national sovereignty. If the right of local self-government, if the dearest of all privileges which Englishmen held as their heritage, that of paying no taxes which they themselves had not imposed, could not be guaranteed them under the ancient kingdom, the time had come for them to establish a new nation. This they proceeded to do, beginning the great Declaration with these impressive words: "We, therefore, the Representatives of the United States of America, in General Congress Assembled, appealing to the Supreme Judge of the world for the rectitude of our intentions, do, in the Name, and by authority of the good People of these Colonies, solemnly Publish and Declare, that these United Colonies are, and of Right ought to be, Free and Independent States."

That which has raised this Declaration to the dignity which it holds among the people of the earth is the genius of George Washington. He did not create the American spirit, but he organized it; he led it, he translated it from solemn declaration into effective action. The words of the delegates were impressive in Congress because they were supported by the army of Washington in the field.

It was some fifteen months from that morning when patriot blood stained Lexington Green to the day when the Liberty Bell first rang in Philadelphia. Some fifteen months away lay Saratoga, a purely American victory, which has been marked as one of a few decisive battles in all history. It was not in high-sounding phrase, or in the voting of resolutions that the Revolution was made or won, but in the service and sacrifice of the people in their homes and above all of the army in the field.

It was not the Declaration but the army which resisted tyranny, which, breaking the power of the King to impose his unlawful will upon the people of the colonies, broke his power to impose an unlawful will upon the people of the realm, and which, preserving the ancient freedom of Englishmen in America, preserved the ancient freedom of Englishmen at home. That army was George Washington. Under him the Americans made a sacrifice for liberty which was not local; it was universal. That sacrifice resisted then, and has ever since been successfully resisting, despotism everywhere. America in its beginnings was doing the work of the world.

True greatness cannot rest merely on a negative. The fame of Washington would be very great if it ended at Yorktown, but both in what he refrained from doing and in what he did after that great event, his fame increases beyond that of a great soldier which is shared by many, into that of a great statesman which is shared by few, and rises to the height of a great patriot which is shared by no one. Washington was first of all an American. He did not refuse the help of foreigners. When, some three years after the conflict began, France made common cause against England, he accepted their assistance gladly and always with the deepest sense of appreciation. But he declared that, if the cause were to be won, it must be won by Americans relying upon themselves. It was this truly American view which not only saved the Revolution but after its conclusion saved what it had won. Washington was a nationalist. That principle lay at the foundation of all his statesmanship. Through the long responsibility of the war he came to know, as no one else could know, the weakness to resist evil of thirteen separate colonies and the power to do good of a united nation. It was the intellectual force of Hamilton which produced the plans and poured forth the arguments, but it was the character of Washington which secured the adoption of the American Constitution. Where Cæsar and Napoleon failed, where even Cromwell faltered, Washington alone prevailed. He wished the people of his country to be great, but great in their own right. He resisted the proposal that he should be set up to rule them. He adopted the proposal that they should be organized to rule themselves. He carried these principles through to the end. Later, when some of his countrymen insisted on adhering to the cause of France, while others insisted on adhering to the cause of England, he insisted on adhering to the cause of America, and, with patience and greatness which were sublime, himself bore the resulting abuse of his country for his country's good.

He was a practical man. If he engaged himself little in proclamation, he engaged himself much in action. To him the Revolution meant an army in the field able to win victories. Knowing where that would lead, he made no haste to claim independence. He made an independent nation. He established a republic under the Constitution, and through two terms as President made its government a reality, with strength enough to preserve order, with honesty enough to meet its financial obligations, and with character enough to win the respect of the world. From henceforth all men, from the most absolute monarch to the most abject subject, were to reckon with what Americans had done and what their country had come to mean.

Under Washington nationality became an accomplished fact. There were those who resisted it then, there were those who would resist it later, through the promulgation of resolutions and finally by force of arms. There were those at home, not confined to any one section, and there were enemies of republican institutions abroad who, for their own selfish reasons, were willing to see the great experiment of self-government fail. But it was not to fail. It was not to diminish. It was to succeed. It was to increase. It was to become all free. We are not to criticise the Fathers because they did not abolish slavery. Progress goes forward step by step. They took their step, and in the pathway of humanity it has a measurement of great length. If they could not acknowledge universal freedom, they declared principles and they adopted institutions which by their very maintenance would establish universal freedom. But it was not only the fact, but the method, which is of importance to us now. There had to be an atonement for slavery. The great evil of its existence had to be resisted by the great sacrifice which was made both by the South and the North for its abolition. It was out of that sacrifice that there came a new birth of freedom, hallowed by the memory of Lincoln. Out of it all there came a most unexpected demonstration of the great strength of free institutions and the power of an awakened conscience in determining the lot of mankind.

It is this same force which sometimes works for a long period silently, with a still small voice, and again goes forth as an army with banners which, for a century now, has shielded the western hemisphere from the menace of Old World aggressions, giving Mexico to the Mexicans and the opportunity for freedom to the islands of the seas.

Our country had proceeded through the course of its history not unmindful of the obligations due to foreign nations, not undesirous of promoting the friendly rivalry of commercial intercourse. It had been not only the merchandise but the word of America which had gone forth into all the world. The name of Washington was known and cherished in all lands, and among all peoples, and his country came to be looked upon as Lincoln saw it, the last, best hope of the world. From it there went out a missionary spirit carrying the promise of general enlightenment, for wherever the American missionary has gone he has carried not only the story of the gospel, but with it the power to establish schools and build hospitals. They ministered to the body, to the intellect, and to the soul. By bearing witness to the truth they supported the cause of freedom. The power of America became a great organizing force wherever it went; but it did not seek foreign conquests, and shrank almost from assuming the government of those dependencies which the doing of duty has intrusted to its care.   Serene in its power, in the doing of justice to all, free from all foreign alliance, having nothing to gain from war, foremost in its organized efforts to promote the peace of the world, it expected and feared no possible aggression.

But unconsciously, almost unwillingly, that nation which had been established by Washington and made free under Lincoln, had become a world-power.   The setting of its own house in order, great as that accomplishment had been, might give it the power to meet its obligations; it could not give it the power to avoid them.   When a military despotism which held in its grasp a great people threatened to destroy the free governments of Europe, when America at last came to realize the issue, the soul of her people was bound to respond.   When the leader of the American Expeditionary Force reached France, I do not know whether as he stood before the tomb of that great Frenchman who had first befriended our country, he said, "Lafayette, we are here," but the event makes the report a reality.   From the day when the prow of the *Mayflower* touched the shores of Massachusetts Bay, wherever any power has sought to substitute the rule of force for the rule of conscience in the affairs of mankind, the soul of America has stood beside the champions of freedom, proclaiming: "We are here."   That spirit of service and sacrifice by which they had saved themselves in the eighteenth and nineteenth centuries called them forth in the twentieth century to cast the deciding weight of their sword into the balance of liberty.

The trial by battle has been decisive. It was as decisive as Yorktown. A stricken and impoverished world has since been struggling to organize and adopt into permanent institutions the results of that victory. Foremost above the desires of all peoples has been the wish to secure new guarantees of peace. No one doubts that the delegates to the Paris Conference were inspired by that noble ideal. Amid all the contending elements they failed to propose a plan which harmonized with the spirit of America. Every one knows that the American soul longed to establish a condition which held the promise of a permanent peace, but its ideal was for a peace not imposed by the major forces of the world from without but maintained by the moral power of the world from within. It saw in the Covenant of the League, whether intended or not, a diminution of its independence, and in its provisions the final sanction not of conscience but of force. It was the American conception that nations, like men, should be free by coming unto a knowledge of the truth, by living in obedience to the law. That was the larger meaning of the war. To translate that meaning into a resolution, to draft it into an agreement, to adopt it as an ordinance, to establish it as one of the fundamental institutions of mankind for the guidance of the society of free nations was a world desire which has tested the statesmanship of civilization.

It was in part in response to this desire that the Washington Conference was called. Men had reached the conclusion that one of the methods of securing peace was by making the necessary sacrifices and performing the necessary services to remove some of the causes of war. It is this which appears to be in harmony with the greater purpose of America. It was not merely the voice of one man, or one party, or one administration, but the true voice of America which proposed, at the opening session of the conference, the scrapping of thirty of its capital ships, aggregating nearly eight hundred and fifty thousand tons, of which fifteen were new ships under construction, on which there had already been spent nearly three hundred and fifty million dollars; and that for a period of ten years the capital ships of this nation be limited to eighteen in number, of a displacement of five hundred thousand tons. It was the same voice which limited the use of submarines and forbade the use of poison gas, which circumscribed the menace of further fortifications in the Pacific, secured justice for China and equal opportunities of participation in her trade and development, and which finally removed the danger of the English-Japanese Treaty—which relied on the sanction of force—and proposed in its place the Four-Power Treaty, which rests on the sanction of justice.

The great strength of this treaty is its simplicity. It does not undertake to establish any artificial relationship; it recognizes the natural relationship between nations. It does not make any new law; it acknowledges the binding force of an eternal law. It is an agreement to respect mutual rights, and whenever those rights are endangered to resort to mutual consultation. This has a sanction to which all force is subject:

"Moreover, if thy brother shall trespass against thee, go and tell him his fault between thee and him alone; if he shall hear thee, thou hast gained thy brother.

"But if he will not hear thee, then take with thee one or two more, that in the mouth of two or three witnesses every word may be established.

"And if he shall neglect to hear them, tell it unto the church: but if he neglect to hear the church, let him be unto thee as an heathen man and a publican."

That rests on the Rock of Ages.

Unto America there has been granted possession of great power which carries with it great obligations. Our domestic burdens are great, but the resources with which they can be met are greater still. We did not suddenly become a great people in 1917, or relinquish our greatness in 1918. The greatness was there, created through long years of endeavor. The occasion revealed its existence. The meaning of America is not to be found in a life without toil. Freedom is not only bought with a great price; it is maintained by unremitting effort. The successful conduct of our economic life is not easy. It cannot be made easy. The burdens of existence, the weight of civilization, cannot be taken from the people. There is no way to establish a better relationship among the people of this nation save through each making great sacrifice. But nowhere does duty done and sacrifice made hold the promise of larger success. The final solution of these problems will not be found in the interposition of government in all the affairs of the people, but rather in following the wisdom of Washington, who refused to exercise authority over the people, that the people might exercise authority over themselves. It is not in the laying on of force, but in the development of the public conscience that salvation lies.

America stands ready to bear its share of the burdens of the world, but it cannot live the life of other peoples, it cannot remove from them the necessity of working out their own destiny. It recognizes their independence and the right to establish their own form of government, but America will join no nation in destroying what it believes ought to be preserved or in profaning what it believes ought to be held sacred. We are at peace with all peoples. We do not deny our duty to continue the making of sacrifices for the welfare of the world. It is not alone for their sake but for our own sake that we should pursue that course. We have adopted toward the world the policy of Washington, not of repression, not of dictation, not of coercion, not of imperialism, but a policy of co-operation, relieving distress, of forbearance, of helpfulness, of sympathy, of forgiveness, a policy which is first of all American, but a policy, above all, of faith in the sanction of the universal conscience of mankind. That sanction is eternal. In it alone is the promise of a larger freedom.

XIV

The issues of the world must be met and met squarely. The forces of evil do not disdain preparation, they are always prepared and always preparing. . . . The welfare of America, the cause of civilization will forever require the contribution of some part of the life of all our citizens to the natural, the necessary, and the inevitable demand for the defense of the right and the truth. There is no substitute for a militant freedom.

ULYSSES S. GRANT

THE world has always worshipped power. As in their humblest beginnings mankind stood in wonder before the forces of nature, so now in their highest development they stand in reverence before the figure of genius. It is in response to an increasing sentiment of gratitude and patriotism that national action has set apart this day to observe the centennial anniversary of the birth of a great American, who was sent into the world endowed with a greatness easy to understand, yet difficult to describe: the highest type of intellectual power—simplicity and directness; the highest type of character—fidelity and honesty. He will forever hold the admiration of a people in whom these qualities abide. By the authority of the law of the land, with the approving loyalty of all his fellow countrymen, in the shadow of the dome of the Capitol which his work proved and glorified fittingly, flanked on either side by a group of soldiers in action, looking out toward the monuments of Washington and Lincoln, this statue rises to the memory of General Ulysses Simpson Grant. It is here because a great people responded to a great man.

Such greatness did not spring into being in a generation. There lay behind it a wide sweep of ancestry representing the blood of those who had set the standard of civilization and borne its burdens for a thousand years. Into his boyhood there came little which was uncommon.

At the Dedication of the Monument to General Ulysses S. Grant, at Washington, April 27, 1922.

He had the ordinary experiences of the son of an average home maintained by a moderately prosperous business. He went to West Point, not so much with the purpose of becoming a soldier as from a desire to secure an education. He liked horses and rode well. He did not appear brilliant, but he had industry. He worked. He made progress. He had that common sense which overcomes obstacles. As a student he is worthy alike of the careful consideration of the young men of the present day and of those who are intrusted with their training.

After his graduation he remained in the army for eleven years, rising to the rank of captain. He served through the Mexican War, part of the time as quartermaster and commissary of his regiment. He demonstrated his personal courage by bearing despatches, on horseback, over a course which was under heavy fire. In 1854 he voluntarily retired from the army, and the secretary of war, Jefferson Davis, refused to reconsider the acceptance of his resignation. Destiny sent him to private life, where he could better feel the rising tide of freedom.

The next few years he spent as a farmer and a business man. He still worked hard, but he did not prosper, scarcely making a living. He had little taste for small things; it required an emergency to call forth his powers.

The great crisis found him in Illinois employed in his father's leather business. "Whatever may have been my political opinions before," he declared, "I have but one sentiment now. That is, we have a government and laws, and a flag, and they must all be sustained." He engaged in recruiting, and offered his services to the War Department, but received no reply. He sought an interview with McClellan, but was unable to see him. Soon, however, being appointed colonel of the 21st Illinois Regiment by Governor Yates, he took command in a speech of five words: "Men, go to your quarters." Within four years he was to be recognized as the greatest soldier in the world.

His regiment was soon disciplined and he was on the march. During the summer Lincoln commissioned him a brigadier-general of volunteers. In the following February, he captured Fort Henry and Fort Donelson. This was one of the first important victories, and it was received with wild enthusiasm. Grant was at once made a major-general of volunteers. During the remainder of 1862 he fought the somewhat ineffective battle of Pittsburgh Landing. A little later he was placed in command of the Department of Tennessee, and was soon making his advance on Vicksburg. This town was surrendered on the morning of the Fourth of July, 1863. Within a week the Mississippi River was under Union control. The nation celebrated the double victories of Gettysburg and Vicksburg. Grant was made major-general in the regular army.

The campaign for the year closed with the battle of Lookout Mountain and the heroic storming of Missionary Ridge, relieving Chattanooga. Here Grant demonstrated his great military genius, both of plan and execution.

The following March he was called to the White House and made lieutenant-general of the Armies of the United States. He took command of the Army of the Potomac. Then followed blow on blow from the Wilderness to

Appomattox.   A campaign of a year brought success and victory.   His losses were great, but they had been greater during three years of failure.   The sacrifices of life had been larger when the result had been little more than a call for more men than they were now, when at last the bands could play "Home, Sweet Home."

He immediately hastened to Washington where he was received by the President and the people with those expressions of joy which only the end of a war can bring. His work finished, though the President had invited him to attend the theatre, he left the city on that fatal evening of April 14.   He mourned the loss of Lincoln, but his first allegiance was to his country.   His attitude toward Johnson was all that could be required of a general toward his commander-in-chief, until the President, seeking to embroil him in his own political disputes, charged him with bad faith.   Although he had received from him a commission as general of the Armies of the United States, and acted a short time as his secretary of war, he was thereafter in sympathy with those who sought to impeach the President.   While Johnson sank in the public estimation, Grant rose, being unanimously nominated and handsomely elected President of the United States.

He had little taste for political manœuvres.   He found his eight years fell on a time of confusion, both of thought and action.   He worked as best he could with the contending elements which made up the Congress.   "I shall have a policy to recommend," he said, "but none to enforce against the will of the people."   He secured a settlement with Great Britain for the *Alabama* claims, and an apology from Spain for the *Virginius* affair.   Although he broke with a well-meaning reform element of his party, which supported Horace Greeley, he was triumphantly re-elected. One of the important contributions which he made to the public service was his veto of the bill which provided for the inflation of the currency by issuing $400,-000,000 in greenbacks. At a time when the political ideals of the country were very low, President Grant held to his own high standard of honorable public service. Through the contested election of Hayes and Tilden, in 1876, he took a course marked by a high spirit of patriotism. "No man worthy of the office of President," he said, "should be willing to hold it if counted in or placed there by fraud. Either party can afford to be disappointed in the result. The country cannot afford to have the result tainted by a suspicion of illegal or false returns." When the man who knew how to command armies took this position for the enforcement of the law, the country stood behind him and peacefully accepted the decision of the electoral commission.

His closing years were marked with great tragedy. Betrayed by one whom he trusted, he saw his property dissipated and large obligations incurred. A lingering and fatal malady added anguish of the body to the anguish of his soul.

Never was he greater than in these last days. With high courage, without complaint, on a bed of pain, seeking to retrieve his losses, he was preparing his memoirs. Congress hastened to restore him to the rank and salary of a retired general of the army. At last his writings were finished. He was still thinking of his country, not as a partisan but as a patriot, not even as the general of the armies he had led but as an American. "I have witnessed since my illness," he wrote, "just what I have wished to see since the war—harmony and good-will between the sections." While he was thus longing for the peace of his fellow countrymen, the great and final peace was bestowed upon him.

Great as he had been, his armies had been greater still. He had been served by officers of commanding ability. He never appeared to maintain for them anything but the most kindly feeling. The greater their ability, the greater was their attachment to him. But the rank and file were more wonderful still. In intelligence, in bravery, in patriotism, and, during the latter years of the war, in military capacity, no armies had ever surpassed those who fought the battles of the war between the States. Their ranks are thin now, but their spirit is undiminished. At an age when others would have quit the field, they remain still holding positions of commanding authority in the service of their countrymen, the soldiers of Lincoln and of Grant. As they supported him in the field, their bronze forms support him here.

Men are made in no small degree by their adversaries. Grant had great adversaries. They fought with a dash and a tenacity, with a gallantry and an enduring purpose which the world has known in Americans, and in Americans alone. At their head rode General Robert E. Lee, marked with a purity of soul and a high sense of personal honor which no true American would ever stoop to question. No force ever quelled their intrepid spirit. They gave their loyalty voluntarily or they did not give it at all. It is not so much the greatness of Grant as a soldier but his greatness as a man, not so much his greatness in war as his greatness in peace, the consideration, the tenderness, the human sympathy which he showed toward them from the day of their submission, refusing the surrender of Lee's sword, leaving the men of the Southern army in possession of their own horses, which appealed to that sentiment of reconciliation which has long since been complete. It was not a humiliation but an honor to remain under the sovereignty of a flag which was borne by such a commander.

It was Lincoln who said of Grant: "I cannot spare this man. He fights." It was Grant himself who said: "Let us have peace."

Our country and the world may well consider the simplicity and directness which marked the greatness of General Grant. In war his object was the destruction of the opposing army. He knew that task was difficult. He knew that the price would be high; yet amid abuse and criticism, amid misunderstanding and jealousy, he did not alter his course. He paid the price. He accomplished the result. He wasted no time in attempting to find some substitute for victory. He held fast to the same principle in time of peace. Around him was the destruction which the war had wrought. The economic condition of the country was depressed by a great financial panic. He refused to seek refuge in any fictions. He knew that sound values and a sound economic condition could not be created by law alone but only through the long and toilsome application of human effort put forth under wise law. He knew that his country could not legislate out its destiny but must work out its destiny.

He laid the foundation of national welfare on which the
nation has stood unshaken in every time of storm and
stress. His policy was simple and direct, and eternally
true.

In the important decisions of his life his fidelity and
honesty are equally apparent. He was a soldier of his
country. His every action was inspired by loyalty.
"Whatever may be the orders of my superiors and the
law," he wrote, "I will execute. No man can be efficient as a commander who sets his own notions above the
law and those whom he has sworn to obey." When the
conflict between President Johnson and the Congress became so acute that it threatened to result in force of
arms, being asked which side he would take he replied:
"That will depend entirely upon which is the revolutionary party." He never betrayed a trust and he never
deserted a friend. He considered that the true test of a
friend was to stand by him when he was in need. When
financial misfortunes overtook him he discharged his
obligations from whatever property he and his family
could raise.

Here was a man who lived the great realities of life.
As Lincoln could put truth into words, so Grant could
put truth into action. How truly he stands out as the
great captain of a republic! There was no artifice about
him, no pretense, and no sham. Through and through
he was genuine. He represented power.

A grateful republic has raised this monument not as a
symbol of war but as a symbol of peace. Not the false
security, which may come from temporizing, from compromise, or from evasion, but that true and enduring

tranquillity which is the result of a victorious righteousness. The issues of the world must be met and met squarely. The forces of evil do not disdain preparation, they are always prepared and always preparing. General Grant gave fifteen years of his life to the military service of his country that he might be prepared to respond to a great crisis. The welfare of America, the cause of civilization will forever require the contribution of some part of the life of all our citizens to the natural, the necessary, and the inevitable demand for the defense of the right and the truth. There is no substitute for a militant freedom. The only alternative is submission and slavery.

The generations shall pass in review before this symbol of a man who gave his service, who made his sacrifice, who endured his suffering for the welfare of humanity. They shall know his good works. They shall look to him with admiration and reverence. They shall be transformed into a like spirit. What he gave, America shall give.

XV

There is no place for the cynic or the pessimist. Who is he that can take no part in business because he believes it is selfish? Who is he that can take no part in religion because he believes it is imperfect? These institutions are the instruments by which an eternal purpose is working out the salvation of the world. It is not for us to regard them with disdain; it is for us to work with them, to dedicate ourselves to them, to justify our faith in them.

THE INSTRUMENTS OF PROGRESS

THE world needs education in order that there may be a better estimation of true values. It is not easy to assemble facts. It is not easy to draw deductions. It is not easy to distinguish between the accidental and the essential. In the complications of modern civilization these are becoming more and more difficult. If world problems are to be solved it will be through greater application, through more education, through a deeper faith and a more complete reliance upon moral forces.

It is only those who cannot see beyond the present, who are lost in particulars, and who have no training to comprehend the greater sweep of events that come to lack the necessary courage to bear their share of the common burden. To a race which claims a heritage of eternity the important question is not where we are but where we are going. Education fails which does not help in furnishing this with some solution. It ought to confer the ability to see in an unfolding history the broadening out of the base of civilization, the continued growth of the power and the dignity of the individual, the enlarging solidarity and stability of society, and the increasing reign of righteousness.

There are two great standards, and two alone, by which men measure progress—creation and redemption. These are not accomplished facts; they are ever-present proc-

Address before the American University, Washington, District of Columbia, June 7, 1922.

esses. While we speak, their work is going on. They are the measure of the dominion of man over himself and over nature, and of his dedication of himself and all his powers to a moral purpose.

Measured by these standards, it would not seem difficult to justify the superiority and the increasing progress of modern civilization. Looking far back, the circumference of the enlightened world was very small. Its light existed, but it was everywhere surrounded by the darkness of ignorance, of superstition, and of savagery. There is no nation existing to-day which does not trace its ancestry back to a primitive people, yet each has come up through all the intermediate gradations to the present state, which it is scarcely too much to designate as world enlightenment. There are still dark places. There are yet remnants of the lower order, but even the Dark Continent is yielding to the light. There have been times when peoples have lapsed, when the march of a certain limited progress which they appeared to represent has ceased, but the cause has never lapsed. The Greek and Roman world lost for a time a part of its power of creation, but the power of redemption was not lost; it was rather increased as the people who inhabited those ancient empires and their dependencies turned to the Christian faith.

It was through that faith, and through the rediscovery of ancient learning by larger and larger masses of people, through the great universities and the teachings of the clergy, that there was brought about the final great reawakening of the Middle Ages, which established and strengthened the mighty creative power of modern science and invention. No one can dispute that power, no one can deny its increased and increasing dominion over all the forces of nature. Science stretches out its hand and reaches instantly any portion of the earth. It has brought under control forces comparable only with the resistless rise of wind and tide. It has weighed the earth in a balance and created instruments so delicate that they can detect a far-off whisper or measure the dynamic force of thought.

The Old World motive for creation, the motive of selfishness, of military aggrandizement, of imperialism, and of slavery, the motive which finally gained the ascendancy over the one-time devotion to moral purposes which characterized the early rise of Greece and Rome, was lost. It was lost because it became a perverted motive. It destroyed itself. A reawakened world rededicated itself to what was sound and true and good in the old motive strengthened and purified by Christian ideals. It was the general acceptance by modern life of this new motive which gave it direction and strength and an increasing creative power.

It was under its inspiration that despotism and slavery have steadily been diminished, and self-government and freedom have steadily been increased. It has been the directing force which has provided the material development of the modern world, established the groundwork of enlightened institutions, and given to humanity the moral character which has been the sustaining power of them all. The supremacy of this motive has marked the great world decisions of recent times. It lay at the foundation of the ambition of Peter the Great to reorganize and direct the energies of the Russian people; it inspired Gustavus Adolphus in his struggle for freedom; it was the deeply cherished sentiment of the parliamentary forces under the leadership of Oliver Cromwell; it was exhibited in the spirit of the French people when they were rousing themselves against despotism; it broke the power of the great Napoleon when he grasped at world dominion. The final consummation of these world forces has been America.

Wherever you may explore the high places of American history you come upon this same motive as the main cause of the action of her people. It was the thought of the early settlers where they raised up their altars and established their schools. It was the meaning of the life of Washington, of the great Declaration, and of the greater Federal Constitution. It is the explanation of Abraham Lincoln and the all-embracing freedom wrought out in his day. Finally, it sent two million men across the sea, that the cause of a Christian civilization might still remain supreme.

The power of creation and the power of redemption have come down through all the ages with mankind in ever-increasing proportions. They are the power to build and the power to endow with righteousness. They represent intelligence and sacrifice, the state and the church, the material and the spiritual. These are the forces upon which mankind can rely. They do not fail; they endure.

The world has been greatly shaken in the past decade. These forces have been tested as they never before were tested. The wonder is not that Russia, under a comparatively new organization which had never reached down to the heart of the people, collapsed; the wonder is that the world as a whole has stood firm, that it is gathering up the threads of existence, resuming its orderly progress, creating and redeeming itself anew. In the doing of this it is doing more, it is striving successfully to reach higher ideals.

The lessons of the great conflict have not gone unlearned. There are, to be sure, disappointment, disagreement, and irritation; but where in ages past such conditions would have made armed conflict inevitable, they are yielding to the power of persuasion and reason, through mutual consultation. There is a general admission throughout the earth of a mutual relationship and a mutual responsibility. There is the League of Nations, which, whether it be successful or not, whatever imperfections may be contained within its terms, is at least the attempted expression of a noble aspiration for world association and understanding. There are the Four-Power Treaty and the covenants for the limitation of the extent and use of armaments—all expressive of an even higher and nobler aspiration and an even firmer reliance upon reason as the foundation for all peace.

All these are creations the like of which the world has never before seen. There is, moreover, the working out of the salvation of mankind through the ever-existing law of redemption through sacrifice.

It would be easy to glance back over recorded history and see how when new institutions are needed they have been brought forth, and how when they have ceased their usefulness they have been cast aside. It would likewise be apparent that when there has been need for leaders they have been raised up to direct and to inspire, and when there has been a requirement for the results of science and invention these have been produced to meet the increasing necessities and to lighten the burden of mankind. Intelligence never rests; ceaselessly it works, building, perfecting, adorning. When creation has been required, creation has appeared.

Along with creation has gone redemption, always through sacrifice. The power of good ultimately to triumph over evil has never failed. When Western civilization was threatened by Attila, Rome and Gaul, in common cause, made that heroic sacrifice which redeemed all subsequent history. When later the followers of Mahomet imperilled Christianity, it was the Frankish hosts who saved it forever at Tours. Always the story runs the same. Whether it be necessary to meet the evil intent of Stuart Kings or the liberty-destroying acts of a Parliament inspired by a mad monarch, or to preserve a nation and rescue it from the curse of slavery, or to overcome the great delusion of world dominion, always there have been those who have made the supreme sacrifice by which these results have been accomplished. Always the cross and always the response. There is a power which moves resistlessly that justifies our faith.

There is scarcely any reliable authority which denies the right of the people to self-government; there is scarcely any dominion which denies obligation to the law of righteousness. Institutions of learning, organized charities, all of the forces of government and of religion, are making their ceaseless contributions to the unbought salvation of the world. The redemption goes on. The moral forces of the world are supreme.

This is the civilization which intelligence has created and which sacrifice has redeemed. We did not make it. It is our duty to serve it. Education ought to assess it at its true worth. It ought not to despise it but reverence it. If there be in education a better estimation of true values, it must be on the side of a great optimism. Under its examination human relationship stands forth as justified and sanctified. There is no place for the cynic or the pessimist. Who is he that can take no part in business because he believes it is selfish? Who is he that can take no part in religion because he believes it is imperfect? These institutions are the instruments by which an eternal purpose is working out the salvation of the world. It is not for us to regard them with disdain; it is for us to work with them, to dedicate ourselves to them, to justify our faith in them. It is a high calling in which to be even a doorkeeper is better than to rule over many multitudes of critics and philistines.

The great service which education must perform is to confirm our faith in the world, establish our settled convictions, and maintain an open mind. The heritage of all the past is neither mean nor insignificant. It is a high estate. The work of the world is neither undignified nor degrading. It lacks neither character nor nobility. It is the means and measure of all real manhood. It is truly the creation and the redemption. Those who are worthily engaged in it are ministers of a holy cause, priests of a divine imposition.

XVI

It is only when men begin to worship that they begin to grow. A wholesome regard for the memory of the great men of long ago is the best assurance to a people of a continuation of great men to come, who shall still be able to instruct, to lead, and to inspire. A people who worship at the shrine of true greatness will themselves be truly great.

GREAT VIRGINIANS

We meet here out of reverence for the past. We come with that resolution, which has characterized Americans, to show by our actions our adherence to those seasoned and established principles which have made our country the greatest among the nations of the earth. It is out of this that there is created the very natural desire to preserve those monuments which were associated with the great names and the great times which laid the foundation of our history.

For more than three generations, now, America has been building, a necessary and desirable operation, worthy of high commendation. This has been a strong index of progress. But to preserve also is to build, and to save is to construct. No people can look forward who do not look backward. The strongest guarantee of the future is the past. Unless that which has been built shall stand with an assured security, the motive for further building is destroyed, and all our structures will go down in ruins.

We need not only the story but the symbols of past history. We can best preserve our institutions by preserving our confidence in the men who did so much to establish them. It is only when men begin to worship that they begin to grow. A wholesome regard for the memory of the great men of long ago is the best assurance to a people of a continuation of great men to come, who shall still be able to instruct, to lead, and to inspire. A people who worship at the shrine of true greatness will themselves be truly great.

It is sometimes assumed that Americans care only for material things, that they are bent only on that kind of success which can be cashed into dollars and cents. That is a very narrow and unintelligent opinion. We have been successful beyond others in great commercial and industrial enterprises because we have been a people of vision. Our prosperity has resulted not by disregarding but by maintaining high ideals. Material resources do not, and cannot, stand alone; they are the product of spiritual resources. It is because America, as a nation, has held fast to the higher things of life, because it has had a faith in mankind which it has dared to put to the test of self-government, because it has believed greatly in honor and truth and righteousness, that a great material prosperity has been added unto it.

This fundamental characteristic of our countrymen is manifest all about us. We can see it in our incomparable charities, in our expanding art and literature, in our philanthropic and patriotic societies, in our tremendous missions, in our religious life. In all these there are revealed the fundamental purposes of our people. They are all the expressions of spiritual ideals.

This is the course of that inspiration which has moved different organizations to gather up the traditions of the past, to mark the location of historic events, to restore and preserve ancient habitations and buildings. It is all intensely American, it is done in the knowledge that where men have worked and wrought righteousness, there is holy ground.

No State is so rich in history and tradition as the Old Dominion of Virginia. The story of the early attempts at its settlement, of its lost colony, and the final success after failure, is all more fascinating than fiction. It has ever been the home of a proud and valiant race of pioneers and their descendants, of the early seventeenth century, strengthened and dignified by a dominant addition of Cavaliers and Huguenots, a sturdy and high-minded people, forever jealous of their rights and intent upon guarding and maintaining their liberties. There was always among them the courage of self-reliance and that true spirit of independence which results in local self-government. It was here in July, 1619, that there assembled the first parliament that was ever convened in America, when the first House of Burgesses met at Jamestown and there began those sessions which, being ever since continual, have made it the oldest of our legislative bodies. While the informal *Mayflower* Compact of November, 1620, holds a high place among the charters of free government, the first formal and authoritative charter which established free government on this continent was that granted to Virginia in July, 1621.

This was the beginning of true representative government. The public authority of the colony was vested in the governor, with veto power, who, together with his council and with the burgesses, made up of two men chosen by the inhabitants of each town, hundred, and plantation, constituted a general assembly, which was to meet each year and make all decisions by a majority vote. The colonies generally acknowledged the authority of the crown. They were always disposed to question the authority of Parliament. How great a step toward freedom and independence this charter was, is disclosed by the provision that when a form of government should be adopted, "no orders of court afterward shall bind the said colony unless they be ratified in like manner in the General Assemblies." Here began an assertion of popular rights carried over into the realm of action which the people of Virginia never relinquished.

When the colony felt itself aggrieved by the navigation laws of Charles II, and an unwarranted interference with its land titles, it did not hesitate to engage in a rebellion in 1676, the principles of which run a very close parallel to those of the American Revolution. It did not result in a final success in the field, but it did demonstrate that here were a people who knew and dared to assert their rights.

Thus was the foundation laid for the great days which were to come when Virginia was to bear an honorable and victorious part in the French and Indian Wars, and following this was to cast the influence of its great resources and great men into the struggle for American independence.

It is the Anglo-Saxon way first to appeal for the maintenance of rights to the courts of law, and it is only when those fail that resort is had to the sword. It was there that John Hampden had first sought protection from the illegal impositions of the King. It was before the judges that James Otis argued the illegality of the British Writs of Assistance at Boston. It was in a Virginia court that

Patrick Henry asserted, in 1763, that the Burgesses of Virginia were "the only authority which could give force to the laws of the government of this colony." It was but two years later that he moved those famous resolutions in the House of Burgesses, asserting chiefly that the general assembly of the colony had the sole right and power to levy taxes on its inhabitants. When these resolutions were adopted, Virginia stood forth as the first colony to declare its resistance to the imposition of stamp taxes.

From that time forth Virginia, at first perhaps unconsciously, was dedicated to the cause of American independence. Massachusetts looked to her confidently as "that ancient colony of whose disinterested virtue this province has had ample experience." Other great Virginians soon joined their names with that of Patrick Henry. There was George Mason, who drew up the Virginia Bill of Rights. This was adopted on the 15th of June, 1776. Two weeks later the new Constitution, which he had prepared, was adopted, so that Virginia declared its independence and set up its own form of government before the momentous action of the Continental Congress taken on the fourth day of the following July. Virginia regarded resistance to illegal exactions as the common cause of all the colonies. She did not fail to send money and supplies to those whom she designated as "our distressed fellow subjects of Boston." "British oppression," declared Patrick Henry, at the opening of the Congress, "has effaced the boundaries of the several colonies. The distinctions between Virginians, Pennsylvanians, New Yorkers, and New Englanders are no more. I am not a Virginian, but an American."

It was a Virginian, Peyton Randolph, who was president of the first Continental Congress. It was another Virginian, Richard Henry Lee, who, on the 7th of June, 1776, moved the adoption of the Declaration of Independence. John Adams, of Massachusetts, seconded the motion. It was another Virginian, Thomas Jefferson, to whom belongs the immortal honor of having drafted the Declaration. It is to the everlasting glory of the Old Dominion that it produced two men of the ability of Mason and Jefferson, one of whom set out in the Virginia Bill of Rights the great fundamental principles of liberty on which our State governments are founded, and the other proclaimed the great truths of our national life in the Declaration of Independence. Along with these great names go Edmund Pendleton, John Marshall, James Madison, and James Monroe.

There was yet another Virginian who towered above them all, who still stands as the first citizen of America, and is yet unsurpassed in greatness by any other man in history. It was he who, as general of the armies, was at times almost the sole support of the Revolution, and it was he who brought it to a successful close at Yorktown. It was he who lent the weight of his great character to the formation and adoption of the Federal Constitution. It was he who, as the first President, organized, established, and gave direction to the present government of the United States of America. In him there is the unusually remarkable combination of a great soldier, a great statesman, and a great patriot.

It is pre-eminently our regard for the memory of George Washington, for all who were associated with him, and for all that they represent that has inspired this gathering. There is standing in this historic city of Fredericksburg a mansion, built about 1752, and named Kenmore, by Colonel Fielding Lewis, the husband of Betty Washington, the only sister of the first President. On its walls are frescos designed by Washington himself, and said to have been executed originally by Hessian artists whom he had taken as prisoners of war during the Revolution. Here he had visited and been entertained with his friends, and here his mother often came during her declining years.

Colonel Lewis was a patriot who sacrificed a fortune in supplying the Revolutionary forces with arms and ammunitions. The mansion not only has these associations, but is a good example of colonial architecture, well fitted to rank in interest with the home of Jefferson, of Mason, of Lee, and with Mount Vernon itself. It ought to be preserved for its own sake. It must be preserved for the sake of patriotic America.

But it must be remembered that these monuments of the past are only the form and not the substance of that which we would perpetuate. They are helps, they are reminders, but of themselves they will not suffice. It is necessary that there be in us a like spirit to that which was in the Virginians of the brave days which we seek to commemorate. There is but one way to demonstrate adherence to principles, that is by acting in accordance with them.

It was not the Declaration which was proclaimed one hundred and forty-six years ago that gave America its independence. It was the action of the army in the field, led by Washington and his generals. It was the support of that army by the people of the colonies. It was the sacrifice made by those who pledged their lives, their fortunes, and their sacred honor to this high purpose.

The institutions which were established in that day, the constitutions which were adopted, the laws which were enacted, did not arise from any new thought. It was the action which was new. It was the people of the colonies, living in accordance with these principles, which constituted a new era in human history. The example of those inspiring times, the eloquence of Patrick Henry, the confidence in the people of Thomas Jefferson, the inspired judgment of John Marshall, the incomparable patriotism of George Washington will all be of no avail unless we shall make the necessary sacrifices to live up to the standard which they acclaimed.

The world to-day is filled with a great impatience. Men are disdainful of the things that are and are credulously turning toward those who assert that a change of institutions would somehow bring about an era of perfection.

It is not a change that is needed in our Constitution and laws so much as there is need of living in accordance with them. The most fundamental precept of them all—the right to life, liberty, and the pursuit of happiness—has not yet been brought into universal application. It is not our institutions that have failed, it is our execution of them that has failed.

The great principles of life do not change; they are permanent and well known. Men are not ignorant of what justice requires. No power can ever be brought into existence which will relieve of obligations. The sole opportunity for progress lies in their faithful discharge.

There is no reason for Americans to lack confidence in themselves or in their institutions. Let him who doubts them look about him. Let him consider the power of his country, its agriculture, its industry, its commerce, its development of the arts and sciences, its great cities, its enormous wealth, its organized society, and let him remember that all this is the accomplishment of but three centuries. Surely we must conclude that here is a people with a character which is not to be shaken. Imperfections there are, violations of the law there are, but public requirements were never so high in the intercourse of society, in the conduct of commerce, in the observance of the law, and in the faithful discharge of public office as at the present time.

There are criticisms which are merited, there always have been and there always will be; but the life of the nation is dependent not on criticism but on construction, not on tearing down but on building up, not in destroying but in preserving. If the American Revolution meant anything, it meant the determination to live under a reign of law. It meant the assertion of the right of the people to adopt their own constitutions, and when so adopted the duty of all the people to abide by them. The colonists of that day had had enough of the reign of force. They had had enough unlawful usurpation of their government, enough of the domination of a military force quartered in their midst. They wanted to escape from the rule of a force imposed from without and live in accordance with the light of reason which comes from within. That is the real mark of progress. That is the true liberation of mankind.

Those who now, under any form or for any purpose, seek to substitute for the reign of public law their own private desire, or any species of force, coercion, or intimidation, are not in harmony with the aims of the great Virginians. The industrial life of the nation cannot stand except on the recognition and observance by everybody connected with it of the fundamental precepts of American institutions. Nothing will ever be settled unless it be settled in accordance with them. Any other attempt will have as its result nothing but confusion, destruction, anarchy, and failure. Virginia has pointed out the way to harmony, to co-operation, to prosperity, and to justice. Her great example must still lead and inspire the nation.

XVII

*Democracy is obedience to the rule of the people.
. . . One of the great tragedies of American institutions is the experience of those who come here expecting to be able to rule without rendering obedience. They have entirely misconceived the meaning
of democracy. But they need not disturb its defenders. To cast it aside could only mean the acceptance of some old kind of rulers which have already
been discarded. The true hope of progress lies only
in perfecting it. Already it is better than anything
else in the world. But it rests entirely on the people.
It depends on their ability both to rule and to obey.
It is what they are. The government is what they
make it.*

THE MEANING OF DEMOCRACY

IT is the common experience of mankind, at first thought, to find their lot disappointing. America has just gone through such an experience in an exaggerated form. Almost in a day nearly the whole population found themselves raised from a condition that they had often regarded as poor and mean to a position of comparative affluence. There was a seller's market. Whatever could be sold brought a fabulous price. The cost of all kinds of commodities and the value of real estate became very high. The compensation for personal service, which is commonly designated as wages, was increased to a point far above what it had ever been before in all history. Incomes which had before been scarcely a hope or a dream to the people at large had suddenly become a reality.

This brought a power, never before possessed, to gratify desires. There was a great rise in the general scale of living. All at once luxuries had become necessities. But the great mass of people, regardless of station, found this extraordinary material prosperity disappointing and unsatisfying. Believing that the cause of their discontent was still a lack of possessions, they reached for more and more until an artificial condition was created beyond the power of the resources of the nation to sustain. The general effort to get more and give less did not work. The

Before the Ninth Annual Industrial Conference at Babson Institute, Wellesley Hills, Massachusetts, August 2, 1922.

inevitable reaction and depression followed. Something was lacking. People had expected that it would be supplied by having more property. It never has been. It never will be. They found that greater wealth, instead of relieving them of the necessity of work, only changed its nature and added to their responsibilities.

During this period there were those who made a wrongful use of their prosperity. They wasted it in extravagance, or worse, but they are not representative of the people as a whole. While they should be regarded with sympathy, the cause of their condition is perfectly apparent. It is the feeling of disappointment in the others which is the cause for concern. If the reason for their discontent be carefully examined, it will be seen that a considerable part of it is the result of their not thinking their problems through. They are the victims not of the want but of the deceitfulness of riches. They have found that having power does not remove from them the requirement of effort. They have found that human existence is not easy, and cannot be made easy. In whatever station, it is bound to be hard. They have found that the possession of everything of value, whether it be liberty or wealth, is held only by meeting the exaction of a price. The greater the value, the greater the price required.

If this discontent is not relieved by additional possessions, the remedy must lie in some other direction, for, surely, mankind has not been created and endowed with reason only to find that existence has been made a mockery without any power of self-satisfaction. If the material things of life are not of sufficient avail, the only resource left is in spiritual things.   If the gathering of possessions has not sufficed, it may be well to examine our attitude of mind toward possessions.   We need a fuller realization and a broader comprehension of the meaning both of political and economic democracy.   In this age of science and invention and organization, there is a special need for a full understanding of the foundations of industrial democracy.

The word democracy is used very inaccurately.   It is often taken to signify freedom and equality.   Many have thought it represented an absence of all restraints.   Others have considered it as providing a relief from all duties. The people of America have long been committed to democracy.   The best thought of the world has been compelled to follow them.   The easy way to understand what may be expected of it is first to understand what it is.

There has never been any organized society without rulers.   The great power of mankind has been created through unity of action.   This has meant the adoption of a common standard.   In most ancient times this was represented in the chieftain.   In modern times it is represented by a code of laws.   The important factor to remember is that it has always required obedience.   Democracy is obedience to the rule of the people.

The failure to appreciate this double function of the citizen has led to much misunderstanding, for it is very plain to see that there cannot be any rule of the people without a people to be ruled.   The difference between despotism and democracy is not a difference in the requirement of obedience, it is a difference in rulers.   He becomes an absolute sovereign by absolute obedience.

He will be a limited sovereign if he limits his obedience.
The criminal loses all his freedom. It is easy to see that
democracy will have attained perfection when laws are
made wholly wise and obedience is made wholly complete.
One of the great tragedies of American institutions is the
experience of those who come here expecting to be able
to rule without rendering obedience. They have entirely misconceived the meaning of democracy. But they
need not disturb its defenders. To cast it aside could
only mean the acceptance of a type of rule which had already been discarded. The true hope of progress lies
only in perfecting it. Already it is better than anything
else in the world. But it rests entirely on the people.
It depends on their ability both to rule and to obey.
It is what they are. The government is what they make
it.

This same principle has been working out in our economic and industrial life. We are slowly, and of course
painfully, arriving at a state of democracy in this field.
In its development it has been analogous to the development in political life. It is not very long ago that the
man who owned an industry assumed to be the absolute
lord over it. He ruled it. He fixed the hours and the
conditions of employment and dictated the amount of
wages. He recognized little or no obligation toward his
employees and had little regard for his customers.

In large enterprises the ownership gradually became
more and more divided with the advent of the corporation. In that case, oftentimes the management was intrusted to representatives, while the owners corresponded
to absentee landlords.

Under this system, as soon as employees could organize and make demands, a condition existed which led to the most violent and bitter of industrial disputes. All hands were eagerly asserting their right to rule, forgetful of their obligation to obey.

Investigation and experience have gradually brought about the recognition of the correct principle. Time and economic development will insure its adoption. Industry is changing from the theory of exclusion to the theory of inclusion. It no longer is content with one small part of the individual, it seeks to enlist all his powers, to recognize all his rights, as well as require the performance of all his obligations. In the ideal industry, each individual would become an owner, an operator, and a manager, a master and a servant, a ruler and a subject. Thus there would be established a system of true industrial democracy.

In very many industries this is already taking place. Employees are encouraged to purchase stock in the corporation and are provided with credit facilities for such purpose. This gives them ownership. They are encouraged to make suggestions for the better conduct of the business. They are requested to apply their inventive ability in the various mechanical operations. Through trade-unions and shop committees they have a large share in the determination of wages and conditions of labor. By the introduction of the sliding scale and piece-work they share in the general prosperity of the concern. This gives them management. Thus industrial democracy is being gradually developed.

There is a principle in our economic life that needs somewhat more emphasis. Long ago James Otis declared that kings were made for the good of the people and not the people for them. It needs also to be remembered that the people are not created for the benefit of industry, but industry is created for the benefit of the people. Those who are employed in it are its chief beneficiaries. Those who have acquired capital provide the plant and machinery for the workman. Those who have acquired skill in organization provide management for the workman. The manager secures the raw materials and markets the product. Capital and management perform this great service for the benefit of the workman. He performs a corresponding service for them. Unto each who contributes in accordance with his ability there is due equal consideration and equal honor. There is no degradation in industry; it is a worthy enterprise, ennobling all who contribute to it. It will be successful in accordance with the opportunity given for the development of all the powers of mankind and the acceptance of the obligation alike to rule and to obey.

The disappointment which has been experienced, at first thought, in the increase of power, whether of wealth or place, has resulted from the expectation that it would bring relief from the necessity of obedience. Neither political nor industrial democracy can relieve mankind from the requirement of obedience. There is no substitute for virtue. Too much emphasis has been put on the desire to rule and too little on the obligation to obey. More and more all social problems must be worked out in accordance with this principle. An obedient nation would possess supreme power.   The law of life, the law of progress, is the law of obedience, the law of service.

"Whosoever will be great among you, let him be your minister; And whosoever will be chief among you, let him be your servant."

XVIII

There is danger of disappointment and disaster unless there be a wider comprehension of the limitations of the law. The attempt to regulate, control, and prescribe all manner of conduct and social relations is very old. It was always the practice of primitive peoples. Such governments assumed jurisdiction over the action, property, life, and even religious convictions of their citizens down to the minutest detail. A large part of the history of free institutions is the history of the people struggling to emancipate themselves from all of this bondage.

THE LIMITATIONS OF THE LAW

THE growing multiplicity of laws has often been observed. The National and State Legislatures pass acts, and their courts deliver opinions, which each year run into scores of thousands. A part of this is due to the increasing complexity of an advancing civilization. As new forces come into existence new relationships are created, new rights and obligations arise, which require establishment and definition by legislation and decision. These are all the natural and inevitable consequences of the growth of great cities, the development of steam and electricity, the use of the corporation as the leading factor in the transaction of business, and the attendant regulation and control of the powers created by these new and mighty agencies.

This has imposed a legal burden against which men of affairs have been wont to complain. But it is a burden which does not differ in its nature from the public requirement for security, sanitation, education, the maintenance of highways, or the other activities of government necessary to support present standards. It is all a part of the inescapable burden of existence. It follows the stream of events. It does not attempt to precede it. As human experience is broadened, it broadens with it. It represents a growth altogether natural. To resist it is to resist progress.

Address before the American Bar Association, San Francisco, California, August 10, 1922.

But there is another part of the great accumulating body of our laws that has been rapidly increasing of late, which is the result of other motives. Broadly speaking, it is the attempt to raise the moral standard of society by legislation.

The spirit of reform is altogether encouraging. The organized effort and insistent desire for an equitable distribution of the rewards of industry, for a wider justice, for a more consistent righteousness in human affairs, is one of the most stimulating and hopeful signs of the present era. There ought to be a militant public demand for progress in this direction. The society which is satisfied is lost. But in the accomplishment of these ends there needs to be a better understanding of the province of legislative and judicial action. There is danger of disappointment and disaster unless there be a wider comprehension of the limitations of the law.

The attempt to regulate, control, and prescribe all manner of conduct and social relations is very old. It was always the practice of primitive peoples. Such governments assumed jurisdiction over the action, property, life, and even religious convictions of their citizens down to the minutest detail. A large part of the history of free institutions is the history of the people struggling to emancipate themselves from all this bondage.

I do not mean by this that there has been, or can be, any progress in an attempt of the people to exist without a strong and vigorous government. That is the only foundation and the only support of all civilization. But progress has been made by the people relieving themselves of the unwarranted and unnecessary impositions of government. There exists, and must always exist, the righteous authority of the state. That is the sole source of the liberty of the individual, but it does not mean an inquisitive and officious intermeddling by attempted government action in all the affairs of the people. There is no justification for public interference with purely private concerns.

Those who founded and established the American Government had a very clear understanding of this principle. They had suffered many painful experiences from too much public supervision of their private affairs. The people of that period were very jealous of all authority. It was only the statesmanship and resourcefulness of Hamilton, aided by the great influence of the wisdom and character of Washington and the sound reasoning of the very limited circle of their associates, that succeeded in proposing and adopting the American Constitution. It established a vital government of broad powers, but within distinct and prescribed limitations. Under the policy of implied powers adopted by the Federal party its authority tended to enlarge. But under the administration of Jefferson, who, by word, though not so much by deed, questioned and resented almost all the powers of government, its authority tended to diminish, and but for the great judicial decisions of John Marshall might have become very uncertain. But while there is ground for criticism in the belittling attitude of Jefferson toward established government, there is even larger ground for approval of his policy of preserving to the people the largest possible jurisdiction and authority. After all, ours is an experiment in self-government by the people themselves, and self-government cannot be reposed wholly in some distant capital; it has to be exercised in part by the people in their own homes.

So intent were the founding fathers on establishing a Constitution which was confined to the fundamental principles of government that they did not turn aside even to deal with the great moral questions of slavery. That they comprehended it and regarded it as an evil was clearly demonstrated by Lincoln in his Cooper Union speech, when he showed that substantially all of them had at some time by public action made clear their opposition to the continuation of this great wrong. The early amendments were all in diminution of the power of the government and declaratory of an enlarged sovereignty of the people.

It was thus that our institutions stood for the better part of a century. There were the centralizing tendencies and the amendments arising out of the War of '61; but, while they increased to some degree the power of the National Government, they were in chief great charters of liberty, confirming rights already enjoyed by the majority and undertaking to extend and guarantee like rights to those formerly deprived of equal protection of the laws. During most of this long period the trend of public opinion and of legislation ran in the same direction. This was exemplified in the executive and legislative refusal to renew the United States Bank charter before the war and in the judicial decision in the slaughter-house cases after the war. This decision has been both criticised and condemned in equally high places, but the result of it was perfectly clear. It was on the side of leaving to the people of the several States, and to their legislatures and courts, jurisdiction over the privileges and immunities of themselves and their own citizens.

During the past thirty years the trend has been in the opposite direction. Urged on by the force of public opinion, national legislation has been very broadly extended for the purpose of promoting the general welfare. New powers have been delegated to the Congress by constitutional amendments, and former grants have been so interpreted as to extend legislation into new fields. This has run its course from the Interstate Commerce Act of the late eighties, through the various regulatory acts under the commerce and tax clauses, down to the maternity-aid law which recently went into effect. Much of this has been accompanied by the establishment of various commissions and boards, often clothed with much delegated power, and by providing those already in existence with new and additional authority. The National Government has extended the scope of its legislation to include many kinds of regulation, the determination of traffic rates, hours of labor, wages, sumptuary laws, and into the domain of oversight of the public morals.

This has not been accomplished without what is virtually a change in the form, and actually a change in the process, of our government. The power of legislation has been to a large extent recast, for the old order looked on these increased activities with much concern. This has proceeded on the theory that it would be for the public benefit to have government to a greater degree the direct action of the people. The outcome of this doctrine has been the adoption of the direct primary, the direct election of the United States senators, the curtailment of the power of the speaker of the House, and a constant agitation for breaking down the authority of decisions of the courts. This is not the government which was put into form by Washington and Hamilton, and popularized by Jefferson. Some of the stabilizing safeguards which they had provided have been weakened. The representative element has been diminished and the democratic element has been increased; but it is still constitutional government; it still requires time, due deliberation, and the consent of the States to change or modify the fundamental law of the nation.

Advancing along this same line of centralization, of more and more legislation, of more and more power on the part of the National Government, there have been proposals from time to time which would make this field almost unlimited. The authority to make laws is conferred by the very first article and section of the Constitution, but it is not general; it is limited. It is not "All legislative powers," but it is "All legislative powers herein granted shall be vested in a Congress of the United States." The purpose of that limitation was in part to prevent encroachment on the authority of the States, but more especially to safeguard and protect the liberties of the people. The men of that day proposed to be the custodians of their own freedom. In the tyrannical acts of the British Parliament they had seen enough of a legislative body claiming to be clothed with unlimited powers.

For the purpose of protecting the people in all their rights, so dearly bought and so solemnly declared, the third article established one Supreme Court and vested it with judicial power over all cases arising under the Constitution. It is that court which has stood as the guardian and protector of our form of government, the guarantee of the perpetuity of the Constitution, and above all the great champion of the freedom and the liberty of the people. No other known tribunal has ever been devised in which the people could put their faith and confidence, to which they could intrust their choicest treasure, with a like assurance that there it would be secure and safe. There is no power, no influence, great enough to sway its judgments. There is no petitioner humble enough to be denied the full protection of its great authority. This court is human, and therefore not infallible; but in the more than one hundred and thirty years of its existence its decisions which have not withstood the questioning of criticism could almost be counted upon one hand. In it the people have the warrant of stability, of progress, and of humanity. Wherever there is a final authority it must be vested in mortal men. There has not been discovered a more worthy lodging-place for such authority than the Supreme Court of the United States.

Such is the legislative and judicial power that the people have established in their government. Recognizing the latent forces of the Constitution, which, in accordance with the spirit of the times, have been drawn on for the purpose of promoting the public welfare, it has been very seldom that the court has been compelled to find that any humanitarian legislation was beyond the power which the people had granted to the Congress. When such a decision has been made, as in the recent case of the child-labor law, it does not mean that the court or nation wants child labor, but it simply means that the Congress has gone outside of the limitations prescribed for it by the people in their Constitution and attempted to legislate on a subject which the several States and the people themselves have chosen to keep under their own control.

Should the people desire to have the Congress pass laws relating to that over which they have not yet granted to it any jurisdiction, the way is open and plain to proceed in the same method that was taken in relation to income taxes, direct election of senators, equal suffrage, or prohibition—by an amendment to the Constitution.

One of the proposals for enlarging the present field of legislation has been to give the Congress authority to make valid a proposed law which the Supreme Court had declared was outside the authority granted by the people by the simple device of re-enacting it. Such a provision would make the Congress finally supreme. In the last resort its powers practically would be unlimited. This would be to do away with the great main principle of our written Constitution, which regards the people as sovereign and the government as their agent, and would tend to make the legislative body sovereign and the people its subjects. It would to an extent substitute for the will of the people, definitely and permanently expressed in their written Constitution, the changing and uncertain will of the Congress. That would radically alter our form of government and take from it its chief guarantee of freedom.

This enlarging magnitude of legislation, these continual

proposals for changes under which laws might become
very excessive, whether they result from the praiseworthy
motive of promoting general reform or whether they reflect the raising of the general standard of human relationship, require a new attitude on the part of the people toward their government. Our country has adopted
this course. The choice has been made. It could not
withdraw now if it would. But it makes it necessary to
guard against the dangers which arise from this new position. It makes it necessary to keep in mind the limitation of what can be accomplished by law. It makes it
necessary to adopt a new vigilance. It is not sufficient
to secure legislation of this nature and leave it to go alone.
It cannot execute itself. Oftentimes it will not be com-
petently administered without the assistance of vigorous
support. There must not be permitted any substitution
of private will for public authority. There is required a
renewed and enlarged determination to secure the observance and enforcement of the law.

So long as the National Government confined itself to
providing those fundamentals of liberty, order, and justice for which it was primarily established, its course was
reasonably clear and plain. No large amount of revenue
was required. No great swarms of public employees were
necessary. There was little clash of special interests or
different sections, and what there was of this nature con-
sisted not of petty details but of broad principles. There
was time for the consideration of great questions of policy.
There was an opportunity for mature deliberation. What
the government undertook to do it could perform with a
fair degree of accuracy and precision.

But this has all been changed by embarking on a policy of a general exercise of police powers, by the public control of much private enterprise and private conduct, and of furnishing a public supply for much private need. Here are these enormous obligations which the people found they themselves were imperfectly discharging. They therefore undertook to lay their burdens on the National Government. Under this weight the former accuracy of administration breaks down. The government has not at its disposal a supply of ability, honesty, and character necessary for the solution of all these problems, or an executive capacity great enough for their perfect administration. Nor is it in the possession of a wisdom which enables it to take great enterprises and manage them with no ground for criticism. We cannot rid ourselves of the human element in our affairs by an act of legislation which places them under the jurisdiction of a public commission.

The same limit of the law is manifest in the exercise of the police authority. There can be no perfect control of personal conduct by national legislation. Its attempt must be accompanied with the full expectation of very many failures. The problem of preventing vice and crime and of restraining personal and organized selfishness is as old as human experience. We shall not find for it an immediate and complete solution in an amendment to the Federal Constitution, an act of Congress, or in the findings of a new board or commission. There is no magic in government not possessed by the public at large by which these things can be done. The people cannot divest themselves of their really great burdens by undertaking to provide that they shall hereafter be borne by the government.

When provision is made for far-reaching action by public authority, whether it be in the nature of an expenditure of a large sum from the Treasury or the participation in a great moral reform, it all means the imposing of large additional obligations upon the people. In the last resort it is the people who must respond. They are the military power, they are the financial power, they are the moral power of the government. There is and can be no other. When a broad rule of action is laid down by law it is they who must perform.

If this conclusion be sound it becomes necessary to avoid the danger of asking of the people more than they can do. The times are not without evidence of a deep-seated discontent not confined to any one locality or walk of life but shared in generally by those who contribute by the toil of their hand and brain to the carrying on of American enterprise. This is not the muttering of agitators; it is the conviction of the intelligence, industry, and character of the nation. There is a state of alarm, however unwarranted, on the part of many people lest they be unable to maintain themselves in their present positions. There is an apparent fear of loss of wages, loss of profits, and loss of place. There is a discernible physical and nervous exhaustion which leaves the country with little elasticity to adjust itself to the strain of events.

As the standard of civilization rises there is necessity for a larger and larger outlay to maintain the cost of existence. As the activities of government increase, as it extends its field of operations, the initial tax which it requires becomes manifolded many times when it is finally paid by the ultimate consumer. When there is added to this aggravated financial condition an increasing amount of regulation and police control, the burden of it all becomes very great.

Behind very many of these enlarging activities lies the untenable theory that there is some short cut to perfection. It is conceived that there can be a horizontal elevation of the standards of the nation, immediate and perceptible, by the simple device of new laws. This has never been the case in human experience. Progress is slow and the result of a long and arduous process of self-discipline. It is not conferred upon the people, it comes from the people. In a republic the law reflects rather than makes the standard of conduct and the state of public opinion. Real reform does not begin with a law, it ends with a law. The attempt to dragoon the body when the need is to convince the soul will end only in revolt.

Under the attempt to perform the impossible there sets in a general disintegration. When legislation fails, those who look upon it as a sovereign remedy simply cry out for more legislation. A sound and wise statesmanship which recognizes and attempts to abide by its limitations will undoubtedly find itself displaced by that type of public official who promises much, talks much, legislates much, expends much, but accomplishes little. The deliberate, sound judgment of the country is likely to find it has been superseded by a popular whim. The independence of the legislator is broken down. The enforcement of the law becomes uncertain. The courts fail in their function of speedy and accurate justice; their judgments are questioned and their independence is threatened. The law, changed and changeable on slight provocation, loses its sanctity and authority. A continuation of this condition opens the road to chaos.

These dangers must be recognized. These limits must be observed. Having embarked the government upon the enterprise of reform and regulation it must be realized that unaided and alone it can accomplish very little. It is only one element, and that not the most powerful in the promotion of progress. When it goes into this broad field it can furnish to the people only what the people furnish to it. Its measure of success is limited by the measure of their service.

This is very far from being a conclusion of discouragement. It is very far from being a conclusion that what legislation cannot do for the people they cannot do for themselves. The limit of what can be done by the law is soon reached, but the limit of what can be done by an aroused and vigorous citizenship has never been exhausted. In undertaking to bear these burdens and solve these problems the government needs the continuing indulgence, co-operation, and support of the people. When the public understands that there must be an increased and increasing effort, such effort will be forthcoming. They are not ignorant of the personal equation in the administration of their affairs. When trouble arises in any quarter they do not inquire what sort of a law they have there, but they inquire what sort of a governor and sheriff they have there. They will not long fail to observe that what kind of government they have depends upon what kind of citizens they have.

It is time to supplement the appeal to law, which is limited, with an appeal to the spirit of the people, which is unlimited. Some unsettlements disturb, but they are temporary. Some factious elements exist, but they are small. No assessment of the material conditions of Americans can warrant anything but the highest courage and the deepest faith. No reliance upon the national character has ever been betrayed. No survey which goes below the surface can fail to discover a solid and substantial foundation for satisfaction. But our countrymen must remember that they have, and can have, no dependence save themselves. Our institutions are their institutions. Our government is their government. Our laws are their laws. It is for them to enforce, support, and obey. If in this they fail, there are none who can succeed. The sanctity of duly constituted tribunals must be maintained. Undivided allegiance to public authority must be required. With a citizenship which voluntarily establishes and defends these, the cause of America is secure. Without that all else is of little avail.

XIX

Without the presence of a great directing moral force intelligence either will not be developed or, if it be developed, it will prove self-destructive. Education which is not based on religion and character is not education. It is a contradiction in terms to suppose that there can be any real intelligence which does not recognize the binding force of right, of justice, and of truth.

THE NEEDS OF EDUCATION

It would be exceedingly difficult to overestimate the important part that teachers take in the development of the life of the nation. They exercise their art, not on the materials of this world which pass away, but upon the human soul, where it will remain through all eternity. It is the teacher that makes the school, that sets its standard and determines its success or failure. Every one is familiar with the assertion of President Garfield that Mark Hopkins, sitting on one end of a log with a student on the other, would constitute a university. He did not particularize about the student, but he was careful to provide that the head of the institution was to be Doctor Hopkins. Only a trained and tried educator could fill the requirements for the head of a seat of learning that was to be dignified by the name of a university. With such a figure occupying that position, the character of the institution would be established.

There no doubt often arises a feeling on the part of the teaching force of the nation that they are lacking in public appreciation. They do not occupy positions which bring them into general prominence. Their compensation is not large in any event and, considering the length of time and the necessary expense required in preparation, is often very meagre. But if their rewards are not large,

Before the County Teachers' Institute and School Directors' Convention, at Reynoldsville, Pennsylvania, December 21, 1922.

they are seldom exposed to that species of criticism, often turning into positive abuse, which is the lot of many elective public servants. If they will but consider the estimation in which they hold those who formerly stood in the relationship of teachers to them, they will, at once, be forced to conclude that, in the opinion of those whose opinion they value, they are not without appreciation and honor. And they must know that whoever can pause for a moment to estimate the value of their work, the importance of their calling, its high requirements in learning and in character, will be moved to admiration for their devotion and their sacrifice.

In addition to this, the opportunity to teach the youth of America, with all the boundless possibilities that lie before each one of them, is a positive guarantee that this calling, continued for any length of time, will bring the teacher into contact with some who are marked with genius and will be known to fame. The opportunity in such a vocation to inspire reverence for the truth and a determination to master it, and live by it, is a compensation of satisfaction beyond what wealth can buy. To lead and infuse the youth of the country in that capacity is to be a minister to the republic.

True education has a twofold purpose. It has two great fundamental objects—the development of the moral power and the development of the intellectual power of the student.

One of the leading characteristics of modern life is its impatience. People are ambitious to secure the result without being willing to pay the necessary price for its attainment. They want the results of discipline without submitting themselves to be disciplined. They desire the immediate accomplishment of an object which, in reality, can only be secured by a long and laborious process. There is a tendency in education to forget the necessity of developing the moral power, the character, the determination to do right, and to place all the emphasis merely on the intellectual attainments. Such an effort cannot meet with success.

The biologists teach us that every individual has to climb up his own genealogical tree. It is a law that each life begins in its lowest form and goes up through all its intermediate stages to its present state of development. If any of the intermediate stages are omitted, development stops at that point. There is the blade, the ear, then the full corn in the ear; but the full corn cannot be secured without, first, the growth of the blade and the ear.

There is, likewise, evidence to support the conclusion that the individual develops as the race has developed. Fundamental requirements for the education of the individual will be found in the fundamental requirements for the development and progress of the race. That which laid the foundation of the intellectual awakening of races and peoples during the progress of history will lay the foundation of any real intellectual awakening of the student bodies of the present day.

The destruction that overtook the civilization which existed at the dawn of the Christian era came only after the predominant peoples of that time had lost their religious beliefs. They had cast aside their ideals. There were still schools and teachers, and people of high intelligence, but they no longer served the cause of righteousness. Might ruled, and might ruled alone, a naked power without sustaining influence. When that comes to represent authority such authority is only apparent, not real. The people at once recognize it as a counterfeit unworthy of their support, and turning from it with disgust, whether it represent a form of civilization, a social order, or a government, they will not protect it, they will not support it, but will be indifferent or rejoice in its destruction. This was the condition and the experience of Western civilization in the period preceding the Dark Ages. The seeds of a new order had been sown, but the old order perished. The moral power which had supplied the conquering vigor of the Roman legions in the day of their patriotic progress was gone. With it went their intellectual vigor. Civilization was waiting for a new light.

Slowly that new light spread over the world. Constantine acknowledged it as the guide of his empire. Gradually it worked its way into the German forests and the British Isles, often commingled and submerged in pagan rites and customs, but still burning with an enduring flame. Its ideals gave cause and direction to the Crusades. But it was not until the great religious revivals of the late Middle Ages that there was laid the foundation for that intellectual awakening which ushered in the modern era of science. The early settlement of New England was a religious movement. Its early government was a religious government. There was, likewise, a profound spiritual revival in the middle part of the eighteenth century, represented by the teachings and philosophy of Jonathan Edwards and the preaching of Whitefield in the Old World and the New, which preceded the successful assertion of the right of self-government and which, beginning its triumphant course in America, has never since ceased in its progress.

It was this great movement, reaching its apex in the early permanent settlement of America, which at once turned its attention to the founding of colleges, the providing of public schools, and the instituting of a general plan of education. The chief cause of these momentous results was the new importance that came to be attached to the individual, arising from a broader acceptance of religious ideals. Man was rediscovered. He was raised up to a new position. The possessor of immortality was no longer to be denied his rights. It logically followed that every avenue of development and achievement must be opened for the people. Freedom, education, culture, and refinement were acknowledged as the inalienable birthright of mankind. It was not education that founded religion, but it was religion that founded education. It was beside the place of worship that there grew up the school.

This important fact cannot be ignored in our development of education. Without its spirit either civilization will fall of its own weight, and that deep and abiding wisdom which supports society will cease to exist, or we shall have a type of mind keen in intelligence, but greedy and cruel, which, armed with the power of modern science in seeking to destroy others, will in the end accomplish its own destruction. Without the presence of a great directing moral force intelligence either will not be developed or, if it be developed, it will prove self-destructive. Education which is not based on religion and character is not education. It is a contradiction in terms to suppose that there can be any real intelligence which does not recognize the binding force of right, of justice, and of truth.

When we turn to the development of the intellect, it must always be kept in mind that the chief purpose of education is to teach man to think. In this field there are two kinds of training. One consists of the development of the power of imitation. This power is very great, and in the young it is very acute. When we remember that it gives to the child the power of speech, with all its complications, we can see how great it is. Carried forward, it is the ability to memorize and to follow custom. If pursued to its logical conclusion, it ends in the creation of a caste system under which the whole race will fall into the senseless condition of being the same that their fathers had been. The accidental and the inconsequential would assume the same importance as the necessary and the essential. Life would be conducted not by reason but by rote. All progress would cease.

Unless we are to be content with the superficial, the cynical, and the immature, something more substantial than this is needed to bring out the best that there is in life. The real constructive power of the mind must be sought. It is necessary to provide a training which will enable a student to assemble facts, draw conclusions, and weigh evidence. Education must bring out these higher powers of the mind, if the result is to be real manhood and real character. The goal is not to be the lower reaches of mere animal existence but the higher reaches of beings endowed with reason. Such a result can only be secured by long and tireless discipline. Courses of study must be pursued which require close application, accurate observation, precise comparison, and logical conclusion. I know of no courses which have supplied these requirements better than the study of mathematics, Latin, and Greek when they are supplemented by contemplation of the great truths of philosophy and a generous knowledge of history. The ideal of education must be not a special training leading to a one-sided development but a broad and liberal culture which will bring into operation the whole power of the individual.

We have witnessed a falling away from this ideal. This has come, in part, from a spirit of pessimism which has gone so far as to question the power of the average individual to reach a high state of development and therefore the ability of civilization to maintain itself. The real problem is not one of intelligence, but one of disposition. The people of the present day are better trained and more intelligent than they were in the past. Sufficient intellectual power has existed to bring the world to its present high state of enlightenment. In spite of many seeming failures, there is no real evidence which warrants the assumption that sufficient power does not now exist to maintain and support the advance of progress. Unless we have this faith, and unless it be justified, we shall come very close to being obliged to deny the existence and reality of the modern era of history. Unless education can be based on a belief in mankind and in the power of the race as a whole to develop by response to the teachings of the truth, education might as well be abandoned. It must assume that a spirit of optimism is warranted.

But while the tendency to discredit the power of the individual has had its effect, a larger contributing cause has arisen from our commercial impatience. There has been a strong demand for that kind of an intellectual training which could be at once translated into dollars and cents. Our country has gone through the most rapid industrial development that the human race has ever seen. It has been a land of pioneers. Men have cut loose from old associations, both of place and of custom. They have moved out into our unoccupied and uninhabited territory and into new and untried regions of production and commerce. These conditions contributed to the very typical success of the American who oftentimes, though he had what was for him the soundest kind of an education and had undergone the severest course of mental discipline in the exacting school of experience, had not had the advantage of attending institutions of liberal culture. Oftentimes this type of man disregards the background and the surroundings of liberal culture without which his own success would have been absolutely impossible, and, forgetting his relation to society, the state, and civilization in general, thinks only of himself and of others as individuals. His argument is likely to run into the statement that he succeeded without attending the schools; many to whom he can point, who had the use of the schools, did not succeed; and therefore, if a liberal education is not a real hindrance to success, it is probably no help and certainly unnecessary.

This argument is often supplemented with the assertion that the methods of education are not sufficiently practical. It is claimed that the learning of the schools does not fit a student to participate in the daily affairs of life. It does not teach the art of earning a living, and therefore, while schools may be good things, they should confine their attention more to the teaching of trades, of occupations, and of the performance of the useful things necessary for self-support and the acquisition of property in the carrying on of the business of modern society.

All of this results from taking too narrow a view of the situation. Great captains of industry who have aroused the wonder of the world by their financial success would not have been captains at all had it not been for the generations of liberal culture in the past and the existence all about them of a society permeated, inspired, and led by the liberal culture of the present. If it were possible to strike out that factor from present existence, he would find all the value of his great possessions diminish to the vanishing-point, and he himself would be but a barbarian among barbarians.

This is not to say that we do not need vocational training, technical schools, and professional learning, where all the practical affairs and arts of life may be taught. There is urgent necessity for them, but they do not displace, they supplement liberal culture. The laws of progress are stern and unyielding. There is no means by which they can be cheated or evaded. Real wisdom will not be developed by pursuing a method of education that leaves out of consideration the human soul, nor will real prosperity arise by relying upon a materialism which leaves out of consideration human ideals. Prosperity is necessary; success is imperative. Too much emphasis cannot be placed on these requirements. But one of the questions with which education deals is how they may be secured. It must be remembered that a liberal culture came first in the effort for progress. It must be placed first. It sets the standard, it provides the ideals without which there can be no material prosperity.

The standards and ideals of society rank first in importance. They must be maintained, if there is to be any real industrial progress. They are, likewise, the foundation of American institutions. In education the whole being must be taken into consideration. It is not enough to train the hand, the eye, to quicken the perception of the senses, develop the quickness of intellect, and leave out of consideration the building up of character, the aspirations of the soul. The fact is that in our industrial life men cannot be dealt with on a purely commercial basis. They are very much more than the mechanical services which they sell in the shop and the market-place, and the attempt to deal with them in our industrial life, without taking all this into consideration, always proves a failure. That is one reason why materialism cannot stand alone. Mankind are reasonable beings. Any human relationship that is attempted to be organized on any other theory is bound to be a failure.

There is the most urgent necessity for a broader understanding of the teachings of history and the comprehension of the height and breadth of human nature, if we are to maintain society, if we are to support civilization. Much of the unrest of the present day, many of the unwise proposals for change in the way of laws, and the large amount of criticism of our government would be completely answered if there were a better general knowledge of history. It is easy to demonstrate that we are very far from perfection. It is natural to assume that, therefore, we must be on the wrong track. Nothing is more instructive and satisfying than to compare our own condition with that which existed in past generations, or with that which is the lot of other peoples at the present day. Progress has a historical and institutional as well as a logical foundation. People cling to their customs, so that the theory of government and society which might be logically sound and perfect, might not find ready adoption by any nation, and what might produce good results in one country would be found to be not workable in another. Especially is it desirable that there should be more accurate knowledge of the causes and events which brought about the settlement of our own land and which went into the formation of its institutions.

Of course there is need of a better understanding of the American form of government. Self-government is still government. There is no such thing as liberty without restraint. My rights are always represented by the duties of others. My freedom is always represented by the obedience of others. Their rights and their freedom are represented by my duties and my obedience. In all the discussion of the American Government that has gone on since its establishment, the chief stress and emphasis has been put upon freedom and liberty. The perfecting of human relationships to which our country has made such an enormous contribution has, in a very large degree, lain in that direction. This possession must be defended, supported, and cherished, for it is of priceless value. But this is not the most necessary for the youth of the land to learn. It is only a part of the story. It is not even the beginning, but rather the end. It is not the cause, it is the result. Any attempt to maintain rights, to secure freedom and liberty for ourselves without the observance of duties and the rendering of obedience toward others, is a contradiction of terms. It defeats itself.

More and more emphasis needs to be placed on the duty of obedience. It must be the first lesson of the child in the home, it must be continued without ceasing in the schools, and it must be established and maintained as the predominant principle of good citizenship.

We are a race of beings created in a universe where law reigns. That will forever need all the repetition and emphasis which can be put on it. Law reigns. It can neither be cheated, evaded, nor turned aside. We can discover it, live in accordance with it, observe it, and develop, and succeed; or, we can disregard it, violate it, defy it, and fail. Law reigns. It is the source of order, of freedom, of righteous authority, of organized society, and also of industrial success and prosperity. To disregard it is to perish, to observe it is to live, physically, mentally, morally, spiritually. It is this principle that requires respect and reverence for authority. It is not sought for the benefit of those who may temporarily represent government or any other example of authority, but for the benefit of the individual himself.

It is perfectly apparent that the needs of education were never greater than they are at the present time. We do not diminish our requirements by raising the standards of civilization. We increase them. In primitive days there was little need of much which is now an absolute necessity. Existence was pitched on a lower scale. It was possible to succeed, according to the standards of that time, with a training altogether different from what is now absolutely necessary. Personal contact was not so close. Life was more solitary. When the struggle for existence was not so exacting, there was less danger that some might do harm to themselves, but less danger that they might do harm to others. The intricate and highly organized society of the present day is only able to give advantages to its members which were unheard of in the past, by insisting on requirements far above those of the past. It is the existence of these necessary conditions which raises the question of whether modern civilization will be able to maintain its progress or whether it is more likely to break down. Certain mental tests have been tried for the purpose of estimating the intellectual capacity of individuals, and there has been an attempt to draw the conclusion that there exists a large body of people endowed with only a moderate mentality. But the capabilities of these people to respond to educational training is still unknown, and no one has yet put a measuring-stick on the possibilities of the human soul. Man is far more than intelligence. It is not only what men know but what they are disposed to do with that which they know that will determine the rise and fall of civilization. There is no evidence that there is a lack of sufficient intelligence to support the present state of society, and no one has ever questioned that there exists in people a sufficient moral power, if only to be used not to destroy but to construct. The realization of progress that has marked the history of the race, the overwhelming and irresistible power which human nature possesses to resist that which is evil and respond to that which is good, are a sufficient warrant for optimism. If this were not so, teaching would be a vain and useless thing, an ornament to be secured by a few, but useless to the multitude.

Our country adheres to quite another standard. It has founded its institutions not on the weakness but on the strength of mankind. It undertakes to educate the individual because it knows his worth. It relies on him for support because it realizes his power. It has not yet been possible for either government or society to provide a college course or university training for all, but there is in existence a system of education which gives a very general access of the public at large to the ideals which are taught in these institutions. They filter out through the primary and secondary schools, through the pulpit and the press into the hearts of the people. We are working toward a greater democracy in our education by providing training that will fit the student for various professions and vocations of life, each in accordance with his own choice. But the chief end of it all, the teaching of how to think and how to live, must never be forgotten.

All of this points to the same conclusion, the necessity of a foundation of liberal culture, and the requirement for broadening and increasing the amount of moral intellectual training to meet the increasing needs of a complicated civilization. Free schools and compulsory attendance are new experiences. No power of government can bring them to success. If they succeed, it will be through the genuine effort and support that can come only from the heart of the people themselves. It is this condition that makes the position of the teacher rise to such high importance.

The standards which teachers are required to maintain are continually rising. Their work takes on a new dignity. It is rising above a calling, above a profession, into the realm of art. It must be dignified by technical training, ennobled by character, and sanctified by faith. It is not too much to say that the need of civilization is the need of teachers. The contribution which they make to human welfare is beyond estimation. In our own country this service was never better performed than at the present day. The earnest conscientious men and women, running from the head of the great university down to the kindergarten, represent a force for good which is immeasurable. The influence which they create for better things, the inspiration which they give for higher ideals, are the chief contributing force to the stability of society and the march of progress. They point the way to the dawn, they lead toward the morning, toward light, toward truth.

XX

We have come to our present high estate through toil and suffering and sacrifice. That which was required to produce the present standards of society will ever be required for their maintenance. Unless there is an eternal readiness to respond with the same faith, the same courage, and the same devotion in the defense of our institutions which were exhibited in their establishment, we shall be dispossessed, and others of a sterner fibre will seize on our inheritance.

THE PRICE OF FREEDOM

It is altogether natural that those who are connected
with religious institutions should be interested in supporting good government. Their interest comes not
merely from the ethical teachings of their faith, which
are always finally on the side of liberty and justice, established through the maintenance of the orderly processes
of the law, but it comes from a realization that in its historical development also religion has laid the foundation
of government. This is pre-eminently true of our American political system. It neither seeks nor claims any
justification for its existence save righteousness. It had
its beginning, it found its inspiration, in the religious beliefs of the men who settled our country, made it an independent nation, and established and maintained its
Constitution and its laws. If it is to endure, it will be
through the support of men of like mind and like character.

The people who laid the foundation of our institutions
had seen a great searching out of minds in the sixteenth
century. It was during that period that there had been
put forth in matters of religion and had come to be acknowledged the principle of private judgment. A remarkable body of men held to this theory with a tenacity
which no persecution was able to shake. Along with it

Before the Evanston Sunday Afternoon Club, at Evanston, Illinois,
January 21, 1923.

went the complementary doctrine of the direct contact of the individual with the Almighty. Here were the standards of intellectual freedom and religious liberty, which have ever since been asserted with increasing acceptance.

It is this principle of individual freedom in religious life, which became established by the final struggles of the sixteenth century, that was carried over into the struggle for individual freedom in political life which took place in the seventeenth century. The settlement of America in increasing numbers was the direct outcome of both of these fundamental developments in the march of human progress. In the impelling force which brought the Pilgrims to Plymouth, the thought of their religious freedom was predominant. While this motive was not absent from the greater and stronger movement which brought many thousands of Puritans to the region at their north, coming at a later time and under different conditions, they were the more strongly influenced by political considerations. But it is impossible to separate the cause of the great migration in those days from the Puritan movement for a free church and a free government which reached a position of temporary power under Cromwell sufficient to be permanently established under William and Mary.

The cause of all this was a great liberal movement, a revolt against authority imposed from without, and the determination to accept for guidance the light of reason which shines from within. It was a groping toward the light of self-government under such free institutions as characterize our republic. In those early days it was the preaching of the clergy rather than the teaching of the magistrates that expounded and maintained the doctrine which, when finally accepted, resulted in our present form of government. Students of that period give a very large credit to that learned clergyman, Thomas Hooker, who first settled with his congregation at Cambridge, but afterward in the pursuit of a larger freedom moved with his parishioners to Hartford. He expressed his faith in free representative government when he said in a letter to Winthrop: "In matters which concern the common good, a General Council chosen by all to transact businesses which concern all, I conceive most suitable to rule, and most safe for relief of the whole." In accordance with the custom of that day, he preached a sermon at the opening of the General Court, in 1638, in which he announced the fundamental principles of democracy which the development of America has established:

The foundation of authority is laid in the free consent of the people,
The choice of public magistrates belongs to the people, by God's own allowance,
They who have power to appoint officers and magistrates have the right also to set the bounds and limitations of the power and place unto which they call them.

Within a short space of time he and his people were living under a written constitution in the Colony of Connecticut, said to be the first which established a complete form of government, and the seed of the American Republic was sown, of which the but partial harvest has been so prolific of human welfare.

Another clergyman of like mind was John Wise, of Ipswich, who had been imprisoned for protesting against the despotic rule of Andros. Early in the eighteenth century he declared: "The end of all good government is to cultivate humanity and promote the happiness of all, and the good of every man in all his rights, his life, liberty, estate, honor, and so forth, without injury or abuse to any," a sentiment which it is not unlikely was familiar to Jefferson, as he set out the immortal Declaration of Independence. By a coincidence, not to be wondered at, another clergyman of Ipswich, Manasseh Cutler, was the author of the Ordinance of 1787, which organized the Northwest Territory and excluded from it the institution of human slavery. It would be difficult to cite action of more far-reaching consequences, more productive of human welfare.

These are some of the prominent examples of the direct influence of religion and religious teachers on the establishment of the American Republic. In this accomplishment they did not act alone, nor were they unsupported by their people. Rather, they were representative of prevailing ideals, to which they gave form and expression. They spoke the word that was in the hearts of their countrymen. From their beliefs there flowed naturally and inevitably those principles and those actions which gave us our form of government and raised this nation to the high position it holds in the world.

They believed in the divine origin of mankind. They saw in him the image of his Creator. Out of the mists of doubt and uncertainty there had come to them a revelation of his dignity and glory. Through a common Fatherhood they perceived a common brotherhood.

From this conception there resulted the recognition that freedom was a birthright. It was the natural and inalienable condition of beings who were created "a little lower than the angels." With it went the principle of equality, not an equality of possessions, not an equality of degree, but an equality in the attributes of humanity, an equality of kind. Each is possessed of the divine power to know the truth.

It is in accordance with these standards that the American people adopted their Constitution and set up their government. In the possession, maintenance, and enjoyment of these rights the individual has the guarantees of public law. Freedom is secured by every means that legislative ingenuity can provide. There are no class distinctions. The government deals with its citizens on the basis of equality. The high estate of mankind is not disregarded. The government and society provide ever-increasing facilities for education, better living conditions, and around the weak there is thrown the protection of humanitarian legislation. The power to legislate is executed through representative bodies, the greatest safeguards of liberty, chosen directly by the people. The administration of justice has been intrusted to courts as free, impartial, and independent as it is possible for human nature to devise. The ultimate decision of all questions of law and justice rests with the people themselves. They have the complete authority to enlarge or diminish, to support or to overthrow. The government is their government, the laws are their laws, the decisions of the courts are their decisions. All speak with their voice. They are in the possession of complete sovereignty.

Along with the solemn assurance of freedom and equality goes the guarantee of the right of the individual to possess, enjoy, and control the dollar which he earns, and the principle that it shall not be taken away without due process of law. This necessarily goes with any theory of independence or of liberty, which would be only a mockery unless it secured to the individual the rewards of his own effort and industry.

These are the ideals which supply the foundation of American institutions. It would be idle to claim that they are always perfectly carried into effect. Before action can be perfect, knowledge must be perfect, and that state has by no means been reached; but it is easy to see what a change in these standards would imply. If we are not to proceed on the assumption of the innate nobility of mankind, then there must be an assignment of some lower estate. If freedom and equality are not to be maintained, then there must be servitude and class distinction. If all the people are not to be permitted to rule, then there must be a rule of a part of the people. If there is not to be self-government, there must be some form of despotic government. If the individual is not to have the dollar which he himself earns, then he must be forced to hand it over to some one who has not earned it. Those who advocate a change in our standards, a change in our ideals, a change in our institutions, a change in our theory of government, can only proceed in this direction. No other course is open to them.

The general results of our institutions would appear to be so obvious as to need little defense. If by the increase of civilization we mean the strength and welfare of organized society, the protection and security of the individual, the growth of self-government, the general diffusion of knowledge, a wide distribution of property, the effective direction of productive industry, and the advance of science and invention, there can be no hesitation in declaring that under the system which America represents there has been a most gratifying progress. This is not to say that in the days of old there were not intellects as keen, nor the perception of truths as profound as any which characterize the modern mind, but no one can deny that at present there is far greater intelligence and a much wider scope of knowledge.

It cannot be disputed that at times the old barbarities break out, and there blazes up the ancient ferocity of the cave and the forest, but these are no longer matters of indifference. Generally they meet with retribution, always with condemnation. The humanity of a common brotherhood asserts itself in the relief of the oppressed and the rescue of the imperilled.

There is not wanting criticism of the character of society and the effectiveness of our laws because the general community has not reached a golden age of indolence and profusion. The truth is that most of the generations which have gone before, could they be transplanted into present surroundings, would feel that they had gone far toward that unattainable goal. When we compare the toil and privations which were in former times the lot of the great mass of mankind, the universal marks of old age which came not from years but from hardship and exposure, and the narrow and contracted plane of existence, the meagre returns for great effort, with the present limited and moderate hours of employment under healthful and sheltered conditions, the broad outlook, the generous compensation, the progress in this direction is abundantly apparent.

The great mistake which is here made is in supposing that under some form of government, or in some advanced state of civilization, people can exist without effort and live wholly at ease. The opposite conclusion would be more nearly correct. It requires less intelligence, less skilful effort, to live among a tribe of savages than to maintain existence under the average conditions of modern society. Independence, liberty, civilization—these are not easy to bear; they are hard to bear. It is not sloth and ease but work and achievement which are the ideals of the present day. It was not long ago that the men who had a competence thought it required them to support themselves in idleness. They sought for lives of leisure removed from any kind of toil. That practice, which tended to breed a class which were selfish, greedy, and cruel, has, for the most part, been discontinued by common condemnation. There came a realization that such an existence led to no opportunity, and furnished no real satisfaction. These are now sought in a higher aim. More and more men are seeking to live in obedience to the law of service under which those of larger possessions confer larger benefits upon their fellow men. The greater their power, the greater their service. The great apostle of this creed was Theodore Roosevelt, who stated it most accurately when he declared: "I wish to preach, not the

doctrine of ignoble ease, but the doctrine of the strenuous
life, the life of toil and effort, of labor and strife; to preach
that highest form of success which comes, not to the man
who desires mere easy peace, but to the man who does
not shrink from danger, from hardships, or from bitter
toil, and who out of these wins the splendid ultimate
triumph."

Civilization is the bearer of great gifts, the source of
ever-enlarging opportunity. It is not the result of a
self-existing plenty, but rather the product of a high
endeavor. It does not rob life of all that is noble, but
inspires it to all that is heroic.

There are two broad theories which have held sway in
the world. They have developed with the development
of the race. One is the system of class and caste, the
system of servitude of body and of mind, of a claim of
divine right of rulers by inheritance—a system where the
individual is nothing and the government is all supreme.
Under such a conception there can be no real freedom,
no independent choice, and therefore no responsibility.
The people look to the rulers. They do what they are
told to do; they believe what they are told to believe. A
bureaucracy will grow up under which will be rigid supervision of every activity, whether public or private. Paternalism will flourish in its worst form. Carried to its
logical conclusion, such institutions might provide, for
a short space of time, a machine of apparent great efficiency. But such a result could be but temporary.
Either the life will go out of such a community, its initiative will vanish, and its society will fossilize into a state
where there is neither hope nor progress, or, undertaking
to extend its dominion by aggression in accordance with

its principle, it will be beset from without and overcome, or, responding to an irresistible urge, its own subjects, casting down this artificial edifice, will assert their true nature in a declaration of their right to be free. Governments apparently stable and a seeming civilization have been reared on this theory, but always their end has been destruction.

There is another system with which every American should be familiar, a system of equality and of freedom, not without the claim of divine right but recognizing that such right reposes in the people; a system where the individual is clothed with inalienable rights, the people are supreme, the government is their agent. Under this conception there is real freedom, real independence, and grave personal responsibility. The rulers look to the people. Their authority is the public will, ascertained in accordance with law. There will be the least possible interference with private affairs. Realizing that it is the people who support the government and not the government which supports the people, there will be no resort to paternalism. Under such institutions there may appear to be a lack of machine-like efficiency, but there will be no lack of character. Private initiative will be stimulated. Self-reliance and self-control will be increased. Society will remain a living organism sustaining hope and progress, content to extend its dominion not by conquest but by service. Such is the system of self-government, the orderly rule of the people, carrying within itself a remedy for its own disorders and the power of self-perpetuation. This is the ideal of America.

No one would say that existence under these conditions

is effortless. Independence is exceedingly exacting, self-control is arduous, self-government is difficult. Always there is the temptation that some element of these should be surrendered in exchange for security and ease. The appeal to passion and prejudice always lies in this direction. The proposal to despoil others of their possessions is a manifestation of the same spirit. This is the reason that to certain of our native-born, and more often to our foreign-born, the American Republic proves a disappointment. They thought that self-government meant the absence of all restraint, that independence meant living without work, and that freedom was the privilege of doing what they wanted to do. It has been a hard lesson for them to learn that self-government is still government, that the rule of the people does not mean absence of authority, that independence means self-support, and that complete freedom means complete obedience to law. They are disappointed more than ever when they learn, as ever they do, that these are so, not because they have been decreed by some body of men, but that they are so by the very nature of things, and all the governments in the world are powerless to change them.

Here again it is perfectly obvious that if the American system is to be cast aside there is only the one other system which can be adopted. The call of the old life of ignorance, of fear, of superstition, of every savage instinct is all toward the old system. The call of the new life of learning, of courage, of enlightened reason, of faith, of religion is all toward the new system. In a contest between these forces it does not seem difficult to judge which are finally to be supreme.

Nevertheless, there is in our country a considerable body of thought which looks upon present tendencies with a great deal of apprehension. Pointing out the high estate of modern civilization, the complicated organization required for its support, the forces which are working against it, they have come to doubt the existence of sufficient intellectual force for the maintenance and advance of progress. Lately they have attempted a quantitative analysis of a cross-section of the people to determine by the application of scientific methods the amount of their intelligence. They have thought that it does not test very high, and that, therefore, civilization is in grave peril of failure. It cannot be denied that there are dangerous tendencies. The fact that one great empire broke down is not to be ignored. But self-government did not break down.

The diffusion of knowledge and the increase in general intelligence are very important. To some it may appear very inadequate. But does any one suppose that it was greater in the sixteenth century, when it was sufficient to sustain a profound spiritual awakening? Does any one suppose that it was greater in the seventeenth century, when out of its abundance there was accomplished a great political revolution which established the sovereignty of the people? Does any one suppose that it was greater in the eighteenth century, when it was adequate for the creation of the American Republic?

While the teaching of ideals has had its source in institutions of higher learning, the motive power of progress and reform has not come from the high and mighty but from the mass of the people. Such movements have their

origin close to the soil. The support for religious freedom came from the people. The army of Cromwell was
altogether wanting in a tinge of nobility. The leaders of
his military force and the prominent figures of his government were tradespeople and artisans, reaching even to
the servant class. The Pilgrims were humble people. For
the most part, the wealth and aristocracy of the colonies
did not follow Washington, but the support of the Revolution came from the farm, from the men of the town
meeting.

The truth would appear to be that only a part of the
power of the people is revealed in any quantitative analysis of their intelligence, however accurate it may be.
It is not the quantity of knowledge that is the chief glory
of man. Great as have been the accomplishments through
invention, large as are the attainments of science, thoroughly established as are many great principles, it is
altogether probable that compared with the discoveries
that are yet to come they will be, in many respects, surpassed. The strength and the glory of man is not to be
sought in quantity but in quality. It is in the moral
power to know the truth and respond to it, to resist evil
and hold to that which is good, that is to be found the
real dignity and worth, the chief strength, the chief
greatness. This power, even in the humblest and the
most unlettered, rises to a height which cannot be measured, which cannot be analyzed. It is this strength of
the people which can never be ignored.

Of course it would be folly to argue that the people
cannot make political mistakes. They can and do make
grave mistakes. They know it; they pay the penalty.

But compared with the mistakes which have been made by every kind of autocracy they are unimportant. It is well also that the people have the power to organize for their industrial protection and advantage. Here too there may be serious errors, but here too such errors have been matched by the errors of those charged with the responsibility of management. Oftentimes the inconvenience and loss fall on the innocent. This is all a part of the price of freedom. We have to bear one another's burdens whether we will or no. We have to make personal sacrifice for the common good. We cannot have what is good unless we pay the price. Unless the people struggle to help themselves, no one else will or can help them. It is out of such struggle that there comes the strongest evidence of their true independence and nobility, and there is struck off a rough and incomplete economic justice, and there develops a strong and rugged national character. It represents a spirit for which there could be no substitute. It justifies the claim that they are worthy to be free.

This is very far from saying that civilization can be maintained without any effort, or that the institutions of our government can exist without the exercise of constant vigilance. We have come to our present high estate through toil and suffering and sacrifice. That which was required to produce the present standards of society will ever be required for their maintenance. Unless there is an eternal readiness to respond with the same faith, the same courage, and the same devotion in the defense of our institutions which were exhibited in their establishment, we shall be dispossessed, and others of a sterner fibre will seize on our inheritance. But this is to say that in the teachings of history and in the divine nature of mankind there is every warrant for the profoundest belief that faith and hope are justified and that righteousness will prevail.

We need to learn and exemplify the principle of toleration. We are a nation of many races and of many beliefs. The freedom of the human mind does not mean the mere privilege of agreeing with others, it means the right of individual judgment. This right our government undertakes to guarantee to all without regard and without punishment to any for following the dictates of their own consciences. It is on this principle that speech is free, the press is free, and religion is free.

But it must be remembered that there are standards of morality, customs of intercourse, and the laws made in accordance with the public will of the people which must be observed if such freedom is to be enjoyed. It ought to be plain enough that what is wrong for the individual to do, it is wrong, by word or writing, for him to advise others to do. There can be no basis for society on the theory that a person may claim the protection of the laws and yet refuse all obedience to the laws. That would not be toleration but anarchy. This situation always yields to the application of the Golden Rule. We should treat with reverence and respect those things which we hold sacred. We need have no fear but that out of such conduct the truth will prevail.

There is an ever-increasing need for teachers who can inspire and lead. They are needed in the schools, in the pulpit, and in the editorial room. Education is the result of contact. A great people is produced by contact with great minds. The requirement for training under those who can see into the heart of things grows greater and greater. Too often the appeal is to weakness, not to strength.

Lieber expressed the correct principle when he said to his former pupils: "You can bear me witness that I have endeavored to convince you of man's inextinguishable individuality, and of the organic nature of society, that there is no right without a parallel duty, no liberty without the supremacy of the law, and no high destiny without perseverance—that there can be no greatness without self-denial." Civilization and freedom have come because they are an achievement, and it is human nature to achieve. Nothing else gives any permanent satisfaction. But most of all there is need of religion. From that source alone came freedom. Nothing else touches the soul of man. Nothing else justifies faith in the people.

XXI

The word of Massachusetts has never been used to utter a narrow and provincial view. Her ideal was correctly voiced by one of her greatest sons, Benjamin Franklin, when he exclaimed: "Above all, Washington has a sense of the oneness of America. Massachusetts and Georgia are as dear to him as Virginia!" It is because Plymouth Rock, Bunker Hill, John Adams, and Daniel Webster represent the nation that they glorify their State. In that faith Massachusetts still lives.

MASSACHUSETTS AND THE NATION

THE place of Massachusetts in the life of the nation has been made by continuing adherence to fundamental principles. This unchanging attitude raised her to primacy in the long struggle for individual liberty and local self-government. The background of her early people peculiarly fitted them for this leadership. They were possessed of an experience, training, and tradition in the art of government which was surpassing. It reached back behind the veil of myth and mystery. While other peoples turned aside, that stock which settled New England, both by reason of their character and environment, swept on from the tribal customs beyond the North Sea to the foremost achievement in human relationship, the Republic of America.

The Pilgrims and Puritans did not come hither empty-handed. They brought with them a perfected conception of rational liberty under the orderly process of public law. They had a clear idea of established rights duly defined and recorded. The heritage which they claimed, that privilege of birth which they had marked out for themselves, was not an estate measured merely by lands and tangible possessions, but a heritage unaffected by these, dowered by inalienable rights of which no government and no power could dispossess or despoil them.

At Washington, before the National Geographic Society, February 2, 1923.
Reprinted by courtesy of the National Geographic Magazine.

This estate they had claimed from days of old. It had been set out in charters, not unstained by the blood of the people, which bore the sanctions of parliaments and the seals of kings. It had been enacted into the statute law of the realm. It carried the approbation and authority of a long line of judicial decisions. But it derived a dominion which surpassed all these from the unalterable convictions of a great people, who had the courage and genius to make whatever sacrifice was necessary to follow right and truth to their logical conclusions.

These founding fathers came of a race which was not without a conception of the supremacy of the people. They had a clear idea of chartered liberty. They understood the principle of parliamentary government and royal authority acting within definite limitations. They were familiar with the jury system and enforcement of civil and criminal liabilities in accordance with existing laws.

The immediate cause of the settlement of Massachusetts was a profound religious movement. Green tells us that in the age of Elizabeth England became a country of one book; and that book was the Bible. When the people took that Book into their hands, the right of personal judgment in matters of religion became established, and from this there was derived the principle of personal judgment in matters of government. The conclusion of the whole matter was individual liberty.

This did not occur all at once. Toleration is not a self-evident truth. Wherever power is lodged in a monarch, always he has sought to maintain and extend it by encroachment upon the liberties of the people. When the more advanced of the Puritans sought to put their principle of freedom into practical effect by separation from the established church, they were met by the notorious threat of the King that he would make them conform or he would harry them out of the land.

In that threat lay the foundation of Massachusetts. That little band, from among whom were to come those made forever immortal by that voyage of the *Mayflower*, sought refuge in Holland, where, by an edict of William the Silent, freedom of religion had been established. What manner of men they were, what ideals they cherished, are described to us by their pastor, John Robinson. "The people," said he, "are industrious and frugal. We are knit together as a body in a most sacred covenant of the Lord, of the violation whereof we make great conscience, and by virtue whereof we hold ourselves strictly tied to all care of each other's good and of the whole by every one, and so mutually. It is not with us as with men whom small things can discourage." In that simple statement is to be found the principle of prosperity, responsibility, and social welfare, all based on religion.

A pride of race and of language determined them to seek out a location for themselves where they would be equally free, and where they would not be in jeopardy of losing their identity, through being absorbed in an overwhelming mass of people. They were of humble origin. The bare necessities of existence had been won by them in a strange country only at the expense of extreme toil and hardship. They did not shrink from the prospect of a like experience in America. "They knew they were Pilgrims," said Robinson, "and looked not much on those things, but lifted up their eyes to heaven, their dearest country, and quieted their spirits." Such was the sentiment cherished by those who were setting out to exert so large an influence in the building of the most powerful empire which the world has ever seen.

They left behind their old pastor, John Robinson, a great man possessed of a great vision and inspired by great piety, not only a clergyman but a statesman. Winslow reports that in his final charge to this congregation he told them: "If God should reveal anything to us by any other instrument of His, to be as ready to receive it as ever we were to receive any truth by his ministry: for he was very confident the Lord had more truth and light yet to breake forth out of His Holy Word," an admonition to keep an open mind, an expression of firm belief in progress.

It was such a people, strengthened by such a purpose, obedient to such a message, who set their course in the little *Mayflower* across the broad Atlantic on the sixth day of September, 1620, old style, which is celebrated under the new calendar as Marne Day.

The country they sought lay around the Delaware River, which was under the charter of the London Company, from which they had secured a grant of land. A providential breeze carried them far to the north, while storms and the frail condition of their ship prevented them from continuing to their destination. They came to anchor off Provincetown far outside the jurisdiction of their own patent and the authority of existing laws.

Undismayed they set about to establish their own institutions and recognize their own civil authority.   Gathering in the narrow cabin of the *Mayflower*, piously imploring the divine presence, in mutual covenant they acknowledged the power "to enacte, constitute, & frame just & equall lawes, ordinances, actes, constitutions & offices," to which they pledged "all due submission & obedience." So there was adopted the famous *Mayflower* Compact. It did not in form establish a government, but it declared the authority to establish a government, the power to make laws, and the duty to obey them. Beyond this it proclaimed the principle of democracy. The powers which they proposed to exercise arose directly from the express consent of all the governed. The date of this document, remarkable for what it contains, but more remarkable still because it reveals the capacity and spirit of those who made it, is November 11, 1620, old style; under the new calendar it is destined long to be remembered as Armistice Day.

Such was the beginning of Massachusetts, men and women humble in position, few in numbers, seemingly weak, but possessed of a purpose, moved by a deep conviction, guided by an abiding spirit, against which both time and death were powerless. It is said that upon the old Colony of Plymouth there is no stain of bigoted persecution. They carried with them the atmosphere of holy charity. Their efforts and their experience stand forth distinctly, raising a new hope in the world.

They were soon to be reinforced by the great Puritan migration which established a vigorous colony at their north, known as the Company of Massachusetts Bay. It was among them that there was worked out more in detail the fundamental institutions of the Old Commonwealth. They had a royal charter granted in 1629, which provided for a governor, a deputy governor, and a council of eighteen assistants, annually to be chosen by the Company. They were likewise given authority to make laws for the government of the settlers, provided they did not conflict with those of England. Here there came into existence the frame of a miniature republic.

One of the main objects of this movement was to provide a retreat for those of Puritan faith in case they were overwhelmed at home by the rising tide of despotism of Charles I. For this purpose men of such prominence as Winthrop and Dudley and their associates, came to the new colony, transferring with them the location of the government. Congregations and clergymen followed. With the arrival of thousands of people churches and towns were established and there began the making of American constitutional history.

These people were of the Puritans. What they have wrought in the Old World and the New is known of all men. Their prime motive was self-mastery. To them the great reality was the unseen world. They had a high disdain for every assumption of earthly authority, whether exercised in the name of the state or of the church. They were guided by the inner life. They rebelled against all government by others, but were humbly solicitous to govern themselves. With that same intensity of spirit with which they scorned kings and bishops, they reverenced the authority which came from on high. They trampled under foot and destroyed despotism in England, but they raised up and established freedom in America.

It was these people, moved by such convictions, that from the day of her settlement guaranteed that Massachusetts should be grandly placed in history.   The Puritan spirit has always worked toward freedom and independence in all things.   Its ultimate goal has not always first been reached within the domain of that Commonwealth.   There have been times when it has seemed to be denied by some of her own people, but the foundation of it was laid there.   The ultimate support for its progress has ever been found there.   If, occasionally, she has been outstripped by those who have gone out from her in the practical application of this spirit which her entire history has illustrated, it is but just to remember that there was located the American source of the original inspiration.

The Puritans cherished as their immediate purpose not a broad latitude in either religious or political life.   Their chief thought was to escape from the intolerable tyranny of Charles and of Laud.   If they were to maintain their safety against the Indians, or their freedom against the King, it was necessary to maintain solidarity in all things. They could not tolerate those who would set over them a tyranny in church or state, or those who, by a division of council lessened the military or political resistance of a weak and exposed outpost.   When to the colony toleration meant extermination, they rejected it, but they held to principles which, when they had the strength broadly to apply them, led to greater and greater freedom.

The leading clergy and many of the Puritans belonged to the established church, yet on reaching Massachusetts they naturally became separatists under the Congrega-

tional form of church government. Religion was their
first thought. They at once built places of worship and
formed church societies on the principle that each congregation was free and independent.

While the early magistrates and clergy were divided
between the principle of aristocracy and democracy in
the government of church and state, the people themselves held to the principle of democracy with a sturdy
and unswerving tenacity. It was the view of Governor
Winthrop that "the best part is always the less, and of
that best part the wiser part is always the lesser," while
the most eminent clergyman of the colony, John Cotton,
probably voiced the opinion of the majority of the profession when he declared he did not conceive democracy
"as a fit government either for church or commonwealth."
These views were more than balanced by such men as
Sir Harry Vane, who was chosen governor in 1636, a
liberal to the point of toleration, and who returned to
England to stand on the side of liberty in the great rebellion, and propose a settlement of government under
Cromwell which would have been on the pattern of the
American Republic. Of a like mind was Thomas Hooker,
pastor of the church at Cambridge, who was later to tell
Winthrop that "in matters which concern the common
good a general council, chosen by all, to transact businesses which concern all, I conceive most suitable to rule,
and most safe for relief of the whole." It was he and his
congregation which moved through the wilderness to
establish Hartford. It was there he preached that remarkable sermon in which he announced that "the foundation of authority is laid, firstly, in the free consent of

the people," and saw at once that doctrine completely recognized and established, in the free republic under a written constitution, of the Colony of Connecticut. Such was the first offspring of the Puritan spirit of Massachusetts. It was possessed of a vitality capable of creating a political structure of great strength and forming free institutions wherever it might go.

The democratic attitude of the people was very early apparent. The freemen of the colony at first undertook in public meeting to administer its affairs. When numbers made this impossible, the authority was lodged with the board of assistants to make laws and elect the governor. But when the inhabitants of Watertown hesitated to pay a small tax which was levied for public defense in 1631, on the ground that English freemen could not be taxed without their consent, the result of the agitation which then arose restored to the freemen the right to elect the governor and gave to each settlement the right to choose their own deputies to a general court. As early as 1644, these deputies, withdrawing from the assistants and forming a second house, became a co-ordinate branch of the legislature. Thus the principle of representative government was developed at once for the purpose of safeguarding the liberties of the people. To gain that end no more capable instrument has been devised by man. It is scarcely too much to say that while the general court then established has sometimes ceased to sit, it has never ceased to exist. From that day to this in Massachusetts it has been the chief repository of the powers of government.

For a period of more than fifty years the Commonwealth was administered under this liberal charter, virtually independent and self-governing in all its affairs, a political training never ceasing, the results of which have been world-wide.

The church having been formed and the government organized, the next thought was of education. An early report states: "One of the next things we longed for and looked after was to advance learning and perpetuate it to posterity, dreading to have an illiterate ministry to the churches when our present ministers shall lie in dust."   In 1636, in order that "the Commonwealth be furnished with knowing and understanding men, and the churches with an able ministry," the general court voted that it "agrees to give four hundred pounds toward a school or college, whereof two hundred pounds shall be paid the next year and two hundred pounds when the work is finished."   Quincy claims that this assembly was "the first body in which the people, by their representatives, ever gave their own money to found a place of education."   Two years later the legacy of a library and seven hundred pounds from John Harvard determined the name of the college.

Conscious of their own purpose, viewing their own accomplishments, believing they were instruments of a divine destiny, it may well be that they felt they were correctly described by Captain Edward Johnson, one of their early chroniclers, when he prophesied: "The Lord Christ intends to achieve greater matters by this little handful than the world is aware of."   A more sober and judicial statement, less in prophecy but greater in history, was made by William Stoughton when he asserted, in his 1668 election sermon: "God sifted a whole nation that he might send choice grain over into this wilderness." The character of the people, their government, their church, their school, all contributed to a great intellectual awakening which was to result in a greater advance and more progress than the human race had ever before accomplished in the same length of time. A government in which the people chose all of their own magistrates, a church in which each congregation determined its own course, a school dedicated to the service of the political and religious life of the commonwealth, all of these partook of a new experience, a new relationship in the affairs of mankind.

Political and theological discussion went on, liberality grew, the franchise was broadened. Under the Halfway Covenant the right to vote was to be extended to those who had been baptized and conducted themselves with propriety, even though they were not communicants. The Old South Church was created as a monument to this liberal principle. Within its walls many a patriot meeting has been held and many a patriot voice has been raised in defense of the rights of the people. It was in this meeting-house that the inhabitants unanimously refused to surrender their charter in the days of Andros. Here in later times gathered those heroes who were to make the American Revolution. From the earliest settlement, every court, council, and town meeting was open to every inhabitant, whether he held the franchise or not. He had the right to appear in person, present his cause, and secure a decision. Local self-government was administered through the town meeting, where the freemen met on terms of equality, a great practical example of democracy.

It was out of all this discussion that there was continued the determination to be free. This determination was strong enough to engage in active preparation for open resistance against the tyranny of Andros when it became apparent that what Charles II had done in England he proposed to do in America. The charter was revoked, self-government ceased, people were imprisoned, congregations were dispossessed, property confiscated, and arbitrary political and ecclesiastical rule was established. At last a signal-fire shone from Beacon Hill, the drums beat, the people rose, Andros was arrested, and a successful revolution was accomplished which only the accession of William and Mary brought to an end.

But this lesson the people never forgot, and the same discussion went on. John Wise, pastor at Ipswich, who had suffered imprisonment under Andros, published a book very early in the eighteenth century, in which he said: "The end of all good government is to cultivate humanity and promote the happiness of all, and the good of every man in all his rights, his life, liberty, estate, honor, and so forth, without injury or abuse to any." By 1765 James Otis declared, "Kings were made for the good of the people and not the people for them," harking back to the day of the high court of justice, which executed Charles I, when its president, John Bradshaw, had said: "There is something that is superior to the law, and that is the people of England." It was no wonder that the regicide judges found comfort and security among the people of Massachusetts.

Such was the preparation for the Revolutionary War, inevitable after the power of France in America had been broken by Wolfe upon the plains of Abraham, a revolution which had its significance not so much in the establishment of independence as in the yet firmer establishment of the principle of governments "deriving their just powers from the consent of the governed." What Cambridge and Watertown and Dorchester had insisted upon at the very outset of their settlement, when the board of assistants undertook to levy taxes, choose the governor, and hold office indefinitely, the men of the Revolution were equally alert to preserve when they rose again to insist on representative government. They had heard from their grandsires of the Court of High Commission, and from their fathers they had heard of Jeffreys and of Andros. More, too, they knew that this kind of a government had always put forth an ecclesiastical hierarchy. When all these spectres began to rise again under George III, Massachusetts had no idea of submission, but sought refuge in rebellion. They believed in principles, but they were a practical people, they always translated theory into action. This time it was not the watch-fire on Beacon Hill, but the lantern in the belfry of the Old North Church that was the signal which brought the men of Massachusetts with arms in their hands to the defense of their liberties.

How far the people of the Commonwealth had advanced between 1620 and the days of the Revolution is indicated by the difference between the *Mayflower* Compact and the Declaration of Rights and the Frame of Government, which is the title of the Constitution adopted in 1780. The Declaration sets out with great precision the fundamental principles of liberty established by law. Article I declares that all men are born free and equal. Article II guarantees religious freedom. Article X asserts the right of protection of life, liberty, and property by the government, and as a corollary the necessity of serving and supporting the government. Article XVIII enjoins "a constant adherence to piety, justice, moderation, temperance, industry, and frugality" as necessary to preserve liberty and maintain a free government. Article XXIX proclaims "the right of every citizen to be tried by judges as free, impartial, and independent as the lot of humanity will admit." Article XXX decrees a complete separation of the legislative, executive, and judicial departments, "to the end that it may be a government of laws and not of men." In between is asserted the sovereignty of the people, the liberty of speech and of the press, the right to trial by jury, and the duty of providing education, together with the other guarantees of freedom. We have come to think of all these principles as natural and self-evident. It is well to remember that we are in the enjoyment of them by reason of age-old effort and the constant sacrifice of treasure and of blood finally wrought into standing law. There is no other process by which they can be maintained.

All of this has been the inevitable outcome of the belief of the Puritans in the rights of the individual. This required education, and the first public school was opened in Boston in 1635. In 1647 the general court enjoined each town of fifty householders to have a primary school, and each of one hundred families a grammar-school. In

1839 a State Normal School was opened, and Massachusetts was the first to have a State Board of Education.

The same ideal that educated the mind protected the health and regulated industrial conditions. In 1836 the first Child Labor Law was passed. In 1842 combinations of workmen made for the purpose of improving their conditions were declared lawful. In 1867 factory inspection was begun. The year 1869 saw the first Railroad Commission and the beginnings of a State Board of Arbitration. It was here that there was established the first State Board of Health, the first State Board of Charities, the first State Department of Insurance, the first Minimum Wage Law for women and children, and the first State sanatorium for the treatment of tuberculosis.

Massachusetts has been the location of an enormous industrial development. It is claimed that the first agricultural show was held there. Certainly it was the home of the Baldwin apple and the Concord grape. There the first railroad was built. Four inventions, most important in modern life, are represented by the telephone, which Bell invented there, the telegraph, the sewing-machine, and the cotton-gin of Morse, Howe, and Whitney, three of her native sons, while inoculation was first used there by Boylston, and the first practical demonstration of the discovery of ether was made in one of her hospitals. There are the greatest fish market, leather market, wool market, and the principal centre for the production of textile machinery, boots and shoes, cotton, woollen and worsted goods, paper, and all government bank-note paper, and the greatest worsted, cordage, and shoe-machinery mills in the world.

Massachusetts has contributed men of great eminence to all the learned professions. Jonathan Edwards preached there, Benjamin Franklin was born there. It has had such scientists as Agassiz and Gray, such preachers as Channing, Parker, Brooks, and Moody. In literature it carries such names as Emerson, Hawthorne, Holmes, Longfellow, Lowell, Whittier, Everett, Phillips, and Julia Ward Howe; in art Sargent, Whistler, Stuart, Bullfinch, Copley, and Hunt; among its lawyers are Story, Cushing, Shaw, Choate, Webster, and Parsons. Among its statesmen have been the Adamses, Webster, Sumner, Wilson, and Hoar. It has been the abiding-place of strong common sense, illustrated by Samuel Adams, master of the town meeting, and Jonathan Smith, the farmer from Lanesboro, who with Adams swung a hostile convention to the ratification of the Federal Constitution. Another clergyman, from Ipswich, was Manasseh Cutler, who drafted the Ordinance of 1787 which Representative Dane of Beverly presented to Congress, thus dedicating a sufficient area to freedom to insure the ultimate extinction of human slavery.

The Commonwealth has furnished pioneers who have gone everywhere. They are represented by such men as General Rufus Putnam, who planned the settlement of southern Ohio; Marshall Field, the great merchant of Chicago; the five students of Williams College who laid the foundation of American foreign missions at the memorable haystack prayer-meeting; Peter Parker, who established the first hospital in China: while in another field of pioneering were Garrison, the abolitionist; Clara Barton, who founded the Red Cross; Mary Lyon, who led the way at Mount Holyoke to higher education of women; Horace Mann, who was foremost in the training of teachers for the public schools. For more than three hundred years there has gone out an influence from Massachusetts that has touched all shores, influenced all modes of thought, and modified all governments. How broad it has been is disclosed when it is remembered that Garfield and Lincoln came of Massachusetts stock.

From the earliest days the people have exhibited a high capacity both for civil and religious government. In 1630 the first general court ever held on this side of the Atlantic Ocean assembled at Boston. In 1637 the first General Council of Churches was held in Cambridge. In 1641 a code of laws for the colony, known as the Massachusetts Body of Liberties, was adopted, forbidding bond slavery. In 1643 the New England Confederacy was formed. This was a league and not a federacy, but it distinctly shows the national tendency. In 1646 there was convened a church synod which adopted the Cambridge Platform. In accordance with its terms the Congregational churches of New England were governed for a long time. All of these were expressions of the fundamental principles of government, not yet in the form of finished product but sufficiently explicit to rank with the great charters of history.

What an important influence the churches and clergymen were in this early life is apparent wherever we turn. To Robinson, who remained at home, were joined others equally prominent who led their flocks to these shores. As Hooker, the early clergyman of Cambridge who, passing on with his congregation to Hartford, set the inextinguishable mark of freedom and local independence under the representative system upon government, so Shepard, who succeeded to his pulpit and was one of the committee of six magistrates and six clergymen chosen to establish the college, set the same inextinguishable mark upon education. It was in their town that the first book ever printed in America came from the press. Wherever a town meeting is held, wherever a legislature convenes, wherever a schoolhouse is opened, the moral power of these two men is felt. The Puritan was ever intent upon supporting democracy by learning, and the authority of the State by righteousness.

It was on the soil of Massachusetts that there first met in unmistakable armed conflict the forces of King George and the forces of the colonies at the opening of the Revolutionary War. That day marks Concord and Lexington, soon to be followed by Bunker Hill. It was under the elm at Cambridge, a few days following, that General Washington formally took command of the first patriot army. The first company to be enrolled, the first men to shed their blood, and the first to reach Washington in response to the call of Lincoln for an armed force came from Massachusetts. One of her regiments went with the first troops to Cuba. Her military organization went in its entirety with the first National Guard division sent to France, and the first National Guard regiment to be decorated for distinguished service in the field was one of these Massachusetts regiments.

In the works of humanity there has been a like promptness. When flood, fire, earthquake, or other calamity has fallen upon a community, relief and charity have been quick to flow from Massachusetts. When Halifax was shaken by explosion, before any other relief could respond, the Public Safety Committee of Massachusetts was on the spot with medical skill, hospital supplies, and trained business ability which met the emergency.

The contribution which Massachusetts has made has been on the side of practical affairs. It has been a demonstration of the method through which the power of intelligence and wealth is to be dedicated to the public service. Always the end in view has been the welfare of the people. In this there has been no class distinction. Properly and truly her designation has been "The Commonwealth." This principle has been applied educationally, industrially, and humanely. It has given not only cultural training, but professional, technical, agricultural, and trade schools; it has used the wealth created in industry not merely to heap up treasure for the few but to provide safe and healthful conditions of employment and reasonable wages through a board of conciliation and arbitration for the many. It has set up a public tribunal guaranteeing to the people the uttermost service that public utilities can render under the compensation which they are to receive. It has adopted preventive measures and ministered to those suffering from disease of the body or of the mind, restoring the deficient, reforming the criminal. It has reached out beyond all of these calls at home to minister in the missionary field of all the world. Faith, hope, and charity have been translated into good works.

While there has come to the sons of the Puritans that progress which results from science and great material resources, their supreme choice is still made in favor of a greater power. The Supreme Judicial Court of Massachusetts, which enjoys a reputation for sound opinions and which makes its decisions more often cited than those of any other court, save the Supreme Court of the United States, recently announced the faith that is dominant still. "Mere intellectual power," the decision runs, "and scientific achievement without uprightness of character may be more harmful than ignorance. Highly trained intelligence, combined with disregard of fundamental virtues, is a menace." Above all else, the people still put their faith in character.

They do not suppose that all virtue landed at Plymouth Rock, that all patriotism defended Bunker Hill. From every people and from every faith there have come Puritans. Every town and countryside has bred devoted patriots. The word of Massachusetts has never been used to utter a narrow and provincial view. Her ideal was correctly voiced by one of her greatest sons, Benjamin Franklin, when he exclaimed: "Above all, Washington has a sense of the oneness of America. Massachusetts and Georgia are as dear to him as Virginia!" It is because Plymouth Rock, Bunker Hill, John Adams, and Daniel Webster represent the nation that they glorify their State. In that faith Massachusetts still lives.

XXII

Freedom is a high estate. It places on the individual grave duties and grave responsibilities. If these be met and performed, success will follow. If they be neglected and evaded, the end will be failure. To a great extent, it is a question of obedience.

PROGRESS TOWARD FREEDOM

This day and this occasion naturally invite our thought to our government. It is a time when we may well consider some of the aims and purposes of those who founded it, and the general success which their principles when carried into effect have brought to all the people.

Very few of the original settlements of the American colonies were made because of a desire for gain. They were a practical people, not unlearned in the art of making a living, not without the ordinary human motive for success, but, broadly speaking, their chief purpose was to escape from a condition of tyranny and create institutions in accordance with their own choice. These settlements were made at a time of extraordinary change. The old order was passing away and the new order was coming in. Both the religious and the political life of the people passed into a new era. Both to the church and the state there came a new freedom.

Before this result had become manifest, during the uncertainties of the struggle which preceded it, many people sought refuge in America, in order that they might accept the chance of securing the privilege of free worship and of free government here, in case despotism should triumph in the Old World. In its very beginnings, America was dedicated to liberty.

At the dedication of a Government Hospital for Colored Veterans of the World War, Tuskegee, Alabama, Lincoln's Birthday, February 12, 1923.

Throughout more than three hundred years her great decisions have been made to this end. The romance of the Pilgrim and Puritan, the Dutch, the Swede, the Quaker, the Catholic, the Cavalier, and the Huguenot runs through it all, as by a separate path each sought a common end. The purpose which they were all seeking to accomplish has not yet been fully attained, but a strong and enduring foundation has been laid by the establishment of great principles, by the constant adherence to which much progress has already been made and great promise lies before us.

Nothing is ever felt to be of value which is not won as a result of sacrifice. The early American colonists had to endure a great hardship in order to accomplish their purpose. In the early seventeenth century, merely the voyage across the Atlantic was a most serious undertaking, but when in addition to that it was proposed to hew out a home in the wilderness, to protect it from hostile natives, to clear the land and cultivate the soil, to be self-existent and self-supporting where neither produce could be sold nor supplies bought, there was required a courage and a determination which could not be surpassed. A people who could engage in that great enterprise and by bringing it to a successful conclusion, establish and cherish institutions of self-government, would soon reach a position where they could never be overcome.

That position had been reached by America at the end of the old French Wars. By the time Great Britain had become the dominant power in North America, the colonists had become so powerful that they were able to direct their own course.   It was then that there was taken one of those great forward steps in the march of human progress for which there had been more than one hundred and fifty years of immediate preparation but for which the whole experience of Western civilization had been the ultimate preparation.   Breaking away from their political connection with the Old World, they were able to realize the dream of their forefathers in the establishment of a government which was not only independent but free.   This in its turn cost the sacrifice of seven years of treasure and of blood.

When the American Constitution was finally adopted, when the government was organized, when it increased in strength and efficiency under a President like Washington, a secretary like Hamilton, a judge like Marshall, and a popular leader like Jefferson, a new power destined to preserve and extend the rights of mankind had come into being.   What this government really was, what powers it possessed, what national character it represented, it was many years in developing.   Liberty is of slow growth, but irresistible.   It took the long debates of Clay, Calhoun, and Webster, and the vigilant action of Jackson, no less than the decisions of Marshall and the wise counsel of Washington, to reveal the true spirit of the nation.

At length the time came for another forward step, another extension of the principle of freedom.   Like all others, it was wrought in sacrifice.   At last the national character of our government was finally established. The fabric of the Union was finally complete.   The rank of citizens was all free.

It was out of this period of suffering and sorrow that there emerged the great statesman Abraham Lincoln, and the two great soldiers Grant and Lee. Each of these represented an American ideal. Lee stands for the power of the States. Grant stands for the power of the nation. But to Lincoln it was given to stand for the power of the people.

It was under him and through him that this power was at last developed and fully revealed. No other figure in all history so understood the people, was so loved by them, or could so enable them to identify their government with themselves. He had a human sympathy that embraced the whole nation. He never recognized any enemies. He did not hesitate to call to his Cabinet those who had opposed him. He had but one motive, which explains all his actions. He was determined to save the Union. He was never influenced by animosity toward any of it. "We are not enemies," said he, "but friends. We must not be enemies." The rule which he followed was the law. The sentiment which he felt was compassion. He was justice and mercy.

The great men of all times baffle all analysis and all description. They rise above all precedent to heights where none may follow. We know that Lincoln was born in adversity. That has been the birthright of many Americans. We know that his youth lacked opportunity for that education which comes from books. This, too, has not been uncommon. We know that he struggled and toiled and studied to perfect himself in learning and in the practice of law. Many others have done the same. We know that he served his local community in the legis-

lature and in Congress. All this was not unusual. We
know that he had a great intellect and a great heart,
great patience and great forbearance. He had a great
soul. He was a revelation. He showed to men their
better selves. He had the power to bind together dis-
cordant elements. He reconciled differences. He was
a universal friend. But all this fails to describe him, for
he was infinitely more.

But we can understand the principles which he announced, the contribution which he made to human welfare, and some of the methods by which he accomplished
his purpose. The chief of these was his belief in the people. "Why should there not be a patient confidence in
the ultimate justice of the people? Is there any better
or equal hope in the world?" he inquired. He there stated
the principle that lies at the foundation of American institutions. His life showed that to this inquiry there could
be but one answer. He never sought to injure any, but to
do good to all. He required the nation to make great sacrifices, not for a partial advantage but for the common
welfare. "In giving freedom to the slave, we assure freedom to the free—honorable alike in what we give and
what we preserve," he explained. He recognized that no
principle could be right which could not have universal
application, and no principle could be maintained which
was not universally applied. To deny right to a part
could end only in denying right to the whole. Whatever
others might do, he chose to follow the truth, trusting
that by his example they would come after him. He defended the rights of mankind because he knew that was
the only means by which he could defend the rights of

any one. Recognizing that "a house divided against itself cannot stand," he removed the cause of division that it might all rest secure on a common foundation.

He re-established the theory of the Fathers, that the government belongs to all the people. He made forever plain and clear the right to individual freedom. The whole power of America now stands unchangeably committed to that principle. The life of Abraham Lincoln gave a new and practical meaning to the right of self-government, which was to grow into a great world of influence.

Americans are not without justification in assuming that this nation has been called into existence to establish, to maintain, to defend, and to extend that principle. In so far as the World War was a conflict between different theories of civilization, it was a conflict between those who supported this principle and those who opposed it. It was the liberty-loving nations of the earth, those most generously committed to the principle of sovereignty of the people, who were victorious. In that victory Abraham Lincoln had a very large share.

Theories are of very little use in this world which cannot be put into practical operation. The theory of freedom would not help any one unless it worked out by bringing greater happiness and success to those who were in the possession of it. There is very much that the people need which cannot be bestowed upon them by the Constitution, or by laws. If they have it at all, they must provide it for themselves. The government can help, but in the last resort every one must work out his own destiny. Freedom is a high estate. It places on the individual grave duties and grave responsibilities. If these be met and performed, success will follow. If they be neglected and evaded, the end will be failure. To a great extent it is a question of obedience. It was the belief of Abraham Lincoln that all people could and would finally rise to these requirements. In the less than seventy years that the negro race in America have been in the enjoyment of freedom, they have made marvellous progress. That progress is shown not only in the property which they have acquired, not only in the talent which they have exhibited in the arts, not only in the professions of the law, of medicine, of the ministry, of teaching, nor yet in the administration of business affairs, all of which have been very great, but most of all in the honest, industrious way in which the great body of their people have performed the plain every-day duties of life. Their greatest contribution lies in the fact that they have helped to do the work of the nation.

When the call came in time of war they were ready and desirous to respond. More than two and one-quarter millions of them were registered under the selective draft. They were more anxious to enlist than they were to evade any service for their country. In spite of every deception or temptation to which public enemies artfully subjected them, they exhibited a loyalty and devotion to the cause of America which was unsurpassed. Nearly 400,000 of them went into military service. The 92d Division was composed exclusively of negro troops. They had 639 commissioned officers especially trained at Fort Des Moines. They furnished 100 medical reserve officers, while the total of their commissioned officers reached about 1,200 in number.

They were brave and courageous in the face of the enemy. Their total casualties were approximately 103 officers and 1,543 enlisted men, of whom 6 officers and 203 enlisted men were killed in action.

The high character of their service is shown by the fact that 14 officers and 43 men received the Distinguished Service Cross, while the First Battalion of the 367th Infantry and the 369th Infantry were awarded the Croix de Guerre by the French.

It was not merely their soldiers in the field but their citizens in the supporting army of production and transportation at home, both men and women, whose efforts contributed to the success of the allied armies. More than that, they gave generously of their resources, purchasing the securities of the government, and contributing to the Red Cross and other war charities. Their patriotism shone forth in every field of action.

They had the commendation of the secretary of war, General Pershing, and former President Roosevelt. Brigadier-General Sherburne, of Massachusetts, who trained and commanded some of the negro artillery, gave me this statement: "Tuskegee, during the war, furnished to the colored artillery regiments some of the finest troops in France. In technical excellence they were unsurpassed. They developed wireless and telephone communication effectively and showed marked ability in the technical lines of artillery. President Moton himself saw the work of the colored artillery and the destruction wrought by it." That is high praise from a man who knew. For the service of the negro race at home and abroad during the war they have the everlasting gratitude of the American people. They have justified the faith of Abraham Lincoln.

Returning home, in common with their comrades, they resumed their peace-time occupations. Like other Americans, they have as a result of their experience a broader outlook, a firmer patriotism, and, like the other peoples of the earth, they are in the enjoyment of a great freedom.

There came also to all Americans, as a result of the war, new duties and new obligations. The first and foremost of these, the one to which the people through their government responded with the greatest readiness and generosity, was the necessity of caring for those who had been injured in the service and for their dependents. There was at once organized the Reconstruction and Restoration Service, under different departments, finally all consolidated in the Veterans' Bureau, to do what was necessary to restore health, provide education, and administer compensation. Very large sums have already been appropriated for these purposes, for which the expenditures are well over $1,000,000 each day. For allowances to families expenditures have been about $300,-000,000. For compensation to those who suffered injuries $675,000,000. For medical and hospital services $262,000,000. Hospital care is now granted to all who request it, at least for a period of observation. For educational and vocational training about $590,000,000. For insurance $90,000,000. For the construction and repair of hospitals about $45,000,000. Other items make a grand total of about $2,500,000,000, all of which has gone directly for these great relief purposes, with the exception of about 4 per cent, which has been the cost of administration.

There are now about 25,000 men in hospitals. During the past year and one-half government-hospital beds have been increased by 9,686, so that they total at the present time 24,759. Money has been provided, and work is in progress, to equip 7,619 additional beds.

More than 232,000 compensation claims and more than 143,000 war-risk term insurance claims are paid each month. There are nearly 550,000 insurance policies in force, representing more than $3,000,000,000 insurance. More than 160,000 men have entered vocational training, of which more than 96,000 are still receiving that instruction. The generosity of the American people reaches directly more than a million service men and their dependents.

It is not possible to administer a great service of this kind without mistakes and delays. The government has had up for consideration more than 1,000,000 service cases of one kind or another. It is the policy to err on the side of the service man. There has been a great expenditure of money and every possible attempt adequately to provide for every service man and his dependents who are entitled to the bounty of a generous and grateful people. The dedication of this hospital, constructed new throughout, at an expenditure of nearly $2,000,000, providing accommodations for 600 cases, exclusively for negro service men, shows the appreciation in which they are held by the government. Here on a beautiful tract of 464 acres there are located 27 permanent buildings, with every facility for the care and cure of those who are afflicted. The government has nothing better anywhere.

Together we are working out, in theory and in practice, that hope of Washington and Lincoln. It is a long, slow, toilsome, and laborious process, accompanied oftentimes with disappointment and delays, but in the progress which has been made there is every reason for encouragement and satisfaction.

It takes time and patience and perseverance to put into practice our theory of human rights. Lincoln knew that. If there was one virtue that he seemed to possess more than another, it was that of forbearance. It is well for us, who must live together as Americans, whatever our race or creed may be, constantly to remember his words: "We are not enemies, but friends. We must not be enemies." Those who stir up animosities, those who create any kind of hatred and enmity are not ministering to the public welfare. We have come out of the war with a desire and a determination to live at peace with all the world. Out of a common suffering and a common sacrifice there came a new meaning to our common citizenship. Our greatest need is to live in harmony, in friendship, and in good-will, not seeking an advantage over each other but all trying to serve each other. In that spirit let us dedicate this hospital and dedicate ourselves to the service of our country. To do that wisely, patiently, tolerantly, is to show by the discharge of our duties our indisputable title to fellow citizenship with Abraham Lincoln.

XXIII

There is very little that is really worth while which can be bought or sold. The desire for gain has made many cowards, but it never made a hero. The country cannot be run on the promise of what it will do for the people. The only motive to which they will continue ready to respond is the opportunity to do something for themselves, to achieve their own greatness, to work out their own destiny.

THE FOUNDATION OF OUR INSTITUTIONS

THESE ought to be days of abiding satisfaction for the American people. There should be steadily accumulating evidences of a deeper devotion to religion, a firmer adherence to the government, a broader acquisition of education, and a wiser use of the resources of an abounding prosperity. Such evidences would establish conclusively the continuing and increasing righteousness of our country and justify a faith in its security and perpetuation.

But instead of this there is a disposition on the part of many observers and students to be disturbed, if not alarmed and discouraged. They think they discover a growing tendency to disregard religion, to violate the law and abandon the government, to substitute for the fundamentals of education catchpenny devices, and for that accurate scholarship which is the product only of sustained discipline a mere superficial knowledge of a scattering range of disconnected facts, to despise sound investment and a constructive expenditure of money, and to seek excitement in wild speculation, wanton extravagance, and all kinds of dissipation. In their opinion they find insufficient reverence and respect on the part of youth, and insufficient loyalty and devotion on the part of maturity. To them there is an apparent lack of moral courage and a decaying spiritual power in the nation.

The New York State Convention of the Y. M. C. A., at Albany, April 13, 1923.

They perceive a decline in the morale of the people which results in a weakening of the forces that bind society together and sustain civilization.

It is never the part of wisdom to minimize the power of evil, but it is far less the part of wisdom to forget the power of good. In the position which those critics of the times have outlined there is altogether too much truth, but it is not the whole truth, it is not even the important truth in respect to conditions as they now are and will continue to be. It was a premature and artificial exaltation which carried us through the war. Some may have expected that it was to be permanent and that we were about to step into the millennium. But war is a destructive force. It not only uses up the material resources of a nation but exhausts its spiritual power. It is sure to be followed by a reaction which can only be remedied by recuperation and reconstruction. It is that process in which we are now engaged.

The world moves in seasons, in periods, in cycles. It advances and recedes. It tries out a certain course only to abandon it. Much it produces is cast aside as unfit. But the fittest always survives, progress always goes on, growth continues. After the entire catalogue of shortcomings is complete, after the worst is candidly recognized and admitted, it does not appear from any reliable assembling of facts or any accurate compilation of statistics that there now exists any permanent condition which justifies alarm or discouragement, but that there is, rather, an abundant justification for faith. The important truth remains that the forces of good, now as always, surpass the forces of evil.

It is not in the results of a day or a year that the Eternal Purpose is revealed. To judge by such short intervals only would result in being lost in particulars. If we are to avoid being dismayed by the accidental, and if we are to contribute anything, it is necessary to take a larger view, to make a wider survey, and work in harmony with those ever-invincible forces which are always advancing the base-line of progress. No one can tell what a day or a year may bring forth. No one can forecast the fortune of an individual or a township. It may be good or ill. But the evidence is all about of what time and mankind, working together, can accomplish. Both experience and reason give warrant to our faith, both what the past has done and what we know human nature to be. There will be no cause to be disturbed by what is superficial if that which is fundamental remains sound.

The fundamental principles on which American institutions rest ought to be clearly understood. Being so understood, they can never lack for defenders. They had been thought out and fought out by the original settlers of the colonies, and whenever they have been in jeopardy they and their successors have not failed to rise and make whatever sacrifice was necessary for their preservation and, from time to time, for their extension. It would be idle to claim that our country has yet reached the goal toward which they plainly lead, but more idle still to deny that the path is open and that the people are continuing to make progress in that direction.

Of all the colonists none had a greater inborn adherence to liberty and independence than those Dutch traders who first settled New York. Their history and tradition run back to the island of Batavia and beyond. They were never conquered by the Romans, but became their independent allies. It was the horsemen of Batavia that saved the day for Cæsar at Pharsalia. Fortunately situated for political and commercial development, they grew up through the centuries with a genius for self-government and commercial prosperity. The arts flourished, culture was abundant. Their land was the home of the illustrious Erasmus, a scholar of profound accomplishments, and of Grotius, one of the most famous names in jurisprudence. The ancient liberties of the land were set out in a charter called the Great Privilege, wrung from the sovereign about 1477. This not only reserved to the provincial estates jurisdiction over new taxes and war, but, what was of chief importance, brought the sovereign under the authority of the law. Haarlem still contests with Gutenberg for the honor of having invented printing, which was rapidly developed. The first English Bible was published in Antwerp, in 1535. Public schools gave opportunity for a diffusion of education. Not only was the country thus early the centre of biblical scholarship, but there then developed a more general reading of the Bible among the common people than in any other land.

It was chiefly during this century that took place the long-continued effort of Spain, which was then the most powerful empire in the world, to destroy the liberties of the Netherlands. It is a story of persecutions and pillage, the destruction of entire cities, the execution of tens of thousands charged with treason and heresy, and of a heroic defense. They gave their lands to the flood and their bodies to torture, but they did not yield. It is estimated that about one hundred thousand people sought refuge in England. The defeat of the Invincible Armada, in 1588, marked the beginning of the downfall of this great power. The absolutism of that day, represented by the King of Spain with the mighty armies of Europe, with the gold and silver of Mexico and Peru, could not break the spirit of freedom and independence which was the ancient heritage of the people of the Low Countries. In 1609 Spain ceased her efforts, and in signing a temporary truce acknowledged defeat. Despotism lost. The material power of the sword, of riches, and of arbitrary rule was vanquished. The spiritual power of freedom of conscience, of personal judgment, of personal responsibility, of religious and political liberty was victorious. These preparations having been made, in that same year Henry Hudson sailed up the river which bears his name. A little later the Dutch began their settlements along its shores.

These settlements were at first trading-stations. They required little in the way of government and absolutely nothing in the way of protecting themselves against any infringement of their rights by the authorities at home. They needed no independent establishment to guard their liberties. They were not unmindful of religion. It is related that after holding a council of peace with the Indians, where the tomahawk was buried, the Dutch promised to build a church over it so that it could not be dug up, an evidence that, in their opinion, peace was supported by religion. Sunday services by reading the Scriptures and the creeds were begun in 1626, and when Van

Twiller came, in 1633, he brought with him Bogardus
the first clergyman, and Roelandsen the first school-
master.   When Stuyvesant arrived, in 1647, he at once
asked money for schools and for finishing a church, which
was granted.   Religion was followed by education.

Some time after the colony had passed under British
rule the first General Assembly of New York, meeting in
October, 1683, adopted a Charter of Liberties, in which
it was declared: "The supreme legislative authority . . .
shall forever be and reside in a Governor, Council, and the
people met in General Assembly."   This charter provided
for freedom in the exercise of the franchise and in religion, and prohibited in express words any kind of taxation "but by the consent of the governor, council, and
representatives of the people in General Assembly."
These important principles the people asserted again and
again, even when at the outbreak of the Revolution a
majority of the Assembly was inclined to disregard
them.

Coincident with the development of the rights of the
people in the Netherlands went on their establishment
in England.   They secured their Great Charter at an
earlier date, due to an earlier breaking out of a similar
conflict.   A corresponding ecclesiastical conflict occurred
in the sixteenth century, which had a like result.   England had its struggle against the forces and gold both of
Spain and France.   It, too, became a Bible-reading country and asserted its right to national independence in
matters of religion, established the supremacy of parliamentary government, and brought its sovereign under the
authority of the law, but it had not yet followed the

Dutch in adopting the broad principles of toleration. It was for this reason that while Hudson was on his voyage of discovery the Pilgrims were seeking refuge in Holland where the conscience of man was free. When they had determined to plant a settlement of their own on the shore of America, they sought for permission to join the Dutch settlement in New York. While they were willing to harbor them at Leyden, the Dutch Government, fearing the displeasure of the English King, was unwilling to promise them military protection in a distant land. The Pilgrims therefore proceeded under a patent secured from the Virginia Company. It was thus that New England was dedicated to freedom. The narrowness of tyranny and bigotry in England broadened the territory of liberty in America. The right redressed the balance of the wrong. How they established their church, started their town meeting, adopted a system of representative government, opened their schools, and founded their college is known to all students of American history.

The wise and sagacious clergyman Thomas Hooker declared the principle that "the foundation of authority is laid firstly in the free consent of the people," and in a letter to Governor Winthrop he said: "In matters which concern the common good, a General Council chosen by all to transact businesses which concern all I conceive most suitable to rule and most safe for relief of the whole." The voice of a clergyman in the Connecticut wilderness, in 1638, speaking the words of empire! Here is that same clear and unmistakable declaration of the principle of democracy and the representative system not only asserted but put into practice at the very outset of the establishment of a government in New England, as it was done a little later in the government of New York.

Joined to these Dutch and English defenders of liberty, differing from them in particulars but agreeing in the broad essentials of human freedom, were the French Huguenots. America became the common meeting-place of all those streams of people, great and small, who were undertaking to deliver themselves from all kinds of despotism and servitude, and to establish institutions of self-government and freedom.

These stupendous results had their source in the great liberal movements of the sixteenth and seventeenth centuries. It was the principle of personal judgment in matters of religion for which the English and Dutch were contending, and which set the common people to reading the Bible. There came to them a new vision of the importance of the individual which brought him into direct contact with the Creator. It was this conception applied to affairs of government that made the people sovereign. It raised up the common man to the place which, heretofore, had been reserved for a privileged class in church and state. It ennobled the people. The logical result of this was the free man, educated in a free school, exercising a free conscience, maintaining a free government. The basis of it all, historically and logically, is religious belief.

These are the fundamental principles on which American institutions rest. When the perception of them was growing dim to European eyes, in the eighteenth century, and the old absolutism, measurably supreme on the Continent, was reasserting itself in England, it was the American colonies that defended and re-established these

ICAPTIONriefOFOUR INSTITUTIONS 291

everlasting truths. They set them out in resolutions and declarations, supported them on the battle-field, wrote them into their laws, and adopted them in their Constitution. The broader freedom which they acquired in that century was supplemented by the broader equality which they established in the nineteenth century.

The great struggle of the twentieth century is still smouldering in the mind of the world. A new kind of absolutism, but with the old method of military force, challenged the existence of liberty everywhere. In the greatest conflict of all the ages freedom was again victorious with a resulting completeness which had never before been secured. No responsible authority now exists in any jurisdiction which would dare to deny that it is derived from the consent of the governed. What further effects it will produce on the fortunes of mankind, time only can disclose.

It would seem as though this broader survey might answer some of the perplexities of the hour. No doubt present existence seems somewhat tame after the lurid events of the Great War. There is not the same thrill in ministering to the starving victims of the Russian Soviet that there was in going to the support of the defenders of Verdun. The enormous toil and effort of endeavoring to pay the debt of the nation, or even of meeting its obligations to its defenders, are not so romantic as arming and sailing away to the battle-fields of France. But there is no reason for discouragement when our country is doing what may seem to be drudgery with equal completeness with which it performed deeds of glory.

The great achievements of the past have always been

the result of a long, slow, and toilsome process filled with disappointments, attended by unavoidable reactions. Human liberty did not perish in the Netherlands, in England, in America, or in France. In the great hours of its peril unexpected reserves, unknown resources have come to its rescue. Because the evil of our own nation or of the world does not all at once yield to the efforts of good intentions or of righteousness furnishes no cause for being alarmed or disturbed. The putting forth of great effort, the making of great sacrifices have never failed to return in due season abundant rewards of human progress. It does not seem unlikely that the world is gathering itself now, in spite of seeming discouragements, for such a forward step.

The great forces of other centuries converged in America. They are working out a new destiny here. It is not for us to view them with too much impatience. It is rather for us to work with them in the full knowledge that there is no easy road to success, no short cut to perfection, and while working maintain our faith.

One of the chief errors of the present day is that of relying too much on the government and too little on our own efforts and on the people themselves. This comes to pass by supposing that, when there is something which ought to be done, we can avoid all personal responsibility by a simple ordinance requiring that hereafter it shall be done by the government. We cannot divest ourselves of our burdens and responsibilities by any such easy method. Where the people themselves are the government, it needs no argument to demonstrate that what the people cannot do their government cannot do.

Another error lies in supposing that great fundamental reforms can be at once accomplished by the mere passage of a law. By law is meant a rule of action. Action depends upon intelligence and motive. If either of these be lacking, the action fails and the law fails. These may be stimulated by rewards or penalties, but whatever else may be their effect, they do not remove the source of evil. It is the mind behind the law that makes it truly effective. Laws are insufficient to endow a nation with righteousness.

Right-thinking people want the results of prosperity, education, and loyalty to the government. The question which is always before us is how these results are to be secured. It is very evident that palliatives fail. The hope of rewards, the fear of punishments do not go very far. There is very little that is really worth while which can be bought or sold. The desire for gain has made many cowards, but it never made a hero. The country cannot be run on the promise of what it will do for the people. The only motive to which they will continue ready to respond is the opportunity to do something for themselves, to achieve their own greatness, to work out their own destiny. It is the motive described with so much eloquence by St. Paul in the eleventh chapter of Hebrews. It is the faith of the men who followed William the Silent, Cromwell, Washington, and Lincoln, and who stood at last at the Marne.

When we explore the real foundation of our institutions, of their historical development or their logical support, we come very soon to the matter of religious belief. It was the great religious awakening of the sixteenth century that brought about the political awakening of the seventeenth century. The American Revolution was preceded by the great religious revival of the middle of the eighteenth century, which had its effect both in England and in the colonies. When the common people turned to the reading of the Bible, as they did in the Netherlands and in England, when they were stirred by a great revival, as they were in the days of the preaching of Edwards and Whitefield, the way was prepared for William, for Cromwell, and for Washington. It was because religion gave the people a new importance and a new glory that they demanded a new freedom and a new government. We cannot in our generation reject the cause and retain the result.

If the institutions they adopted are to survive, if the governments which they founded are to endure, it will be because the people continue to have similar religious beliefs. It is idle to discuss freedom and equality on any other basis. It is useless to expect substantial reforms from any other motive. They cannot be administered from without. They must come from within. That is why laws alone are so impotent. To enact or to repeal laws is not to secure real reform. It is necessary to take these problems directly to the individual. There will be a proper use of our material prosperity when the individual feels a divine responsibility. There will be a broadening scholarship when the individual feels that science, literature, and history are the revelation of divine truths. There will be obedience to law when the individual feels that government represents a divine authority.

It is these beliefs, these religious convictions, that represent the strength of America, the strength of all civilized society. They are not a power which is diminishing but a power which is increasing. The standard of conduct which they require was never before so universally recognized and accepted. It sanctifies every place of worship, it is revealed in every institution of learning, it supports every activity of government, it sustains every economic structure. In domestic affairs, in international affairs, it is more and more the reliance of mankind. The evidences of it are increasing, the results of it are accumulating. More and more the people are living under the conviction that it is righteousness alone which exalteth the nation. Surely the recognition of this fact, which stands out above all others, ought to make these days of abiding satisfaction and of continuing faith and determination for the American people.

XXIV

The greatest accomplishments of mankind are not accidents. Almost without exception they represent the leadership of one man. We may not say he was indispensable. Knowing what is in man, we can but realize that there is many a "Cæsar guiltless of his country's blood," and many a "mute, inglorious Milton," for it is the Cæsar and Milton in men which respond to the inspiration of leadership. This does not diminish, but increases the glory of our heroes. It does not weaken, but strengthens the admiration which is their due.

WILLIAM McKINLEY

A NEW century and a new generation has come since
the stirring scenes which you are gathered to commemorate. The nineteenth century seemed to end for America with the Spanish War, and those new ideals and that
broader outlook under which we now live began to form.
The men of the former generation were just passing off
the stage, the generation of those who preserved our
country by their sacrifices, and developed it by their
effort and their wisdom. It was the day of those who
rededicated America to a larger and, at last, complete
freedom, and in that spirit began the development of her
great resources which have created wealth, enlarged
population, and made America the greatest and most
powerful nation of the earth.

The greatest accomplishments of mankind are not accidents. Almost without exception they represent the
leadership of one man. We may not say he was indispensable. Knowing what is in man, we can but realize that
there is many a "Cæsar guiltless of his country's blood,"
and many a "mute, inglorious Milton," for it is the Cæsar
and Milton in men which respond to the inspiration of
leadership. This does not diminish, but increases the
glory of our heroes. It does not weaken, but strengthens
the admiration which is their due.

The formative period of our country was presided over

At the Convention of Spanish War Veterans, Saunders Theatre, Harvard
University, Cambridge, April 17, 1923.

by Washington. Other generals might win victories while he was suffering defeat; other statesmen might propose measures while he remained in seclusion, but through it all, he was the background of the Revolution. Massachusetts, no less than Virginia, looked to him. Pennsylvania, no less than New York, followed him. Whatever victories were won, were won because of him. Whatever measures were adopted for the purpose of accomplishing the Revolution could not have been adopted without him. As he was the genius of the Revolution, so Hamilton was the genius of the formation of the Federal Government. He perceived its necessity. He harmonized contending elements into the proposal of the Constitution. By his illuminating arguments he secured its ratification. By his statesmanship he made it, financially and politically, an established government. The judicial side of our national institutions was the conception of John Marshall. He raised the Supreme Court of the United States into the greatest tribunal of the world and by the breadth of his decisions guaranteed the legal integrity of the nation. It was Thomas Jefferson who brought to bear upon national questions the force of public opinion, and through his skill retained for our institutions the principle of popular government. When there was need of argument and example to defend the principle of the integrity of the Union, there came the eloquence of Webster; the action of Jackson. When argument turned to arms, when at last there came the great conflict for nationality and a larger freedom, men turned to the leadership of Lincoln the great statesman and Grant the great captain.

This work completed, the men of the intervening period came into action and eminence. One of the most interesting of these was your Commander-in-Chief, the President of the United States, William McKinley. In character he was gentle, generous, true, seeking the welfare of his fellow men by eloquent counsel, by sound measures promoting prosperity, reuniting and strengthening the national sentiments, raising his country from provincialism to a world-power. He represented the policy and later supplied the leadership for those principles which are characteristic of this period. America has always preferred to take her great men from the soil. Rarely has she bestowed her choice on those nourished where city pavements separate them from the mother of us all. McKinley was born amid formative industry. His earliest boyhood was thrown among men struggling in response to the instinct to produce, to create. They were men and women of imagination and character. He belonged to the race of pioneers. A lusty, hardy stock, who leave well-trodden paths for the outposts of the frontier; to whom there is born, not only those who lead the advance of civilization, over the face of the earth, but who lead in the advance of ideas, for they are pioneers likewise of the spirit and the soul. To strength of body they add strength of mind. They have vision. Seeing the end, they "press on toward the mark of the high calling." It was among such a people that William McKinley was born. Around him was a religious home. He grew up conscientiously attentive to the lessons of his Bible class, amid domestic surroundings where sobriety reigned, where there was industry, thrift, and integrity, where, if opportunity for education came, it came as a result of sacrifice.

When the call of Lincoln came for volunteers, William McKinley, a youth of eighteen, was one of the first to volunteer, starting his military service on June 11, 1861. He was not too young, however, soon to be given responsibilities and to command confidence. When Sheridan made his way through the Union army after his ride from Winchester, McKinley was by his side, where he saw that which has happened but rarely in military history—an army in retreat turn and win a victory. When he finished his service in July, 1865, he had the rank of major, which he bore through life, though he was more familiarly known, by those with whom he had served, by the endearing title of Comrade McKinley.

Returning to civil life, he was soon admitted to the bar, where he won fame as a prosecuting attorney and as an advocate in the trial of jury cases. Prominence was a part of his being. It came to him. He did not seek it. He could not avoid it. In 1876 he was chosen a Representative in Congress. He determined to make himself a master and authority in some subject of legislation. He had a desire for service, he believed in his country, he believed in his countrymen. He believed in the development of the resources of the land and the resources of mankind. Who shall say what directed him, in choosing to become a master of the theory and practice of the protective tariff? Whatever called to him from his surroundings at home, from his knowledge of the needs of his country, or from out of the infinite, attentively he listened, he heard, and he obeyed. The soldier of Lincoln was in him still.

The country was recovering from the losses of the war. It was retiring the national debt and turning an invincible energy to the conquest of our vast domain. McKinley knew the needs of formative industry—he had been brought up with it. He knew not only from study and observation, but from family tradition, why peoples had crossed the sea, what conditions they had left behind, what aspirations they cherished here. His desire was to protect them from the hard existence of the Old World and give them the opportunity of an undreamed-of development and prosperity in the New World. His advocacy of this cause brought him to the Ways and Means Committee when Garfield left it for the presidency. From that time until he laid down the burdens of life he was known as the chief advocate of a tariff for protection.

These were times when the spirit of party ran high. Being the shining mark, he never failed to draw the fire of the opposition. Within his· own party he held his place without opposition until 1890, when he became chairman of the Committee on Ways and Means and the leader of his party on the floor of the House. It was at this time that he presented, and the Congress enacted into law, that tariff meas ire which bore the title of the McKinley Bill. In the great reaction which came in the middle of the term of President Harrison, though his district had been gerrymandered so as to be Democratic by three thousand, he came within three hundred votes of election.

He did not falter in defending his cause, he did not lose faith in the soundness of his principles; he said the country would return to them, and he saw it return under his own banner.

Divested of office, he was not divested of rank or leadership. What his opponents had thought to be his undoing turned out to be his promotion. That destiny, for which his discretion and diligence had prepared him, touched him and led him on. He was chosen governor of Ohio. That election was national in its effect. Two years later he was again returned by eighty thousand over his nearest competitor.

In the meantime, the country had its experience with an attempted tariff-reform policy. Grover Cleveland was a brave, conscientious, public servant. He liked candor and faith in the performance of public business. Chosen, as he believed, to secure tariff reform, he wished to see that policy carried out fairly and honestly. The bill which the Congress of his party sent to him he characterized as tainted with party perfidy and party dishonor. It became a law without his signature. In the wreck of business produced by the prospect of this law and the disorganization of the currency, there ensued the panic of 1893. President Cleveland will ever live as a man who maintained the authority of the law against the violence of disorder, and the integrity of the United States Treasury against the opposition of his associates. In maintaining these he broke his party. The business of the country demanded relief. The economic intelligence of the country demanded a sound currency.

It was at this time that the business interests of America took a decided stand in relation to public affairs under the leadership of Marcus A. Hanna. He organized the campaign which nominated McKinley at the first ballot, on a platform which declared for protection and the gold standard. After a great campaign of education, McKinley was chosen President. He at once revised the tariff and strengthened the law establishing the gold standard. Prosperity immediately returned. There was not only a domestic market but immense exports. The foreign trade increased more under the first term of McKinley than it had ever increased in any other four years.

This man who had set out to study the tariff that he might better the condition of his fellow men had seen that hope not only accomplished but, because he had been faithful to that trust, had the increased satisfaction of firmly re-establishing the finances of his country. Through being faithful over a few things, he had seen his countrymen make him ruler over many things.

War had no attraction for this President. He had seen four years of it. "Peace," he said, "is the national desire and the goal of every American aspiration. The best sentiment of the civilized world is moving toward the settlement of differences between nations without resorting to the horrors of war. Let us ever remember that our interest is in concord, not conflict; and that our real eminence rests in the victories of peace, not those of war. We love peace better than war, and our swords never should be drawn except in a righteous cause, and then never until every effort at peace and arbitration shall be exhausted." Holding these views, it was the tragedy of his administration that conditions forced on his country a war with Spain. He resisted it to the end, and finally submitted to it with tears. When it was over, he insisted on giving freedom to the Antilles and to the Philippines. He was charged with embarking upon a course of imperialism. Perhaps his own character was the best answer to this charge, but guiding the people by going with them he moved on. He wanted ever to build, not to destroy. The instinct of his people to produce, to create, followed him yet. "The prophets of evil were not the builders of the Republic," he said, "nor in its crises since, have they saved or served it." His domain was extended. A ruler over many things, he became a ruler over more things.

On him and on his statesmanship the people again set their mark of approval. He was returned in triumph at the national election. Under responsibilities he had grown and broadened. His vision now beheld his country first, but it reached beyond our own shores. He sought in trade and commerce a world relationship. His last public utterance, made at Buffalo, advocated reciprocal trade relations, which he knew had no basis without protection. At the same time he urged an Isthmian canal to unite our own coasts with the Latin-American Republics. The next day he was struck down. He died as he had lived, on his lips a prayer.

There is no better interpretation of the character of a great man than the plain narrative of his life. There is no adequate portrayal of his personality. He must be seen. There is no satisfactory description of his eloquence. He must be heard. All our attempts to reveal William McKinley to his fellow men seem poor and mean beside the man himself. With all our efforts we do but reflect ourselves. His genius, his greatness elude us.

We can describe the period during which he lived and wrought. He represented that youth of the country, stalwart in their patriotism, sincere in their devotion, followers of the truth, which made up the armies of Lincoln. He cherished the best aspirations of ambition, he sought the awards of professional life through intense application, guided by a high sense of honor. With gentleness, with courtesy ever he led the nation on.

The driving force of American progress has been her industries. They have created the wealth that has wrought our national development. They have attracted immigration. They have builded great cities. They have spanned the continent with railroads. Without them, the great force of agriculture would be now where it was in the eighteenth century.

As we look back, we can see the unfolding of the plan for the making of America. We can see the struggle of its early settlers; their deep, religious convictions; their aspirations for liberty; the long years of preparation through military experience, through the education of the public mind by pamphlet and speech, for the bringing in of the Revolution. At last independence was established. The Constitution was adopted and defended until, under Lincoln, the land stood all free. All this was the making of a form of government, the adoption of principles, the settling of policies. The groundwork had been laid for a great material advance.

When all these things were done, the time was ripe for the great economic and industrial development of our country. It was this situation, this opportunity, that called forth William McKinley. Taking up again the work of Hamilton and Clay, because commercial problems necessarily had been laid aside for the solution of the more fundamental problems of freedom, McKinley re-established their principles, and under his leadership the government readopted their policies.

It was his policy, the application of his principle of a protective tariff, which furnished the initial opportunity for the laying down of the great industries of America and the development of her entire resources. These benefits have been reciprocal. They have been felt at the forge and the spindle, on the farm and in the marts of trade. It was under the stimulation of this policy that American production came to lead the world. No one will deny that to secure all this America has had to pay the price. It has tended to diminish the shipping industry. There have been abuses. It has increased the cost of certain lines of commodities, but McKinley long ago pointed out that cheap goods meant cheap men. What country is there on earth that, to secure our results, would not have been willing to pay the price many times over? The benefits which have come cannot be counted. Whole peoples have been raised from degradation to affluence. The material foundation has been laid on which has rested the spiritual progress of the American people.

There was nothing of the materialist in William McKinley. In his being he had no selfishness. Riches did not tempt him. Military conquest was his abhorrence. If power came to him, it was not of his seeking, he used it not for himself, but for his country. He did not desire to give selfish advantages to those who might immediately benefit from the policy of protection. He was looking to the general welfare. He sought to enlarge and strengthen an empire for the glory of its sovereign, the people. He thus defines his "special interest": "I am for America, because America is for the common people." He never undertook to substitute a part for the whole. He looked beyond outward appearances. He saw into the very soul of things. "I believe in the common brotherhood of men," he declared. "I believe that labor gets on best when capital gets on best, and that capital gets on best when labor is paid the most. Every attempt to array class against class, 'the classes against the masses,' section against section, labor against capital, 'the poor against the rich,' or interest against interest in the United States, is in the highest degree reprehensible. The most un-American of all appeals is the one which seeks to array labor against capital, employer against employed." These were his counsels. They are not born of the flesh, but of the spirit. He was the "advance agent of prosperity," that he might be the prophet of the intellectual and moral forces of mankind. He turned the hand of man to production, that he might lift up his soul. He turned the thought of man to creation, that he might reveal his own divine image.

Following his administration came the period of the regulation and control of the great economic forces which he had created. That work is being done. The problem now is to move forward in one harmonious whole along the paths that he has pointed out. America has not neglected to follow his precepts. When liberty has been assailed, she has continued to defend it. With his vision, she has looked beyond her own shores. Even now, she is mindful, as he was mindful, in his last message to his countrymen, of the impelling duty of the establishment of peace through justice and mutual prosperity through trade, among all the peoples of the earth. The nations will ever have need of a McKinley, who shall re-establish them as he re-established America. They need some one who can inspire them with his confidence in a sound currency, who can encourage them to promote their welfare through peace and industry, who can continue his great work of liberation.

It is in harmony with these principles that America is to-day using its influence in the world. It holds the leadership in sound finances, enlarged industry, peace and concord, the promotion of a better understanding, not by force but by conference, and that justice tempered with mercy which has characterized the great liberal movements of mankind. All of this is in accord with the spirit of your great captain. The foundation of peace, prosperity, and of broad human liberty on which he wrought with such a mighty hand is continually being strengthened. That work ever goes on as he carried it on, in plain and homely things; in a universal industry and honesty, which built the character of William McKinley; in the acceptance of an abiding faith in the right and the truth.

Although there was never greater heroism displayed, and the forces by land and sea were never led with greater precision and success, looked at as a whole, the work of the Spanish War was not so much a feat of arms as the beginning of a new American spirit. In so far as it placed our country in the position of a world-power, it was the beginning of a new world spirit. It was the beginning of a new recognition of the right of people to be free, reaching from the near Atlantic to the farther shore of the Pacific. It was a new awakening throughout the earth. It brought out in America the determination to secure a broader distribution of the rewards of that great industrial prosperity which had grown up in the day of McKinley. It was the end of a true reconstruction period and the beginning of a liberal movement the end of which is not yet. The sentiment which it fostered has been of inestimable value to mankind, giving a new warrant to hope, a new sanctification to faith, and new bonds to human brotherhood. In this spirit the world is working out a new salvation.

XXV

The times which built this church and succeeding history have been productive of progress, because they have represented a spirit of liberality, of toleration, and of freedom. They have permitted the people to be the masters of their own destiny and the individual to be the keeper of his own conscience.

THE OLD NORTH CHURCH

The doings of mankind always hold for us a vast interest. Any two hundred years of which we could secure the record would not be lacking in this vital element. It represents a very substantial period. It is more than one-tenth of the Christian era, and two-thirds of the time since the coming of the Pilgrims to Massachusetts Bay. But when those years lie between 1723 and 1923, because of the contribution which they have made not only to the progress of our own country but to that of the world, their interest becomes, for us, one which is predominant. There are few organized institutions and still fewer buildings in all the land that go back to that day. The continuity of some religious bodies has been kept up, but in nearly all else there has been a break. This building stands with the Old South Church, the old State House, King's Chapel, and Faneuil Hall as the sole remaining public buildings of Boston constructed before the Revolution.

The period around 1723 is one in which the interest centres in the activities of peace rather than war. Massachusetts was then a loyal colony of the British Empire. The Treaty of Utrecht had been signed a few years before, preserving the brilliant victories of Marlborough and leaving to the British navy the long-to-be-main-

At Boston, celebrating the Two Hundredth Anniversary of the establishment of Christ Church, known as the Old North Church. April 18, 1923.

tained supremacy of the seas. George I had succeeded Queen Anne. The old Whig aristocracy was in control of the government. The King, being unable to speak English, ceased to attend cabinet meetings. A passion for speculation arose which reached its height in the South Sea bubble. When this collapsed, Sir Robert Walpole became First Lord of the Treasury and Chancellor of the Exchequer, in 1721, to restore financial order. The strength of his personality and the foreign language of the King brought about a responsible cabinet under parliamentary government, and the beginning of the prime ministry. The policy of the empire at this time was national unity, toleration, peace, and commercial development. It was not an era of warfare, but rather one in which were being harvested practically all those results which warrant warfare in behalf of human liberty.

In the colonies somewhat similar conditions existed. Indian warfare had for the time ceased to be an overwhelming peril. The narrowness of the old theocracy of Massachusetts, under Cotton and the Mathers, in the administration of the local government had given way to a more liberal spirit. The Old South Church stands as a monument to the beginning effectiveness of this new light. This society was formed by those who insisted on the broadening of the franchise under the "Halfway Covenant" to include those who had been baptized and led decorous lives, even though they might not be church communicants. While the theocracy was intolerant at home, it had the virtue of being independent abroad. It was just as defiant of English tyranny as it was of colonial disbelief. In fact, it narrowed the franchise to church communicants in order that it might keep out of any control of its government representatives of the established church, which meant to them representatives of the tyranny of Laud and the Stuarts, the Court of the High Commission, and the Star Chamber.

The days of Andros had come and gone. The old charter had been taken away, under which Massachusetts had been practically autonomous for more than fifty years. The new charter, granted by William III, required of voters only a property qualification and reserved to the crown the appointment of the governor and the right to veto laws passed by the colonial legislature. Thus was laid the foundation for that long struggle between the provincial legislature, which had the power of the purse, and the royal governors, who held the power of the sword, which was finally to be decided only by the American Revolution. One of these unending squabbles was in process at this time, so that Governor Shute sailed away in disgust in the last days of 1722, because the Assembly had haggled over his salary and refused to appropriate money with which to provide protection from the Indians, leaving the office to Lieutenant-Governor Dummer, who continued as acting governor for about six years. But after the fall of the Stuarts, the rebellion against Andros, the seating of William and Mary and their successors on the British throne, these quarrels were more or less incidents of administration. There was no apparent deep-seated organized resistance to British authority until, after the expenditures made necessary by the French and Indian War, Parliament thought it necessary to lay taxes and regulate trade in America to reimburse the home treasury for the cost of colonial defense.

In the old days Episcopal services had not been tolerated in the colony, but Andros took possession of the Old South Meeting-House by royal order for that purpose, often keeping the minister and his parishioners waiting outside. At that time the building of King's Chapel was started. The disturbing feature of this to the colonists was not a question of toleration, but the fact that this, in their eyes, represented a part of the tyranny of the Stuarts, and they suspected it to be the forerunner of an assault on their own liberty of worship. No such condition existed in 1723. Under the reigning dynasty at that time there was no apprehension of the loss of their political liberty or unwarranted interference with the religious views of Congregational churches. Judge Sewall relates that Doctor Increase Mather "much bewail'd the Connecticut Apostacie; that Mr. Cutler and others should say there was no minister in N. E.," but the public does not appear to have joined in this sentiment, and the old man was gathered unto his fathers and laid at rest in yonder burying-ground before this church was opened by the installation of Reverend Doctor Timothy Cutler, who had been to England to receive his ordination from the Episcopal bishops. Had the tendencies of the time not been liberal, there would have been no founding of the Brattle Church, where Benjamin Coleman preached, requiring for admission no examination by the presiding clergy but merely a subscription to the Westminster creed. The proposal for a religious test for the president and fellows of Harvard College, made at the end of the seventeenth century, would not have failed. The Reverend

Samuel Willard would not have succeeded Doctor Mather
in the performance of the duties of president of Harvard,
and he, in turn, would not have been followed by John
Leverett, who was associated with the extremely liberal
clergy of that day. At Northampton Reverend Solomon
Stoddard would have required for admission to com-
munion more than baptism in infancy.

Another evidence of the awakening of the public mind
was the reaction which had arisen against the witchcraft
persecutions. Many of those who had been concerned
in them, either as officers or witnesses, laity or clergy,
had expressed the belief that they had been in error, and
made public renunciation. That state of terror which
had held the land for more than two generations, arising
from a fear of Indian attacks at home and the peril of
ecclesiastical and political tyranny from abroad was at
last dissipated. The people were returning to that normal condition of public mind which is the result of an
untrammelled freedom for self-expression. They were beginning to seek development, not through the monotony
of a dead uniformity, but through the variations of individual choice and inclination.

But while there was a distinct reaction in matters of
religion, there was at the same time a rising Tory flavor
in the community. One of its leading spirits was Joseph
Dudley, who had been thrown into prison with Andros,
whom he had served under and supported to the extent
of declaring that the people of New England had no privileges left except not to be sold for slaves. But public
opinion had softened since 1687, so that he had acted
twelve years as a royal governor, beginning in 1702, with-

out public protest. He represented a second generation, who were very active commercially, had become people of wealth and influence, and were attached to the old form and the old ritual. They were the rising tide of aristocracy. He was opposed to Doctor Mather, who had led the town meeting in the Old South in defiantly refusing to surrender the old charter, but was on good terms with those who were inclined toward liberality in religion, perhaps because Doctor Mather and his party also disagreed with them. These people were naturally drawn toward the established church. Their aspirations were to move in an atmosphere of culture under the domination of the customs of polite society.

The community was interested in the advancement of learning. The Commonwealth had just appropriated funds for the erection of Massachusetts Hall, at Harvard, built under the administration of Governor Shute, which is still standing. This spirit was prevalent in Connecticut, where a college had recently been located at New Haven and named for a native of Massachusetts, Elihu Yale. It is said that the Mathers looked upon this more conservative institution with some sympathy, which may have been modified when the rector and president of the college, Doctor Cutler, became the first clergyman of this church. There was as yet little in the way of literature, though Anne Bradstreet, wife of the old governor, had written verses which were republished in London and were not without admiration. The narrative of Governor Bradford and the history of Governor Winthrop had, of course, been written but not published. There were journals and chronicles, and of sermons there was no lack.

Edward Johnson's "Wonder-Working Providence" dates from 1654. These sporadic works, which are of great value now, were probably little regarded at that time. Among the books on religion and government which were published and well distributed, one of the most famous is that of Reverend John Wise, of Ipswich, entitled "A Vindication of the Government of New England Churches," printed in 1717. This was an arsenal in the demonstration of the freedom and the equality of man, which did valiant work in supporting the principles of the Revolution. This patriot author, who had been fined and imprisoned under Andros, could have looked down with satisfaction on Bunker Hill and could have seen the influence and almost the language of his writings in the Declaration of Independence.

Of newspapers there were as yet very few in all America. The Boston *News Letter* was started in 1704. There was a Boston *Gazette* in 1719. James Franklin started the New England *Courant* in 1721. This paper apparently held to a critical attitude. Judge Sewall refers to it as a "virulent libel," because it quoted Watts's "Psalms" against judges. On account of their theological views, the Reverend Mather Byles characterized the men who edited this paper as the "Hell-Fire Club of Boston." But when criticism was made of the Assembly, fine, imprisonment, and suppression followed, making future publication necessary under the new name of Benjamin Franklin, the brother of James. It was out of this circumstance that Benjamin was released from his indenture to his brother James, so that in 1723 he was making that journey, at the age of seventeen, with all that it was to imply to learning, to science, and to liberty, to his new home at Philadelphia.

Another young man, Jonathan Edwards, was just rising to a great place in the world at this time. He was about to become a tutor at Yale, "helping to overcome the shock," Doctor Allen tells us, "to the College and the community caused by the secession of its Rector Mr. Cutler, Mr. Johnson one of its tutors, and others, to the Episcopal Church." In the years to come he was to preach the Great Awakening at Northampton, in which he was to be joined by Whitefield, the Episcopalian from England, the great revivalist of that day. A little later he writes: "On January 12, 1723, I made a solemn dedication of myself to God . . . engaging to fight with all my might against the world, the flesh, and the devil." Franklin and Edwards indicate to us the quality of manhood which these times were raising. What they were to do in behalf of the freedom and regeneration of mankind is now known to the world. In nine years George Washington was to be born. These names declare a spirit dedicated to truth deep-rooted in the beginnings of the eighteenth century.

It was under such conditions that some of those of the Episcopal faith in this town, finding King's Chapel was no longer adequate for their accommodation, associated themselves together for the building of this church. They were a people of devotion, of patriotism, ready to defend liberty, probably with a healthy primal instinct for the support of the existing order of things. They represented that conservatism which is the strength of all civilization. Considering the change which time has wrought in this portion of the town, there is a significance in the text from which Doctor Cutler preached the opening sermon, when he chose a verse from Isaiah, which declares: "For mine house shall be called an house of prayer for all people." This was a church of dignity and importance. It numbered among its pewholders the names of Vassall, Sewall, and Thomas Graves, who was the first senior warden and chief justice of the Superior Court of the province. Professional men, merchants, and ship-owners were among its parishioners. The church still has a Bible and prayer-books, presented by King George II, in 1733, and it installed the first chime of bells that was set up in this country, bearing the date of 1744. It has been adorned by the enterprise of American privateers in the French wars. Although this was a parish of the established church of England, the clergy and membership of which were generally inclined toward loyalty to the King, we read in the diary of Ezra Stiles of "Doctor Byles' little Flock which are more for liberty than any Episco. Congregation North of Maryland." One of its parishioners, Captain Daniel Malcom, was a stanch opponent of the revenue acts and a leader of the patriots. This attitude, no doubt, was partially the reason that Doctor Byles was formally separated from the parish on the eighteenth day of April, 1775, the day that has given to this church and its steeple so much of enduring fame.

It was from that steeple, one hundred and forty-eight years ago to-night, that the signal-lanterns gleamed, warning the watchers on the Charlestown shore that the British troops were on the move toward Lexington and Concord. There seems no doubt that these lights were

displayed by the sexton, Robert Newman. Probably he
was assisted in entering the church by Captain John
Pulling, Jr. Back of this activity and directing it was
Doctor Joseph Warren, who was within three months to
give his life for his country at Bunker Hill. He had two
messengers that he despatched on this night to warn
Hancock and Adams, who were at Lexington, and arouse
the countryside to resist the advance of the hostile forces.
One of these was William Dawes, whom he sent out over
Boston Neck, and the other was Paul Revere. It was
Revere who arranged for the display of the signals which,
as it turned out, were unnecessary, because he himself
coming directly from Doctor Warren was stealthily rowed
across the river, almost under the British war-ships, to
Charlestown. He had been one of the moving spirits in
a band of mechanics at the North End, organized to
watch and report on all British actions. He knew what
was acting, as he himself said, but had he been intercepted
in crossing, as he feared, the lanterns would have conveyed the correct message to his confederate, Colonel
Conant, who was waiting and received him on his landing. It is because his ride on this night was the consummation of a long period of watching and working, largely
under his immediate oversight, that Paul Revere rises to
the plane of true heroism. It was his plan and his preparation, as well as his execution of it, that gave him the
authority in that eventful hour to speak

"A word that shall echo forevermore!"

And yet it was because his word was received and acted
upon that he rose to so grand a place in history. He

became a hero only because the land was filled with heroism.

It was from the same lofty belfry tower that General Gage looked out across the water on the historic day of Bunker Hill. Twice he saw his troops reel back in disaster under the terrible execution of the patriots' fire. In their last charge he saw them prevail at the expense of one of the bloodiest hours in warfare. It was in this last assault that Pitcairn, the old major of marines, who always rested under the charge, which he denied, of having first fired on the minute-men at Lexington, received his death-wound. He was buried under this church. Alone, among British officers, he had dealt fairly with the townspeople. Although a monument rises to commemorate him in Westminster Abbey, there is strong probability that his bones still rest here, where out of the common sacrifice of American and Briton the liberty of the world was made more secure.

The old church was closed now, its congregation nearly all away supporting the patriot cause. It did not meet the fate of at least one other church and many buildings, of being pulled down by the British for lumber and firewood. It did not become training-quarters for horsemen like the Old South. It was reopened again, after Washington had driven the British from Boston, by Reverend Stephen Christopher Lewis, who, though he had been deputy chaplain in Burgoyne's regiment of light dragoons, took the oath of allegiance to the colonial cause. He was directed by the parish "to prepare a proper form of Prayer for the Congress of the United States, for the several States, and for their success in the present important

contest, to be used Daily in the Church." Prayer-books
and liturgy were accordingly changed, and this was the
first Episcopal Church in New England that transferred
its form from the "Church of England" to the "Protestant
Episcopal Church of America." Truth here had been
supreme. Duty had not faltered.

That spirit had now reached maturity which was to
send Samuel Nicholson, one of the parishioners of this
church, to be the first commander of the frigate *Constitution*, known in song and story as *Old Ironsides*. The
conflicts of those days have been decided. The contests
of arms and of principles have been won as America would
have them won. Into her keeping there is more and
more intrusted the support and defense of those immortal
truths which make for the progress and salvation of the
world.

The old days are gone. The Green Dragon, where
Paul Revere and his fellow mechanics met and watched
and worked for freedom, is no more. But the voice of the
common people has not been weakened. They are still
ready when need be to meet the counsel and rise in the
spirit of the stout old patriots. The belfry lanterns are
dimmed, but the light of inspiration which has gleamed
from this chancel for two hundred years has not paled.
It still sheds its radiance over the way of patriotism, truth,
and righteousness. It still throws out its signal warning
good to resist evil. The nation and the government which
were the product of all these experiences still remain
strong and vigorous.

There are voices which are counselling the destruction
of the rights of the individual which our institutions were

established to maintain, some by out-and-out revolution. But these need only to be brought into the light of publicity to wither away. There are others which are more insidious, more dangerous, which come under the guise of government activity instigated for the general good. Our fathers sought for an enlarged freedom, for the right to enjoy the rewards of their own industry. They had felt the oppression of government regulation, competition, and monopoly. They wished to be rid of these restrictions. That most precious privilege they gained. They can maintain it only upon one condition, that they use it righteously. It is the abuse of liberty which warrants oppression. If the people will pursue a course of economic and industrial righteousness there will be no motive for interfering with their liberty by drastic government regulation, or sequestration of their property by government operation, or a confiscation of the results of their industry in the name of taxation. It is the existence of a wrong public sentiment, a wrong standard, whether expressed in private economic relations or in government attempt to remedy what cannot be remedied by law, which causes the evil. In either case, there is a harmful curtailment of freedom. In the teachings of religion lies the fundamental remedy.

The times which built this church and succeeding history have been productive of progress because they have represented a spirit of liberality, of toleration, and of freedom. They have permitted the people to be the masters of their own destiny and the individual to be the keeper of his own conscience. They have given to the world the inestimable stimulant of making persons think for themselves, act for themselves, and be responsible to themselves. This is the spirit of knowledge, of science, and of true wisdom. These are the fundamentals upon which human welfare depends. Their increasing maintenance will mean increasing industrial peace and commercial development.

It is because this church, irrespective of its connection with the stirring events of local history, stands as a monument to these principles that it survives, and has reached the day when it may glory not only in its good works but in its antiquity. It is a representative of the realities of life, without which all else is vain. It has stood now for two hundred years, ministering to the spiritual needs of the community. As an influence for sound government, ordered liberty, righteous living, peace and good-will among men, it will endure forever.

XXVI

But if our republic is to be maintained and improved it will be through the efforts and character of the individual. It will be, first of all, because of the influences which exist in the home, for it is the ideals which prevail in the home life which make up the strength of the nation. The homely virtues must continue to be cultivated. The real dignity, the real nobility of work must be cherished. It is only through industry that there is any hope for individual development.

THE DESTINY OF AMERICA

THE soldiers and benefactors of Northampton make a long and honorable list. They represent a strong and devoted citizenship. The early settlers were trained in arms from military necessity. Their first-born child, Ebenezer Parsons, fell in King Philip's War. The first train band was organized in 1658. The latest National Guard company is now in process of organization.

In between lie many generations of history. Their sons have served in all the wars from the local New England struggle against the Indians under King Philip to the last great world conflict which has just closed. One of her early citizens, Colonel John Stoddard, was the principal influence in this valley in the first half of the eighteenth century. Contemporary with him was that eminent divine, Jonathan Edwards, many years pastor of the church, a philosopher, a theologian, and one of the greatest intellects ever produced in America. Of special military fame was General Seth Pomeroy, who fought in the Indian Wars, took part in the capture of Louisburg, was one of the patriot band at Bunker Hill, and died an old man, with the confidence and respect of Washington, while serving in the opening years of the Revolution. Another patriot of those days was Major Joseph Hawley. He was one of the moving factors of the Revolution. His legal mind perceived the unconstitutionality of the acts

The Memorial Day Services at Northampton, May 30, 1923.

of Parliament, his statesmanlike vision saw that the colonists must fight, and that the necessary outcome must be union and independence. A wise counsellor, of whom John Adams said: "His character shines like burnished gold." A close associate of his, a delegate who helped frame the National Constitution, was Caleb Strong, one of the first United States senators, eleven years governor of the Commonwealth, always a supporter of ordered liberty. Three other residents of Northampton have been Massachusetts members of the United States Senate, Eli Porter Ashmun, Elijah Hunt Mills, and Isaac Chapman Bates.

This patriotic tradition has never ceased to be maintained in public service and private life in time of peace, and by officers and men in time of war. The lengthening list is now so great that it can no longer be given in detail. It is represented by that brilliant military record of Colonel Joseph B. Parsons, descendant of the Joseph Parsons who, as clerk of the train band, was the first military officer in town, made by his years of service as one of Lincoln's soldiers, by Rear-Admiral Cook, commander of the battleship *Brooklyn* in the naval battle which destroyed Cervera's fleet, and by such a rank and file as made up old Company I, which, going to the front in the Spanish War, was in the engagement which resulted in the capture of the city of Santiago, was in the first National Guard division to go across the sea, and a member of the 104th, which was the first National Guard regiment to be decorated in France for distinguished service. All these are representative, in their life and service, of the thousands of others who have made, and are making, the patriotic devotion of the people of the city of Northampton.

Patriotism is easy to understand in America. It means looking out for yourself by looking out for your country. In no other nation on earth does this principle have such complete application. It comes most naturally from the fundamental doctrine of our land that the people are supreme. Lincoln stated the substance of the whole matter in his famous phrase, "government of the people; by the people, and for the people." The authority of law here is not something which is imposed upon the people; it is the will of the people themselves. The decision of the court here is not something which is apart from the people; it is the judgment of the people themselves. The right of the ownership of property here is not something withheld from the people; it is the privilege of the people themselves. Their sovereignty is absolute and complete. A definition of the relationship between the institutions of our government and the American people entirely justifies the assertion that: "All things were made by *them*; and without *them* was not anything made that was made."

It is because the American Government is the sole creation and possession of the people that they have always cherished it and defended it, and always will. There are two fundamental motives which inspire human action. The first and most important, to which all else is subordinate, is that of righteousness. There is that in mankind, stronger than all else, which requires them to do right. When that requirement is satisfied, the next motive is that of gain. These are the moral motive and the material motive. While in some particular instance they might seem to be antagonistic, yet always, when broadly considered or applied to society as a whole, they are in harmony. American institutions meet the test of these two standards. They are founded on righteousness, they are productive of material prosperity. They compel the loyalty and support of the people because such action is right and because it is profitable.

These are the main reasons for the formation of patriotic societies. Desiring to promote the highest welfare of civilization, their chief purpose is to preserve and extend American ideals. No matter what others may do, they are determined to serve themselves and their fellow men by thinking America, believing America, and living America. That faith they are proud to proclaim to all the world.

It is no wonder that the people are attached to America when we consider what it has done and what it represents. It has been called the last great hope of the world. Its simple story is a romance of surpassing interest. Its accomplishments rise above the realm of fable. To live under the privileges of its citizenship is the highest position of opportunity and achievement ever reached by a people.

If there be a destiny, it is of no avail for us unless we work with it. The ways of Providence will be of no advantage to us unless we proceed in the same direction. If we perceive a destiny in America, if we believe that Providence has been the guide, our own success, our own salvation require that we should act and serve in harmony and obedience.

Throughout all the centuries this land remained unknown to civilization. Just at a time when Christianity was at last firmly established, when there was a general advance in learning, when there was a great spiritual awakening, America began to be revealed to the European world. When this new age began with its new aspirations and its new needs, its new hopes and its new desires, the shores of our country rose through the mist, disclosing a new hemisphere in which, untrammelled by Old World conventions, new ideals might establish for mankind a new experience and a new life.

Settlers came here from mixed motives, some for pillage and adventure, some for trade and refuge, but those who have set their imperishable mark upon our institutions came from far higher motives. Generally defined, they were seeking a broader freedom. They were intent upon establishing a Christian commonwealth in accordance with the principle of self-government.

They were an inspired body of men. It has been said that God sifted the nations that he might send choice grain into the wilderness. They had a genius for organized society on the foundation of piety, righteousness, liberty, and obedience to law. They brought with them the accumulated wisdom and experience of the ages wherever it contributed to the civilizing power of these great agencies. But the class and caste, the immaterial formalism of the Old World, they left behind. They let slip their grasp upon conventionalities that they might lay a firmer hold upon realities.

Wherever we examine the work of these founding fathers we find them attached to the same general principles. In the old dominion of Virginia, which was to

play such an important part in defending liberty in later
times, we observe, as early as 1619, the establishment of
a representative assembly elected by the people, the first
legislature of Englishmen ever to convene upon this continent. When the Pilgrims landed, in 1620, they brought
on shore with them the *Mayflower* Compact, declaring the
right of all the people to form a government and enact
laws, and acknowledging the binding obligation of obedience to the authority of laws so made. A little later
the Puritans established at Massachusetts Bay what remained under their charter for nearly sixty years, virtually a free republic, choosing their own governor, electing
their own legislature, making their own laws, imposing
their own taxes. But it remained for the State of Connecticut, in 1639, to establish a democratic republic under
a written constitution, which embodied the American
principle of government. These are all actions of the
utmost significance, declaring the right of self-government and the subordination of public office to the will of
the people, based, for the most part, upon religious belief
and generally proposed under the inspiration and guidance of the clergymen of that day.

It cannot be too often remembered that the early settlement of our country and the foundation of its institutions was, to a large extent, a religious movement. They
claimed a right of free choice of religious worship for
themselves. While at first they denied this right to
others, the principle they professed led straight to toleration. They lived in a day that had just discovered, as
a result of the Renaissance, the importance of mankind.
It was the beginning of the end of the slavery of the body

and the slavery of the mind. Out of their religious beliefs came the conviction that mankind was born with a
right above all others to be free. This conviction led
straight to the right of self-government. As a necessary
corollary there came the privilege and requirement of
education.

A beginning was made in 1621 by the Virginia Company to provide, as they said, "for the education of children and grounding them in the principles of religion . . .
whereof both church and Commonwealth take their
original foundation and happy estate." The next year
raising money to found a university was begun, but was
not completed, when some of the friends of the movement
were killed by Indians and others were removed from
office. Harvard College had been founded in 1636 that
there might be maintained learned magistrates and
learned clergy. The next year a printing-press was set
up at Cambridge. In 1692 the college of William and
Mary was founded in Virginia, and Yale University dates
from 1701. Along with these went the public schools,
especially in the North.

The people of these early days gave much thought to
religion, government, and education. They were discussed in the pulpit, in the town meeting, and in the
Legislative Assembly. They were argued and debated in
the occasional book and the very frequent pamphlet. It
was under the inspiration of these times that Connecticut
bred Jonathan Edwards, and Massachusetts raised Benjamin Franklin. What the men of those days believed
they did not hesitate to put into action.

It was with such a background that the colonies approached the Revolution. The British Government undertook to lay taxes on them. When these were resisted an army was sent to enforce their payment. The people denied that there existed any constitutional authority to impose taxes upon them, save by the consent of their own representatives. Beyond that they appealed to their natural rights. "The people," said John Adams, as early as 1765, "have rights antecedent to all earthly government." It was mainly on that principle that they finally took their stand. They had but one choice, either to submit or fight. They chose to fight. General Washington, on his way up from Philadelphia to take command of the Continental forces at Cambridge, being met by the despatches from Bunker Hill, inquired whether the militia had fought. When told they had not only fought but fought well, he replied: "Then the liberties of the country are secure."

In a little over a year the Declaration of Independence had been adopted, asserting a principle which was not new, but which had never yet been put into effect, that governments derive their just powers from the consent of the governed. The seven years' revolutionary conflict, with all its sacrifice, was required to demonstrate that a people holding this opinion could not be conquered, before Great Britain was forced to acknowledge the independence of the American Colonies. In 1788 the Federal Constitution, praised by Gladstone as the greatest work ever struck off by men at a given time, was adopted, creating that form of government for which all the experience of the colonies had been preparing them. It is not a government above the people, superior to them, oppressing them, which they are required to serve; but a government under the jurisdiction of the people, obedient to their will, which is required to serve them, providing that broader freedom which the forefathers sought. It may be well to remember that it was established as a result of war. It was because the men of that day held what they believed right to be dearer than life that the American Republic lives.

Great actions have always required great leaders. The Revolutionary period was richly furnished with men of that character. Chief of them all was Washington, a man of consummate wisdom, a soldier qualified to rank with the great captains of history, a statesman endowed with a clear vision, with ability and character alike both to perceive the needs and inspire sufficient confidence in his associates to secure their co-operation in providing for the government of his country; and last of all, a patriot, a great example of one who served himself by serving his country, refusing a crown himself that he might bestow upon his countrymen kingly powers; without rank himself, yet outranking all nobility. Of his able assistants the chief of all was Hamilton, a profound lawyer, a financier of the first rank, an advocate through the spoken or written word surpassing all his contemporaries, sharing with Madison the great work of drafting the Constitution, securing its adoption by the convention and, by the exposition of it in those masterly papers since known as *The Federalist*, its ratification by the several States. As the first secretary of the treasury he ordered the public finances with national honesty and success. He had a large share in the conception of what the Constitution should be and how the government should be organized. Along with these went Jefferson, who drafted the Declaration of Independence, the great exponent of popular government, the ablest advocate of liberalism in his day.

What these men were in the legislative and administrative side, Marshall became on the judicial side of the government. A soldier under Washington, the chief force in the Virginia Convention for the ratification of the National Constitution, secretary of state under Adams, chief justice for many years, his decisions determined that the Constitution should stand as the supreme law of the land, which neither the acts of State legislatures nor of the Congress had power to contravene. As Hamilton found the Constitution merely a plan on paper and made it a living organism of government, so Marshall found the Constitution seemingly exposed and unprotected, and by his decisions and interpretations left it an invincible defense of liberty. He demonstrated that the Supreme Court was the chief guardian of the rights of the people, chief defender of their established government.

The question of the respective rights of State and National Governments had not yet been settled. Sometimes it was States in the North, as in the time of the embargo and the War of 1812, which led to the Hartford Convention; at other times it was some State of the South, as in the time when South Carolina, under the leadership of Calhoun, undertook to nullify the tariff law. It was the word of Webster, who, by demonstrating the supremacy of the Constitution and the laws enacted by its authority, became thereafter known as the Great

Expounder, and the action of Jackson, who, in proposing the toast, "Our Federal Union—it must be preserved," and ordering land and naval forces to Charleston, threatened those who resisted the national law with treason, which left the Federal Government, for the time, supreme.

Still the great question of the supremacy of the Union was not fully and finally determined. Economic questions of embargo and tariff had not been sufficient seriously to jeopardize national authority. But now the great moral question of slavery was agitating the people. Lincoln had said that the nation could not endure half slave and half free, but the Union was not to fail—it was to triumph. The nation again realized its destiny. After the great sacrifice of four years of civil strife Providence again blessed her people with a broader freedom. Liberty and union were at last secure, never again to be challenged. This, too, was established as the result of war. It was because the men of that day held what they believed right to be dearer than life that the American Republic not only lives but is all free.

After this came an era of unprecedented industrial development. The great natural resources of the country began to be utilized. There was an enormous expansion in the building of railroads, in the construction of manufacturing-plants, in the opening up of mines, and in turning vast tracts of land to agricultural purposes, all of which brought great expansion, not only of trade and commerce but of population, while the great increase in production brought to the people increased means for providing the necessities and conveniences of life, raising the standard of living through the resulting prosperity to a point never before reached. This era was represented by McKinley. His name became the synonym for prosperity, and his policies came to represent increasing opportunity for employment, brought the highest rate of wages in the world, and great business expansion.

It was under his administration that the Spanish War was fought. This again resulted in the extension of a broader freedom to the people of the West Indies and the Philippines, and brought America into the recognized position of a world power.

The genius of this day was not altogether material. It had its spiritual side, deep and significant. The country sought prosperity that the people might be raised up. With the utmost reluctance it engaged in warfare, which it turned more to the advantage of others than itself. Prosperity came to the people that they might have the resources for more of the refinements of life, more for the needs of education and religion, more to minister to the things of the soul. Power came to the nation that it might the better serve its own citizens and bear its share of the burden of civilization. McKinley knew that the nation could not live unto itself alone. His last word was a plea for co-operation and helpfulness in international industrial development by reciprocal trade agreements among the peoples of the earth.

This was followed by the policy of the regulation and control not, as is sometimes said, of great aggregations of capital but of the men who had the management and direction of such capital. They had come into the possession of very great and far-reaching power—rightly used, capable of conferring great benefit; wrongly used, capable of doing great injury. It was inevitable that such combinations should be brought under the authority of national law, which should insure, so far as possible, that they should be used not for the selfish purpose of serving merely their owners and managers but for the generous purpose of serving the public welfare. This was the policy of Roosevelt. Carried too far, no doubt, in some respects, not far enough in others, it is still somewhat in its experimental stage. But the principle that the resources both of men and materials of the country must be conducted for the public welfare, and that there is no power which is above the authority of the law, is absolutely sound. The government of the people must always remain supreme.

In this way America developed, with all that it came to mean to its own people and to the world. It represented the reserve power of civilization. Referring again to Lincoln, it has been "conceived in liberty and dedicated to the proposition that all men are created equal," while he and the men of his day had demonstrated that all men are likewise created free. The great question of his day has been, is, and will be, whether "any nation so conceived and so dedicated can long endure." Despotism has forever had a powerful hold upon the world. Autocratic government, not self-government, has been the prevailing state of mankind. It needs to be remembered that the record of past history is the record not of the success of republics but of their failure. Those now in existence have escaped from overthrow, time and time again, by an exceedingly narrow margin. A government of the people is not easy to maintain—it is the most difficult of all governments to maintain. Some forget that "eternal vigilance is the price of liberty." Some forget the ultimate sufferings and hardships that the people are obliged to bear under an autocratic rule, and turn to it as the easy way. There is scarcely a word in the constitution of any of our States or of the nation that was not written there for the purpose of protecting the liberties of the people from some servitude which a despotic government had at some time imposed upon them.

In so far as the World War was a contest between forms of government—and that was the chief element in that great struggle—it was a contest to determine whether despotism or democracy, the rule of a class or the rule of the people, autocratic government or self-government, should be the present lot of mankind. That great question had again to be determined by war. It was because the men of this day held what they believed right to be dearer than life that the American Republic not only lives and is all free but its underlying principles have become the accepted theory of government among all the great powers of the earth.

The main characteristics of those principles, from which all others are deduced, is a government of limited and defined powers, leaving the people supreme. The executive has sole command of the military forces, but he cannot raise a dollar of revenue. The legislature has the sole authority to levy taxes, but it cannot issue a command to a single private soldier. The judiciary interprets and declares the law and the Constitution, but it can neither create nor destroy the right of a single individual. Freedom of action is complete, within moral bounds, under the law which the people themselves have prescribed. The individual is supported in his right to follow his own choice, live his own life, and reap the rewards of his own effort. Justice is administered by impartial courts. It is a maxim of our law that there is no wrong without a remedy. All the power and authority of the whole National Government cannot convict the most humble individual of a crime, save on the verdict of an impartial jury composed of twelve of his peers. Opportunity is denied to none, every place is open, and every position yields to the humblest, in accordance with ability and application.

The chief repository of power is in the legislature, chosen directly by the people at frequent elections. It is this body, which is particularly responsive to the public will, and yet, as in the Congress, is representative of the whole nation. It does not perform an executive function. It is not, therefore, charged with the necessity of expedition. It is a legislative body, and is, therefore, charged with the necessity for deliberation. Sometimes this privilege may be abused, for this great power has been given as the main safeguard of liberty, and wherever power is bestowed it may be used unwisely. But whenever a legislative body ceases to deliberate, then it ceases to act without due consideration. That fact in itself is conclusive that it has ceased to be independent, has become subservient to a single directing influence or a small group, either without or within itself, and is no longer representative of the people. Such a condition would not be a rule of the people, but a rule of some unconstitutional power. It is my own observation and belief that the American Congress is the most efficient and effective deliberative body, more untrammelled, more independent, more advised, more representative of the will of the people than any body which legislates for any of the great powers. An independent legislature never deprived the people of their liberty.

Such is America, such is the government and civilization which have grown up around the church, the town meeting, and the schoolhouse. It is not perfect, but it surpasses the accomplishments of any other people. Such is the state of society which has been created in this country, which has brought it from the untrodden wilderness of three hundred years ago to its present state of development. Who can fail to see in it the hand of destiny? Who can doubt that it has been guided by a Divine Providence? What has it not given to its people in material advantages, educational opportunity, and religious consolation? Our country has not failed, our country has been a success. You are here because you believe in it, because you believe that it is right, and because you know that it has paid. You are determined to defend it, to support it, and, if need be, to fight for it. You know that America is worth fighting for.

But if our republic is to be maintained and improved it will be through the efforts and character of the individual. It will be, first of all, because of the influences which exist in the home, for it is the ideals which prevail in the home life which make up the strength of the nation. The homely virtues must continue to be cultivated. The real dignity, the real nobility of work must be cherished. It is only through industry that there is any hope for individual development. The viciousness of waste and the value of thrift must continue to be learned and understood. Civilization rests on conservation. To these there must be added religion, education, and obedience to law. These are the foundation of all character in the individual and all hope in the nation.

While these are some of the requirements on the part of the citizens, there are other requirements on the part of the government. One of the most fundamental is the preservation of order and security against either domestic or foreign violence. To "insure domestic tranquillity" and "provide for the common defense" are two of the six purposes declared in the preamble of the Federal Constitution. The people of old Northampton were not unfamiliar with the necessity of maintaining that principle. Their soldiers had fought in King Philip's War and King William's War in the seventeenth century, in Queen Anne's War, Father Râle's War, King George's War, and the French and Indian War in the eighteenth century. We are not an old nation, though our flag is one of the oldest. That flag we have carried in the war of the Revolution; actual, though not declared, war with France; war with the Barbary pirates; war with Great Britain; war with Mexico; war with the Confederate States; war with Spain; actual, though not declared, war with Mexico; and war with Germany and Austria. We want no more war. You men and women who have seen it or have been engaged in it want war least of all. We want peace with justice and with honor. But this does not justify the government in disregarding history, in leaving the people undefended against national peril at home or abroad. Not for defiance, but for defense; not for aggrandizement, but for protection; not as an appeal to force but to insure the administration of justice we need an adequate army and navy. The forces of evil and of despotism have ever been gathering. Our safety and security lies in their realization that this nation has such a force and such a spirit that they can attack American rights only at their peril. America represents the greatest treasure that there is on earth, the greatest power that there is to minister to the welfare of mankind; to leave it unprepared and unprotected is not only to disregard the national welfare, but to be no less than guilty of a crime against civilization. The day of competitive armaments, we hope, is passing, but we cannot yet see when the day will be past for adequate military preparation.

A growing tendency has been observed of late years to think too little of what is really the public interest and too much of what is supposed to be class interest. The two great political parties of the nation have existed for the purpose, each in accordance with its own principles, of undertaking to serve the interests of the whole nation. Their members of the Congress are chosen with that great end in view. Patriotism does not mean a regard for some special section or an attachment for some special interest, and a narrow prejudice against other sections and other interests; it means a love of the whole country. This does not mean that any section or any interest is to be disproportionately preferred, or disproportionately disregarded, but that the welfare of all is equally to be sought. Agriculture, transportation, manufacturing, and all the other desirable activities, should serve in accordance with their strength and should be served in accordance with the benefits they confer. A division of the people or their representatives, in accordance with any other principle or theory, is contrary to the public welfare. An organization for the purpose of serving some special interest is perfectly proper and may be exceedingly helpful, but whenever it undertakes to serve that interest by disregarding the welfare of other interests, it becomes harmful alike to the interest which it proposes to serve and to the public welfare in general. Under the modern organization of society there is such a necessary community of interests that all necessarily experience depression or prosperity together.

They cannot be separated. Our country has resources sufficient to provide in abundance for everybody. But it cannot confer a disproportionate share upon anybody. There is work here to keep amply employed every dollar of capital and every hand of honest toil, but there is no place for profiteering, either in high prices or in low, by the organized greed of money or of men. The most pressing requirement of the present day is that we should learn this lesson and be content with a fair share, whether it be the returns from invested capital or the rewards of toil. On that foundation there is a guarantee of continued prosperity, of stable economic conditions, of harmonious social relationships, and of sound and enduring government. On any other theory or action the only prospect is that of wasteful conflict and suffering in our economic life and factional discord and trifling in our political life. No private enterprise can succeed unless the public welfare be held supreme.

Another necessity of the utmost urgency in this day, a

necessity which is world-wide, is economy in government expenditures. This may seem the antithesis of military preparation, but, as a matter of fact, our present great debt is due, in a considerable extent, to creating our last military establishment under the condition of war haste and war prices, which added enormously to its cost. There is no end of the things which the government could do, seemingly, in the way of public welfare, if it had the money. Everything we want cannot be had at once. It must be earned by toilsome labor. There is a very decided limit to the amount which can be raised by taxation without ruinously affecting the people of the country by virtual confiscation of a part of their past savings. The business of the country, as a whole, is transacted on a small margin of profit. The economic structure is one of great delicacy and sensitiveness. When taxes become too burdensome, either the price of commodities has to be raised to a point at which consumption is so diminished as greatly to curtail production, or so much of the returns from industry is required by the government that production becomes unprofitable and ceases for that reason. In either case there is depression, lack of employment, idleness of investment and of wage-earner, with the long line of attendant want and suffering on the part of the people. After order and liberty, economy is one of the highest essentials of a free government. It was in no small degree the unendurable burden of taxation which drove Europe into the Great War. Economy is always a guarantee of peace.

It is the great economic question of government finances which is burdening the people of Europe at the present

time. How to meet obligations is the chief problem on
Continental Europe and in the British Isles. It cannot
be doubted that high taxes are the chief cause for the extended condition of unemployment which has required
millions to subsist on the public treasury in Great Britain
for a long period of time, though the number of these un-
fortunate people has been declining. A government
which requires of the people the contribution of the bulk
of their substance and rewards cannot be classed as a
free government, or long remain as such. It is gratifying
to observe, in our own national government, that there
has been an enormous decrease in expenditures, a large
reduction of the debt, and a revision of taxation afford-
ing great relief.

But it is in peace that there lies the greatest opportunity for relief from burdensome taxation. Our country is at peace, not only legal but actual, with all other
peoples. We cherish peace and good-will toward all the
earth, with a sentiment of friendship and a desire for
universal well-being. If we want peace it is our business
to cultivate good-will. It was for the promotion of peace
that the Washington Conference on the Limitation of
Armaments and Pacific Questions was called. For the
first time in history the great powers of the earth have
agreed to a limitation of naval armaments. This was
brought about by American initiative, in accordance with
an American plan, and executed by American statesmanship. Out of regard for a similar principle is the proposal to participate in the establishment of a World
Court. These are in accordance with a desire to adjust
differences between nations not by an overpowering dis-

play or use of force but by mutual conference and understanding in harmony with the requirement of justice and of honor.

Our country does not want war; it wants peace. It has not decreed this memorial season as an honor to war, with its terrible waste and attendant train of suffering and hardship which reaches onward into the years of peace. Yet war is not the worst of evils, and these days have been set apart to do honor to all those, now gone, who made the cause of America their supreme choice. Some fell with the word of Patrick Henry, "Give me liberty, or give me death," almost ringing in their ears. Some heard that word across the intervening generations and were still obedient to its call. It is to the spirit of those men, exhibited in all our wars, to the spirit that places the devotion to freedom and truth above the devotion to life, that the nation pays its ever-enduring mark of reverence and respect. It is not that principle that leads to conflict but to tranquillity. It is not that principle which is the cause of war but the only foundation for an enduring peace. There can be no peace with the forces of evil. Peace comes only through the establishment of the supremacy of the forces of good. That way lies only through sacrifice. It was that the people of our country might live in a knowledge of the truth that these, our countrymen, are dead. "Greater love hath no man than this, that a man lay down his life for his friends."

This spirit is not dead, it is the most vital thing in America. It did not flow from any act of government. It is the spirit of the people themselves. It justifies faith in them and faith in their institutions. Remembering all that it has accomplished from the day of the Puritan and Cavalier to the day of the last, least immigrant, who lives by it no less than they, who shall dare to doubt it, who shall dare to challenge it, who shall venture to rouse it into action? Those who have scoffed at it from the day of the Stuarts and the Bourbons to the day of the Hapsburgs and the Hohenzollerns have seen it rise and prevail over them. Calm, peaceful, puissant, it remains, conscious of its authority, "slow to anger, plenteous in mercy," seeking not to injure but to serve, the safeguard of the republic, still the guarantee of a broader freedom, the supreme moral power of the world. It is in that spirit that we place our trust. It is to that spirit again, with this returning year, we solemnly pledge the devotion of all that we have and are.

XXVII

We review the past not in order that we may return to it but that we may find in what direction, straight and clear, it points into the future.

THE GREEN MOUNTAINS

WE do not meet to-day so much to think new thoughts as to rehearse old stories. Our purpose is not to survey new courses, but to relocate ancient landmarks. We review the past not in order that we may return to it but that we may find in what direction, straight and clear, it points into the future. We do not come here burdened with regrets or depressed by any memories of faded splendor, but to rejoice in the possession of hope fulfilled and to glory in the vision of desire realized. The promise which attended the founding and settlement of the city of Burlington has been abundantly redeemed.

The recorded beginnings of this locality lie far back on the verge of American history. When the Cavalier was struggling to plant the first colony in Virginia, just as Henry Hudson was entering the bay of New York, or ever the prow of the Pilgrim *Mayflower* had been turned toward Plymouth Rock, the great Champlain undoubtedly landed here in 1609. He determined, in no small part, by his fateful collision with the dominant Indian power of this region on the farther shore of the lake, which made them ever after hostile to France and friendly to England, that the prevailing civilization of this country was to be not Latin but Anglo-Saxon. For one hundred and fifty years the tide of conflict rose and fell,

One Hundred and Fiftieth Anniversary of the Settlement of the City of Burlington, Vermont, June 12, 1923.

357

leaving inextinguishable marks and names, until the banners of the old régime passed down the lake forever to encounter Wolfe on the plains of Abraham, holding the master-key to this new continent.

So the time passed when this alluring territory was to be famed chiefly as the meeting-place of the contending forces of native Indians or invading white men and was to become the permanent habitation of a peaceful civilization. The days of conflict were not all gone, but the days of sufficient tranquillity for stable development had come. The power and influence of France, with its devotion and loyalty to church and King, were not to be swept away, for the good does not perish, but whatever it had wrought for good was to be merged in a new order. A new day was rising, a new life was stirring, a new era was opening for the Western world.

The beginnings of this city were tinged strongly with the dominant spirit of the times. The people of the land were for the first time coming to be consciously American. To a reassertion of the old rights there was beginning to be added the assertion of new rights. The colonists had come to feel their power and were reaching out to exercise it with a new boldness. Stronger impulses and broadening opportunities were rousing the old spirit of the pioneer. The country was on the eve of a new birth of freedom.

The territory now comprising most of the State of Vermont made a strong appeal to these sentiments. At first it was supposed to be under the jurisdiction of New Hampshire, which granted charters to many towns within its borders, under which the settlers held title to their lands; next, with the support of crown and Parliament, claimed by New York, which not only asserted political jurisdiction but undertook to deny the legality of the title to any lands not conveyed by its authority. These contentions brought on conflicts, both before the court and in the country, which resulted in the inhabitants, now hostile to the British rule that proposed to confiscate their homes, declaring their independence and organizing the new State of Vermont, and in that condition they maintained themselves, in spite of the constant opposition of powerful adjoining States, the threats of the Congress to send the army against them, and all the peril of war with a mighty empire, until finally admitted to the Union. Those days furnished no example of more heroic devotion than that which was exhibited by the unconquerable defenders of the Green Mountain State.

It was amid such conditions that Burlington came into being. Though her territory was little vexed by all these conflicts, those who founded the town, whose names were early associated with its settlement and development, bore a dominant part in the brilliant and thrilling history of those significant times. One of these was that romantic figure, Ethan Allen, picturesque in word, dashing in action, a typical pioneer. Another was Remember Baker, a skilful mechanic, a trained woodsman, a brave officer, one of the trusted leaders of the settlers. Associated with them was Thomas Chittenden, a man of sound judgment and a strength of character that commanded the confidence of his fellow men. Joined with this band, though never directly connected with your city, was Seth Warner, wise, brilliant, cautious, a soldier gifted with the ability to command. Surpassing them all in breadth of intellect was Ira Allen, a man of affairs, a diplomat and a statesman. This group of pioneers, all Burlington proprietors except Warner, laid the foundation of the State of Vermont, and performed untold service in the promotion of the American cause.

Burlington was chartered by Governor Wentworth of New Hampshire, June 7, 1763, apparently to parties nearly all resident of New York. A few years later the Onion River Company, composed of four of the Allens and Baker, appear as the proprietors. They cut a road through from Castleton to Colchester in 1772, and Ira Allen made the first survey of land within the town September 30 of that year. The first settler was Felix Powell, who came in 1773. He owned land at Apple Tree Point, on which he built a log house. He had also been the first settler in Dorset. In 1778 he sold his rights to James Murdock, of Saybrook, Connecticut, and so, having gained the fame of being the first settler, left others to finish what he had so well begun. In November, 1774, Stephen Lawrence of Sheffield and others bought land in town, but did little in the way of settlement. During this year and the following Lemuel Bradley and others established themselves on the Intervale, but in the summer of 1776 these settlements, in common with all north of Rutland County, were abandoned on account of the impending war.

The first meeting of the proprietors was held at Salisbury, Connecticut, March 23, 1774, of which Thomas Chittenden was the moderator and Ira Allen the clerk. During the ensuing year more meetings were held at

Fort Frederick, which was a blockhouse they had built on the Colchester side of the river to protect the settlements, the last being May 1, 1775. Although this meeting stood adjourned to the first Monday of the following September, it was never held. Only a few days before news had come of the momentous events at Lexington and Concord. The land was aflame. No longer could men turn their thoughts to the peaceable affairs of territorial development. They listened to a sterner call than that which comes from commercial enterprise, yet they accorded to it an even more ready response. No other meeting of the proprietors was held until that of January 29, 1781, which met at the house of Noah Chittenden in Arlington.

A few days after the May meeting Ethan Allen was at Bennington sending for Baker and Warner, who were at Fort Frederick, to join him in the surprise attack on Ticonderoga and Crown Point, which they did. Allen captured Ticonderoga May 10, and Warner took Crown Point on May 11. These victories, with their capture of ammunition, arms, and about two hundred pieces of cannon, were to have a result all out of proportion to the small force engaged in their accomplishment. Just how important this operation turned out to be was best realized by the British when one morning in the following March they saw the cannon which Allen had captured so mounted on Dorchester Heights as to command their positions in the city and harbor and force them to evacuate Boston.

After the war the inhabitants began to return. Stephen Lawrence moved his family into town in 1783. Settle-

ment proceeded rapidly. The first recorded town meeting was held in Burlington, March 19, 1787, when Stephen
Lawrence, Frederick Saxton, and Samuel Allen were
chosen selectmen. They voted to raise a tax of twopence
on the pound to purchase town books, and the same for
the repair of highways and bridges, but this later was
reduced to one penny at a meeting held the first Monday
of the following May. The first freemen's meeting on
record was held the first Tuesday of September, 1794.
The last Tuesday of the following December occurred the
first recorded election of a representative to Congress.
The first recorded marriage is that of Lucy Caroline, a
daughter of Ethan Allen, to Samuel Hitchcock, May 26,
1789, and the first recorded birth is that of their daughter,
Loraine Allen Hitchcock, on June 5, 1790. So now the
government of town, of State, and of nation was pro-
ceeding in accordance with public law. Immediately
began that general development toward a modern city
which has since continued without ceasing.

It is altogether probable that Ira Allen perceived the
possibilities for the development of Burlington as a centre of population, transportation, and commerce, by
reason of its location and natural advantages. He supported his judgment with his resources, which at that
time were very considerable. He owned, at different
periods, a large portion of all the land within the limits
of the town. He was instrumental in locating here the
University of Vermont, to which he made generous contribution. Although his residence was across the river
in Colchester, his chief interests and chief efforts were
here.

The old names early associated with the town now began to appear—Ferrand, Catlin, Van Ness, Buel, Pearl, Sawyer, and others. The first store, always an important meeting-place in a new and small community, was built by Stephen Keyes and opened in 1789. Professional men, doctors and lawyers, soon joined the growing community, which became of sufficient importance and accessibility that the legislature met here in 1803.

The desire formally to organize the religious life soon appeared. About 1795 the Reverend Chauncey Lee preached here for some time, and was followed by Reverend Daniel C. Sanders, who preached at intervals until 1807. In 1799 the town voted to raise two hundred dollars, "to be paid in grain, beef, pork, butter, and cheese, to be delivered to the minister who shall be hired in Burlington for the year ensuing," and it was further voted, on June 15, 1805, to form themselves into a religious society, known as the First Society of Social and Public Worship in the Town of Burlington. In 1810 this society was divided on the line of liberal and conservative. The conservatives took the name of the First Calvinistic Congregational Society, ordained Reverend Samuel Clark on April 19, 1810, and built the Unitarian Church in 1816. These were followed by the Methodist, Baptist, Episcopal, Catholic, and other churches, which now minister to the religious well-being of a devout people.

The cause of education must have had very early attention, for at the March meeting in 1790 it had been sufficiently developed so that it was voted to divide the town into school districts. In 1812 a system of graded schools was apparently started, and some years later the

Burlington Academy took over the high-school work, which it continued until 1849, when the Union School superseded it. The Burlington Female Seminary, an institution which was of great importance, started in 1835. There were also other schools for young women. The University of Vermont was chartered and located in Burlington in 1791, a lot of fifty acres was assigned to it, and a building was begun in 1794 and completed in 1798. In 1799 citizens of the young town gave 2,300 pounds sterling to this enterprise, when the entire grand list of the town, as then figured, was but 2,174 pounds sterling, and the whole number of polls but 224. The Reverend Daniel C. Sanders was chosen president, October 17, 1800, and the university formally admitted four young men to its courses. The charge for tuition was established at ten dollars a year. The town was thus early equipped to provide that liberal education which is one of the foundations of an enlightened civilization.

One of the oldest newspapers in Vermont, known as *The Sentinel*, began to be published here in 1801. This was followed by *The Free Press*, which was started in 1827. The town has been, almost from its beginning, well provided with the best that could be had in the way of newspaper publications and has benefited through the tremendous influence which they wield for good by informing the public mind. Newspapers are one of the strongest supports of the republic.

Navigation was an early contributing force to the material welfare of the town. In early days it was carried on with a fleet of sailboats. The second steamboat in the world in actual point of construction, was built at

Burlington, christened *Vermont,* and launched in June, 1808. By 1814 regular communication had been established with Boston by four-horse coach. The Champlain Canal, opened in 1823, connected the lake with the Hudson River, which left Burlington one of the chief ports on the continuous waterway from New York City to Montreal, while the coming of the railroads in 1849 opened up the overland route to Boston.

The early settlers and proprietors had nearly all some share in the Revolutionary War. Some of them, like the Allens and their close associates, played a most heroic and important part. But this glory must all be shared with other places, for it represents not so much a local production as an importation. The next conflict was on a different basis. The War of 1812 and its causes were not popular issues in New England. A very considerable commerce was at stake, but beyond that the substantial element of this section preferred the conservatism of Great Britain to the radicalism and imperialism of France in that era. On February 2, 1809, the town unanimously adopted resolutions which declared its loyalty to the National Constitution and its government, but condemned the embargo policy of the Federal administration. Nevertheless, Burlington responded eagerly to every requirement for national defense when the actual need arose. Colonel Isaac Clark, being sent here, called out the local militia, purchased and fortified the Battery, which dates from that time, for the protection of the town. Captain Thomas MacDonough of the navy was stationed here. He had very valuable assistance from the people in winning the great naval battle at Plattsburg, September 11, 1814, by which he regained entire control of the lake. Captain Horace B. Sawyer, a native of the town, was made prisoner when the British captured the *Growler* and *Eagle*, but returned to serve on the famous frigate *Constitution*, taking part in her remarkable victory over the *Cyane* and *Levant*.

When the call came from Lincoln, in April of 1861, the Burlington company, under Captain David B. Peck, at once responded. Their example was followed by a host of others who served with distinction until the close of the war. The part which was taken by this town in the lesser contest with Spain and the brilliant and effective contribution made to the success of the Great War demonstrated that, in military spirit and power, it retains its ancient vigor. One of your townsmen, a graduate of the Naval Academy, Lieutenant-Commander Jonas H. Holden, was on the battleship *Maine*, but was rescued only to be lost on the vessel which mysteriously disappeared in the Gulf of Mexico during the World War. Another, Lieutenant Devere Harden, with the regular army, was the first American officer wounded in France, while still another, Admiral Henry T. Mayo, had the merited distinction of being commander-in-chief of the Atlantic fleet.

In the comparatively short space of time of a century and a half Burlington has steadily advanced from the day of Felix Powell, the lone settler on the northern frontier, to the day when it is the metropolis of an extensive and cultivated region of activity and industry. It became the centre of an important foreign and domestic commerce, and has ranked as one of the chief lumber ports of the nation in bygone times. The falls of the Winooski, on its border, have been a valuable source of water-power, which has supported the industrial interests of the region. Manufacturing has contributed to make this not only a source of distribution but a source of production. It provides employment for thousands of wage-earners and its annual output reaches many millions of dollars. In its material development Burlington has become a city marked by enterprise and wealth.

Men of ability and fame have given an added distinction to these surroundings, already honored by reason of the quality of its citizenship. It has been often represented in the governor of the State, in the national House and Senate, and in the high diplomatic stations of our country abroad. The first to be governor was Cornelius P. Van Ness, who also served as minister to Spain, and the last was Urban A. Woodbury; Heman Allen was minister to Chili, and that learned scholar George P. Marsh was minister to both Turkey and Italy, while Edward J. Phelps was ambassador to Great Britain. One of the men who ranked very high as a United States senator, a profound lawyer, and an able statesman, was George F. Edmunds. One of your present citizens, a leading figure of the Vermont bar, Charles H. Darling, has been an assistant secretary of the navy.

The material resources and wealth of the community, the ability of distinguished men, the high character of the people, and the practical application of the teachings of religion, have all combined to make this city well-governed, well-educated, and richly endowed with many charities. All these forces have united to create a moral and spiritual power, the influence of which has been felt in the uttermost parts of the earth. The world is not what it would have been without that influence. It has increased the vigor of health, the strength of intellect, the power of character, and extended the domain of everlasting righteousness.

To-day we behold the wonder of all these accomplishments. We realize that they have been wrought by the hand of man working in harmony with the will of Divine Providence. When we inquire what manner of men they were, what principles they represented, what character they developed, the answer is revealed in their work. They were active, enterprising men, intent upon conducting a successful. business. They were endowed with imagination and vision, but their chief guide was that hard common sense which is the result of continued experience with hardships and difficulties, always the heritage of the pioneer. They had come up out of much tribulation. Their methods were bold and direct, the very essence of all that was practical. They believed in common honesty and simple justice. They were determined to be free. It was in accordance with these standards that they fashioned their town and established their Commonwealth. The local public policy of that day is declared in the town charter. All the fit pine-trees were reserved for masting the royal navy. Of the seventy-two shares provided for in the charter, one was reserved for the incorporated society for the propagation of the gospel in foreign parts; one for the glebe for the Church of England; one for the first settled minister of the gospel; and one for the benefit of a school in the town.

Although the perils of war had left the region of Burlington bare of inhabitants, compelling the people to take refuge in more thickly populated and better-protected settlements at the south, they did not cease to exert a powerful influence over the destiny of those rebellious days. The founders of this city appear as leaders in the records of the public actions which established the State of Vermont. At the convention held in Dorset, September 25, 1776, Burlington was represented by Lemuel Bradley, and those present who were connected with the Onion River Company were Thomas Chittenden, Ira Allen, and Heman Allen. When the convention reconvened at Westminster Chittenden and the two Allens were present. Here, on January 16, 1777, they adopted the momentous resolutions asserting their readiness to do their "full proportion in maintaining and supporting the just war," but declaring that they should hereafter be "a separate, free, and independent jurisdiction or state." Chittenden was a member of the committee that drafted this declaration, and the Allens were on committees instructed to plan for further proceedings. The claim of independence that they set forth they made a reality by their future action.

When the convention met at Windsor, July 2, 1777, undoubtedly Chittenden and the two Allens were there, although almost the only record is the Constitution, which on July 8 was adopted. That document asserted that government was "derived from and founded on the authority of the people only," forbade slavery, adopted manhood suffrage, recognized that conscience, speech, and press should be free, undertook to guarantee the protection of life, liberty, and property, prescribed trial by jury, provided for town and county schools and a State university, admonished the people to observe the Sabbath, maintain religious worship, and remember that "a firm adherence to justice, moderation, temperance, industry, and frugality are absolutely necessary to preserve the blessings of liberty and keep government free." Those who held these opinions were not likely tamely to submit or long to be deprived of success.

The charter of the town and the constitution of the State recognized religion as the foundation of human relationship. They acknowledged that their obligation of spreading the gospel was world-wide. Having contributed to the clergy at home and the missionary abroad, they extended liberal support to the cause of education. They knew that learning belonged to the people. In sustaining the royal navy they were not only providing for the defense of the realm but extending the domain of commerce. They were well aware that the observance of the plain virtues of life is not only the source of all individual character but the foundation of all national greatness. The principle of freedom and equality was not a visionary doctrine with them but a rule of action to be put into practice. Within the State of Vermont no person could ever be held as a slave and no man was ever too poor to have a vote.

These rights were neither secured nor maintained without the exaction of supreme sacrifice. Whatever property interests the inhabitants had in Burlington at the outbreak of the war were rendered practically valueless. The leading men of the region risked their lives in the capture of Ticonderoga and Crown Point. Remember Baker was killed by an enemy bullet in the closing days of the summer while leading a scouting party toward Canada. Ethan Allen, a month later, was captured in his attempt to take Montreal. Transported across the sea in irons, he was held for nearly three years in British prisons. It is probable that the house of a Felix Powell in Pittsford, which was plundered and burned in his absence, was that of your original settler. Mrs. Powell looked on, hidden in the woods near by. In such destitution she bore a child before the next morning. Some fell in the disaster at Hubbardton, others on the victorious field at Bennington. They all showed such a spirit that Burgoyne reported them to be the most active and most rebellious race on the continent, that hung like a gathering storm on his left. That storm, more violent than his forebodings, swept him to destruction at Saratoga.

That same spirit had been exhibited in every hour of peril in all their history. They had established a reputation which gave entire credibility to Ethan Allen, when he declared: "I am resolutely determined to defend the independence of Vermont . . . and rather than fail will retire with the hardy Green Mountain Boys into the desolate caverns of the mountains and wage war with human nature at large." Washington, who knew the power of their soldiers, issued a warning against any attempt by the Congress to subdue the State with the army. He knew, and plainly said, that such a people, occupying such a territory, could not be conquered. Besides, Washington admired courage, believed in freedom, and loved justice. It was said that he looked with

sympathy on the cause of the struggling little State of
Vermont.

Yet these people were neither quarrelsome, lawless, nor
violent.   They had that respect for constituted authority
which had been bred in their race by more than a thousand years of liberty under the law.   It has been their
characteristic to submit their cause to the courts, as John
Hampden submitted his cause, as James Otis submitted
that of his clients; and only when the plain requirements
of justice were denied did they determine to meet an
illegal decision with righteous resistance.   So the settlers of the Green Mountains, under the leadership of
Ethan Allen and his associates, submitted their cause
to the determination of the royal court at Albany.

When the court, which apparently had a personal interest in its own decision, found against them, and the
opposing authorities intimated that it would be wise to
submit because might oftentimes made right, it was
found that the settlers were by no means inclined to
yield to the application of that principle.   Such a course
might be decreed at Albany, but it would not be executed
in Vermont.   Allen remarked grimly, "The gods of the
valleys are not the gods of the hills," and further offered
to make his meaning clear to those who would come up
to Bennington.   To those who went up with the unau-
thorized writ of this court, his word was kept.   They
were chastised with the twigs of the wilderness and sent
home, bearing on their backs, as the test of the higher
authority of this jurisdiction, the unmistakable imprint
of the beech seal, in the hope that those who considered
irrelevant and inadmissible the Warrant of the King, an

Order of Council, and the Broad Seal of the Royal Province of New Hampshire might recognize the weight of this more impressive evidence.

Outlawed, with a price set on their heads, in constant peril of death, yet through all this conflict, though they met threat with threat, they never inflicted loss of life upon any one; they never resisted the execution of either civil or criminal process which they considered lawful. Such was the character of the men of that day, such were their works. The first moderator of the Onion River Company, Thomas Chittenden, became the first governor of the State, holding the office many years. The first clerk, Ira Allen, became the first State treasurer, ranking as a benefactor of mankind. Another member, Ethan Allen, became a national hero, holding forever the applause of his countrymen. They were supported by the invincible forces of truth and justice. They were destined to immortality.

The standards which the men of that day adopted, the principles in accordance with which they acted, have the power to supply their own vitality. They are self-perpetuating. Had the authorities of New York been content to exercise political jurisdiction over the Green Mountain region and leave undisturbed the land titles acquired and paid for in good faith, instead of using their power to further the unjust speculations of some of their high officials, undoubtedly the settlers would have remained a contented part of the Empire State. The desire to locate farther away from the molestations of Albany would not have sent the proprietors of the Onion River Company into this locality. The power of leadership which they developed would have been used for some other purpose than to defy the governor of New York and the King of Great Britain. The city of Burlington, with its population, its wealth, its commerce, its university, and the State of Vermont, with all its romantic history and its glorious contributions to liberty, would not have come into being. Ticonderoga and Crown Point might still hold a British garrison. There might have been no evacuation of Boston, no victory at Bennington, no decisive battle at Saratoga, and no final success at Yorktown. It was the overreaching greed for gain and an overmastering desire to impose an autocratic rule that raised up the makers of Burlington and set in her midst a crowning citadel of knowledge and of truth which will defend the cause of justice and liberty for all mankind forevermore.

When Ethan Allen and his eighty-three Green Mountain Boys stood within Fort Ticonderoga, in the dawn of that May morning, this man, some time to be charged with the darkness of infidelity, did not fail to utter the word of light when he demanded the garrison captain surrender "in the name of the Great Jehovah and the Continental Congress." He there gave expression to the faith and the cause for which he and his fellow patriots ever stood ready to make the supreme sacrifice. For God and country. That faith has been justified. That cause has been prospered. Could there be any better description of the purpose which has created the city of Burlington? Could there be any firmer foundation on which its influence will stand through all eternity? The same sun is above us which lighted the morning of that day with all that it has come to mean. The same gleaming waters remain. The same shadowy mountains tower around us. The same dream city rises from the shore, now a reality. In those who shall continue to behold them, let them inspire the same spirit, the same abiding faith, the same power, through sacrifice, to minister to the same great cause. For God and country.

XXVIII

We do not need more material development, we need more spiritual development. We do not need more intellectual power, we need more moral power. We do not need more knowledge, we need more character. We do not need more government, we need more culture. We do not need more law, we need more religion. We do not need more of the things that are seen, we need more of the things that are unseen.

THE THINGS THAT ARE UNSEEN

THE educational institutions of our country act in a public capacity. Although oftentimes privately endowed, they exist under the authority of a charter granted by the government, defining and limiting their powers under the law. They were established to support the State, intellectually and morally. They are not for the private advantage of the individual but for the public welfare of the citizen.

This ideal is old, but America has made a new application of it. Formerly there was an educated class. From among their membership were drawn the magistrates and the clergymen. It was their province to furnish instruction and leadership for the people. They filled the pulpits, administered the offices, and conducted the schools. But in our country the ideal is no longer that of a highly educated few but of a broadly cultured and enlightened people. Education is no longer the privilege of a class but is recognized as a common duty necessary for all.

The old idea of training a few for leadership has been superseded by the modern idea of universal education to increase national harmony and unity of action. This ideal has not yet been fully realized, nor can it be for a considerable length of time. With all the resources with which America is endowed, they are not sufficient, as

At Wheaton College, Norton, Massachusetts, June 19, 1923.

yet, to provide for all our inhabitants a liberal education, although they are sufficient and are providing a very general and increasingly broadening elementary training. This leaves somewhat of the old necessary duty of service and leadership imposed upon those who have been fortunate enough to secure the advantages of the higher institutions of learning.

Broad as this class has now become, they are still the ones who have been selected to be foremost in advancing the cause and bearing the burdens of an enlightened civilization. They have come into the possession of an increased intellectual power. They have acquired training and skill that they may the better minister to the needs of humanity. It is this purpose lying behind all our endeavor for education that requires, first of all, that it should represent a moral training. It is not the skill of a Fagin that is sought, it is not the mere power to exist, but, rather, the wisdom of a Madame Curie, the enlightened disposition to serve. An education which does not accomplish this result is not a real education. It may provide a higher degree of cunning, a more intensified selfishness, and may add another prehensile claw with which to lay hold of the things of the world, but unless it results in the cultivation of the higher nature, unless it strengthens the spiritual power, unless it develops into real character, it will be without any final satisfaction.

No doubt the need always exists for self-confidence. That is strengthened by an exact and scholarly knowledge. But it is also desirable to be able correctly to estimate values. A comprehension of the little that we know, or can know, not only of all the universe or of our own earth, of science, of literature, of history, of philosophy, or of their various subdivisions, compared with all that is to be known, is useful for the cultivation of an appropriate humility. This virtue is not thought to be overestimated by the youth of the present day. But it is only in the spirit of true humility that there is any approach to the better things of life.

After all, education is the process by which each individual recreates his own universe and determines its dimensions. As civilization advances, the need becomes not less but more. The present industrial methods, with all their dependence upon invention, with all their subordination to science, are yet narrowing rather than broadening in their effect upon the general mass of employees. The requirement of efficiency has reduced much of modern industrial life to a mere mechanical operation. Those engaged in it are no longer able to draw on inspiration from their work.

Under more primitive conditions this was not the case. Those who were perhaps entirely untrained in the schools found ample opportunity for complete personal expression in their daily employment. Such was especially the condition in the industries of those days. The arts and crafts were what their names signified. A masterpiece was a graduating essay, by which the apprentice, after years of training, demonstrated his fitness to be admitted to the ranks of the master workmen. The skilled hand, the true eye, the designing mind were all employed in producing the useful and the beautiful. All the faculties had daily opportunity for artistic expression in the common employments.

These conditions were not without a marked effect on the character of those who came under their influence. At a very early date the tradespeople and artisans of London became stanch defenders of order and liberty. They were a people educated in no small part by means of their employment. They created a vigorous and enterprising citizenship which made a very pronounced contribution to human welfare.

The tendency in modern industry has been to change these conditions very materially in the direction of reducing the arts to the position of a trade. This in no degree detracts from the dignity of work, but it has produced a kind of work which is very different in its effect on the development of the individual. In addition to this, there has been introduced into our system of education the vocational and trade schools. These have a rightful place and make a very valuable contribution to individual efficiency in industrial life. This whole scheme of things does not diminish but enlarges the requirement for a liberal education, the liberal culture which is taught in the schools, and the maintenance of the opportunities for broader culture, apart from the trades and vocations of livelihood outside the schools. The machines of the shops have a tendency to make machines of the employees. This must be offset, it must be met by a counter tendency. There is but one—some kind of cultural activity.

Our country has very well learned the value of the results of a material prosperity derived from a narrow but very intense skill and the technical use of the applied sciences. All of this has not only relocated but has intensified the burden of maintaining the ideals, which are the foundation of all else, upon the institutions of liberal culture and those who have been their direct beneficiaries. In a sense it reopens the old field and restores the old necessity for active leadership not only in the religious life, political life, and the school life but in that which we term the every-day life of modern civilization.

The satisfactions of life arise from the art of self-expression. If these are not found in the occupational life, they must be sought and provided from some other source. Modern industry has its rich compensations. It not only tremendously increases production, which on the whole has greatly reduced prices, placing the necessaries, conveniences, and even luxuries of life almost within universal reach, but has very much reduced the required hours of labor and at the same time greatly increased the remuneration. This has provided both the time and means for the people at large to engage in outside beneficial and cultural studies and activities. The American people are nothing if they are not energetic. They have accepted these conditions with their usual enthusiasm and used their resources in endless effort in an attempt to provide themselves with amusement, diversion, and recreation, a considerable part of which takes the form of lavish expenditure of money for many purposes which, after a while, are no longer able to please. Carried to its logical conclusion, the end is greed and envy.

One of the chief requirements of the liberally educated of the present day is that they should contribute to a better art of living. There is an enormous opportunity in this direction, by example and precept, for the educated womanhood of the land. They have the power to set a standard which would be far-reaching in its effects. In number they are already considerable. They are increasing rapidly and they have an opportunity to wield a vast influence for good.

Our country is beginning to give more public attention to the development of the fine arts. More thought is bestowed upon the architecture of public buildings, the laying out of streets, with a provision for public squares and parks with suitable statuary and appropriate adornment. More attention is being given to the beautifying of private residences and grounds, to formal gardening and the more artistic use of flowers, shrubberies, and trees. While these things are taking place out of doors, there is a corresponding movement inside. The art of home-making is being cultivated. Under trained supervision and guidance, there is coming to be harmony of decorations and furnishings as a result of more cultivated taste. Good pictures are more and more appreciated. Music, which has the power of making such a universal appeal and arousing such instant response, is being taught in the public schools, studied under private direction, and developed as a community activity. There is a periodical literature of high quality and great profusion, which reaches into every corner of the land. The use of library books is increasingly large. The possibilities of the moving picture are just beginning to be realized. It has popularized a high quality of dramatic portrayal. Even the automobile, by contributing to a much wider range of vision, is removing whatever was left of a shut-in provincialism. The increasing membership of seasoned fraternal and patriotic societies shows the desire to fulfil the requirements of a more intimate social relationship. The American people are starting to supplement a mechanical age with artistic expression.

All of this is an indication of the direction in which future progress and development lie. In these outside activities and interests those who are engaged in the industries have every opportunity for artistic expression. It is along these avenues that they can employ their latent talents and find a more satisfying existence. It is in the leadership of this social side of life that there is an especial opportunity and requirement for those of liberal education and culture.

It will readily be observed that all of these activities, all of the service and leadership which they require, partake of the nature of a charity. That is always a necessary requirement. The higher and better things of life, without which existence would be altogether vain and empty, can neither be bought nor sold. Unless they are done because they ought to be done, without any direct remuneration, they will not be done at all. In its nobler aspect, like eternal life, civilization is a gift. We cannot say we have more merit or are more worthy than those born to the darkness of ignorance and barbarism. We did not acquire our position through our own individual efforts. We were born into it. It is the gift conferred by the sacrifices of past generations. It can only be maintained by the sacrifices of this generation.

Yet it is not possible to receive its higher benefits passively. It is only by active co-operation, it is only by intense application that the individual comes into the enjoyment and possession of the heritage of civilization. It is in this sense that there must be a re-creation. The wonders of civilization do not exist for us unless we make them our own. All the science and art, all the mathematics and literature, all the discoveries of nature and the truths of philosophy are not for us unless we appropriate them. We learn of each other through the contact of mind with mind. There has never been any system of education that did not require clergymen; there has never been any system of government that did not require magistrates and leaders.

It is on this side of life that the liberally educated should apply themselves. They have been given the power to hold up the torch that lights the way. It has always been through their efforts that civilization was created. It will always be through their efforts that it will be maintained.

This is in no wise a limitation of the American ideal; rather it represents the chief application of it. This ideal does not diminish the recognition of the usefulness and necessity for learning and culture, but from the earliest days has been most careful to provide for it, to cherish it, and to admonish all those in authority to maintain it. This has been written into the fundamental laws of the land. It has been adopted in the provisions of our constitutions by the people and enacted into statutes by our legislatures. The American ideal requires that learning and culture should be extended to all the people. In broadening the old theory of a privilege to be held by a few into the new theory of a right that it is necessary to supply to all, it does not pull down education and culture but undertakes to raise the people up to their standards.

It is in this direction that America exhibits its greatest incompleteness, for it is readily recognized that the direct benefits of a liberal education are very far from reaching all the people. The indirect benefits, of course, are universal and more than sufficient to justify public support. They speak from every schoolhouse and every pulpit, and from every learned profession in the land. They set up and maintain the ideals which provide the standards of all conduct. They are the source of liberty, enlightenment, and civilization. But the present great need of our country is an extension of the direct benefits of a liberal culture.

It has sometimes been said that education unfits people for the ordinary tasks of life. This does not appear to me to be the case—rather it is ignorance that unfits them for carrying on their ordinary vocations. It is not dissatisfaction with our work but dissatisfaction with ourselves that is the cause of the unrest and discontent which is always manifesting itself in one form or another. We think we want to change our employment, when we really want to change ourselves. It is a lack of ability to appreciate the real dignity of any useful occupation, to realize that it is an integral part of the greater whole that is necessary for promoting the welfare of civilization, that makes some think of their daily task as poor and mean and sordid. Unless the coal be mined, the northern schoolhouses will close. Unless the sewers be dug, the public health will suffer. Yet the man in the mine or sewer does not recognize himself as one who is ministering to the cause of education and of health, as in some degree a teacher and a physician; he thinks he is

only a shoveller of coal and a digger of ditches. They
need to visualize; they need to see their duty. It is not
ignorance but a greater enlightenment that reveals to
us the true nobility of all toil which contributes to the
conduct of the necessary activities of the world. It is
not in ignorance but in enlightenment that contentment
will be found. It will only be through greater enlightenment that the work of the world can be done.

This era has come to be recognized as the scientific age.
The world has come into the possession of more discoveries and inventions than ever before existed. They
have combined to place in the hands of mankind a power
they never had before. It is scarcely too much to say
that the elements have at last been conquered. It was
only the other day that a man flew from New York to
San Francisco in about twenty-four hours. A reproduc-
tion of the human voice has been sent by radio from
Schenectady to England. There are in the world to-day
more people with a scientific training, ranging all the way
from a workman pursuing his trade at the bench up to
the genius of an Edison, than at any other period. On
this side of life the world is wildly alive and thoroughly
interested. It is making larger and larger demands of
the schools, of the press, and of every other avenue that
provides technical skill and scientific knowledge.

Yet, when success in this direction is not secured, or,
being secured, it fails somehow to satisfy, there is a tendency to begin to criticise our institutions and the standards of society, as though they were in some way to
blame. Sometimes this goes so far as to advocate a
complete change in the attitude of the government toward

property rights. More generally this takes the form of some proposal for extended government control and regulation and a radical change in the theory of taxation. The fundamental purpose sought in these proposals is said to be more equal distribution of the results of industry. Our country is an exceedingly good example of the fact that if production be encouraged and increased, then distribution fairly well takes care of itself. Other countries, by their actions in stopping production, in penalizing industry and economy, and rewarding indolence and extravagance, have been able to bring about a very general and equal distribution of misery, but no other country every approached ours in the equal and general distribution of prosperity. The tendency, at the present time, is all in the direction of a distribution of industrial income among the employees, rather than retaining it as an accumulation of capital or distributing it to stockholders. Perhaps it is well to remember that some of the greatest fortunes in America have been voluntarily given away and dedicated to charitable purposes. Our institutions all seem ultimately to function in the direction of charity, in the direction of civilization.

It is not on this side of our life that we need to put the emphasis at the present time. We had our day of laying the foundation of modern industry, the consolidations, and the intense stimulation of production in the closing decades of the last century. We had our day of bringing these great agencies under public control and regulation, in the opening decades of the present century. We have looked to our industries. We have looked to our government. We may well let a season of adjustment and experience disclose the results of the theories which have been adopted in the past forty years. Present appearances would indicate that there is little more to be hoped for by extending our course in that direction.

The time appears to have arrived when we may more properly look to the people, when natural laws may well be left to supplement artificial laws. It is necessary always to give a great deal of thought to liberty. There is no substitute for it. Nothing else is quite so effective. Unless it be preserved, there is little else that is worth while. In complete freedom of action the people oftentimes have a more effective remedy than can be supplied by government interference. Individual initiative, in the long run, is a firmer reliance than bureaucratic supervision. When the people work out their own economic and social destiny, they generally reach sound conclusions.

This is by no means saying that we have reached perfection in any province; it is merely a consideration of some of the things that the liberally educated ought to do to promote progress. We have reached the antithesis of the asceticism of the Middle Ages. There is no tendency now to despise self-gratification or to hold what we call practical affairs in contempt. To adjust the balance of this age we must seek another remedy. We do not need more material development, we need more spiritual development. We do not need more intellectual power, we need more moral power. We do not need more knowledge, we need more character. We do not need more government, we need more culture. We do not need more law, we need more religion. We do not need more of the things that are seen, we need more of the things that are unseen. It is on that side of life that it is desirable to put the emphasis at the present time. If that side be strengthened, the other side will take care of itself. It is that side which is the foundation of all else. If the foundation be firm, the superstructure will stand. The success or failure of liberal education, the justification of its protection and encouragement by the government, and of its support by society, will be measured by its ability to minister to this great cause, to perform the necessary services, to make the required redeeming sacrifices.

XXIX

A PRIZE ESSAY
(1895)

IN CALVIN COOLIDGE'S SENIOR YEAR AT AMHERST COLLEGE, THE SONS OF THE AMERICAN REVOLUTION OFFERED A PRIZE OF A $150 GOLD MEDAL FOR THE BEST ESSAY ON THE CAUSES OF THE AMERICAN REVOLUTION. THE CONTEST WAS OPEN TO SENIORS OF ALL AMERICAN COLLEGES AND UNIVERSITIES. THE JUDGES OF THE CONTEST AWARDED TO CALVIN COOLIDGE THE FIRST PRIZE.

A PRIZE ESSAY
(1895)

WHEN history looks beyond the immediate cause of the American Revolution for the justifying principles, it is very soon brought back to the spirit of English liberty. It is the same genius for freedom that has led the race from the primeval forests of Germany to the Thirteenth Amendment of the Constitution.

Such an honorable antiquity of political ideas has made the race very conservative of self-government. The idea is prehistoric. It is the descendants of those very freemen described by Tacitus, who not only dictated the policy of Edward the Confessor but extorted the great charter of human rights from King John in the thirteenth century.

And during the next four hundred years, too, this spirit was not dormant, but came to the surface on three great occasions—the confirmation of the Magna Charta by Edward I, the Petition of Right to Charles I, and the Revolution that drove James II from his throne.

Although it is characteristic of Englishmen to have great love for a king so long as he respects the liberties of the people, yet the fact that they drove out one king, rebelled against two and executed three, shows clearly enough that there was always a strong idea of the divine right of the people as well as of kings.

Precedents, then, are by no means wanting among Englishmen for the successful resistance of arbitrary despotism whenever it encroached upon their liberties.

Another fact that must be noted is the character of the colonists, and especially those of Massachusetts. These were the Puritans, who had fought the wars of liberty in England. Then, because they were not satisfied with church ordinances, they were driven by Archbishop Laud to seek religious freedom across the sea.

Of all the race they were the most tenacious of their rights and the most jealous of their liberties. The American Revolution was not, then, any struggle for emancipation from slavery; and the colonists were free men. Nor was it at first so much for gaining new liberties as for preserving the old.

Nor can it, as is often thought, be called a war between different nations. Both sides were Englishmen who gloried in the name of England. William and Mary had, moreover, given the colonists a full share of the rights of British subjects. Another fact showing the same thing is that almost the ablest advocates of the colonial cause were members of the British House of Parliament, while the most ardent adherents of the King were colonists.

The real object of resistance was to gain security from Parliamentary encroachments. This was the chief cause for which the Revolutionists contended, but by no means all they obtained. The war was finally fought out on principles as far-reaching as the history of nations. It was a struggle for the retention of those great institutions that check oppression and violence.

The colonists were contending for the principle of a representative government of chartered rights and constitutional liberties. They were defending themselves against the military despotism of George III and struggling to change the foundation of government from force to equality.

The defense of the principles set forth above involves scarcely anything more than a narration of the leading events that culminated in the Declaration of Independence. It has been said that the separation of America from the mother country was the logical outcome of the French and Indian War. However this may be, it is quite certain that the condition of England at the close of this war forced a new colonial policy that would not have been thought of before 1763, and could not be executed until after that date.

For, instead of wanting new taxes and new restrictions upon their commerce, the colonists were already breaking away from the old restrictions by their systematic evasions of the navigation acts. These laws of trade were merely commercial regulations and not at all for revenue. But because the colonists were no longer trading-stations in their relations to the central government, they resisted even these restrictions.

Instead, however, of noting these tendencies, Grenville made a leading part of his scheme of government the passage of laws for raising revenue in America. He proposed to enforce the trade laws, which meant that the interests of a few merchants in England were to be considered before the welfare of the King's subjects in America; he proposed to quarter soldiers here, nominally for the purpose of defending the colonies, which meant force and a military despotism; he proposed to raise a tax on the authority of the English Parliament, which meant the disfranchisement of three million British subjects, and the surrender of all those rights laid down in the Magna Charta.

The means Grenville adopted for the raising of this tax was the notorious Stamp Act. This, however, met with so much disapproval that it was soon repealed, but at the same time Parliament passed the Dependency Act, which declared that the repeal did not include the principle involved. This was followed by Townsend's Revenue Act, laying duties on imports. Again the colonies protested and the ministry attempted coercion.

This measure was too expensive, so once more all revenue taxes were repealed, except the one on tea, which was left to maintain the principle. During an interval of some four years that followed, from 1770 to 1774, there were several acts of violence on the part of the colonies in their resistance to these imports, including the Boston Massacre, the burning of the *Gaspee*, and the Boston Tea Party.

Again Great Britain had recourse to acts of coercion. First, it closed the port of Boston, thus destroying the property of thousands.

Second, it declared void certain parts of the charter of Massachusetts, following a policy begun in New York in 1767, and so it virtually attempted to annihilate the protection of chartered rights and chartered liberties that has always been so dear to Englishmen. Free government was destroyed, too, in another way.

Judges, courts, sheriffs were made almost the puppets of the King. They were placed in his direct pay and made subject to his pleasure. Town meetings were forbidden, and thus the old familiar forms of self-government were entirely swept away. The governor was made as absolute as a despot, and the form of government that was thus thrust upon Massachusetts was despotism such as Englishmen would not have endured even in the days of Henry VIII.

Third, the British Government sent nearly all criminals to England for trial.

Fourth, soldiers were quartered upon the inhabitants, so that a military government was set up in the colonies.

Fifth, Parliament passed the so-called Quebec Act, to separate the French from any bond of sympathy with the colonies.

The governor stood over them like a viceroy. In his command was the army. If a soldier should murder a citizen, he was sent to England for trial. If a citizen should become a criminal, he, too, might be sent across the sea, in order that in both cases the government might have the advantage. It was a military despotism. There were no popular meetings, no criminal courts, no habeas corpus, no freedom of the press. The question was no longer one of taxes; that was a mere figment now.

Though the injustice of taxation without representation made a good war-cry, it is, in the last analysis, a dangerous principle. But it is easy to grasp, and the common people no doubt fought the war largely on that issue. The fact is, it is a duty to the state to pay taxes, and it is equally a duty to vote. It does not follow that because the state requires one duty it shall require the second.

But there is another side where the requirement of the state runs over into tyranny. Only on this ground can resistance to taxation be justified. So long as the colonies were a part of the state of Great Britain—and they were so by their charters and by the action of William and Mary—that state had the right to demand not only their property, but their service in the army, and, in the last extremity, their lives. It cannot be, then, that the American Revolution was fought that colonists might escape paying taxes. The great struggle that they passed through must make such a duty seem insignificant. The real principle was not one of the right of the state or the duty of citizens; it was a question of government, a question of form and method.

It is this that is meant above, in the statement that the struggle was not between nations, or for new principles. It was not so much a revolution, a propagation of new ideas, as the maintenance of the old forms of representative government, of chartered rights and constitutional liberty. England had fought for this in 1688 and imagined it was secured. But it was so only in name.

George III was by nature a despot; at heart he was another Stuart. He had the Parliament almost completely under his control in its legislation upon English questions, but in regard to the King's colonies his will was supreme.

He forced a policy of government upon America that he could not, and dared not, force upon England, though his disposition was strong enough. Were the descendants of Cromwell's Puritans going back to submit to a Stuart régime?

That is what is meant when we hear that America fought at once the battle of freedom in the colonies and in England. That is what England's great statesman meant when he declared on the floor of Parliament that he rejoiced in the resistance of the colonists. The Earl of Chatham knew that the government of George III, in whose ears was ringing the admonition of his mother "to be King," was undermining the constitution of Great Britain and bringing the state back to the form of monarchy that had existed in the time of the Stuarts and the Tudors.

But if the leading principle was the preservation of the English constitutional government from the encroachments of King and Parliament, there is another principle, as far-reaching as the development of the state in government. Sovereignty is always finally vested in the people.

It may need a theocracy to lead a people out of barbarism; this may develop into a despotism with the power divided between kings and bishops; but a struggle is sure to come, and the people will gather about the King to make him a monarch, like Louis XIV, who really was an objective realization of the state. This, too, will be but temporary; the people will realize more and more that the sovereignty is with them and will finally assert it.

England had asserted it against the Stuarts, but George the Third forgot it, and it took the loss of the colonies by the American Revolution to remind him of it.

If the King could have accommodated himself to the existing state of affairs for America as he managed to do for England, there would have been the limited constitutional monarchy that Great Britain finally reached in 1832. But this was impossible, and so the colonies were driven to assert by war what the Commons of England partly gained by legislation sixty years later.

There was further gained in the United States a recognition that quality, not quantity, is the basis of the peerage of man, and accordingly all men were declared free and equal.

Still, there is another factor that must have eventually led to separation. The great land of America had a part to play in the history of the world that could best be performed by making it an independent nation.

England's great work was to plant colonies; America could not aid in that work. It was her place to found a great nation on this side of the Atlantic and bring out the conception of free government.

And when this was done, then America stretched out her hand over the sea to aid the oppressed of Europe, to furnish them a place of refuge, and, as soon as they could assume the duties, make them citizens not alone of our United States but of the world.

XXX

A VETO

My oath was not to take a chance on the Constitution; it was to support it. When the proponents of this measure do not intend to jeopardize their safety by acting under it, why should I jeopardize my oath by approving it?

A MESSAGE TO THE LEGISLATURE OF MASSACHUSETTS ACCOMPANYING THE GOVERNOR'S VETO

THE COMMONWEALTH OF MASSACHUSETTS
EXECUTIVE DEPARTMENT, BOSTON, May 6, 1920.

To the Honorable Senate and House of Representatives:

A bill entitled, "An Act to Regulate the Manufacture and Sale of Beer, Cider and Light Wines," being House No. 38, is herewith returned under the provisions of the Constitution without approval.

There is little satisfaction in attempting to deceive ourselves. There is grave danger in attempting to deceive the people. If this act were placed on the statute books of this Commonwealth to-day it would provide no beer for the people. No one would dare act upon it, or if any one did he would certainly be charged with crime. Similar laws in other States are to date ineffective. I am opposed to the practice of a legislative deception. It is better to proceed with candor. Wait until the Supreme Court of the United States talks.

The proper authorities have declared the Eighteenth Amendment to the United States Constitution adopted. Under it Congress has passed legislation. Should the claim that the amendment is void be sustained, our present high-license law remains in effect and this act then will be a dead letter. No one would defend it. Should the act of Congress be declared void, then let Congress

405

pass a new law. No one can say this act does not now or will not in the future conflict with United States law. It does not even pretend to be an act to enforce the Eighteenth Amendment. By the solemn adoption of an amendment to the fundamental law of the land jurisdiction over this subject has been placed in Congress. It ought to be left there until it is declared with equal solemnity by the Supreme Court that such amendment is void.

When I took office I gave an oath to support the Constitution of the United States. That Constitution and the laws of Congress are declared to be the supreme law of the land. It may be that the Eighteenth Amendment and the act under it are one or both void. So far as any court has decided I understand the amendment has been sustained. They have been before the Supreme Court for some time, where up to now they both stand as law. That which the court hesitates to decide I shall not hasten to declare. It would be extremely improper to undertake to influence that decision by the action of the lawmaking power of Massachusetts. Do not anticipate it, await it. My oath was not to take a chance on the Constitution; it was to support it. When the proponents of this measure do not intend to jeopardize their safety by acting under it, why should I jeopardize my oath by approving it?

We have had too much legislating by clamor, by tumult, by pressure. Representative government ceases when outside influence of any kind is substituted for the judgment of the representative. This does not mean that the opinion of constituents is to be ignored. It is to be weighed most carefully, for the representative must represent, but his oath provides that it must be "faithfully and impartially according to the best of his abilities and understanding, agreeably to the rules and regulations of the Constitution and laws." Opinions and instructions do not outmatch the Constitution. Against it they are void. It is an insult to any Massachusetts constituency to suggest that they were so intended. Instructions are not given unless given constitutionally. Instructions are not carried out unless carried out constitutionally. There can be no constitutional instruction to do an unconstitutional act.

The authority of the law is questioned in these days all too much. The binding obligation of obedience against personal desire is denied in many quarters. If these doctrines prevail all organized government, all liberty, all security are at an end. Force alone will prevail. Can those intrusted with the gravest authority set any example save that of the sternest obedience to law? Can Massachusetts afford to take any position which may turn out to be, which can anywhere be interpreted to be, an act of nullification? If rights are infringed the way to the court is open. The cases are pending which will undoubtedly decide the question here raised. Let the Supreme Court of the United States talk. The Massachusetts method of determining the authority of the law ought always to be by litigation and never by nullification, which is legislative direct action.

INDEX

INDEX

Adams family, 262
Adams, John, 178, 245, 266, 324, 331
Adams, Samuel, 262
Advance of civilization, 72, 78
Agassiz, 262
Agriculture, 78, 108, 113, 261
Alabama claims, 154
Albany, N. Y., 283, 373
Alexander, 65, 74
Allen, Ethan, 359, 361, 371, 372, 373, 374
Allen, Heman, 367
Allen, Ira, 360, 362, 369, 373
Allen, Lucy Caroline, 362
Allen, Samuel, 362
America a young country, 37 *ff.*
America becomes a world-power, 144, 147 *ff.*
America, ideal of, 5, 379 *ff.*
American Bar Association, 195
American Classical League, annual meeting, 1921, 57
American Expeditionary Force, 144
American Legion, convention, 1921, 85
American University, Washington, D. C., 163
Amherst College, 393
Amherst College Alumni Dinner, 1920, 3 *ff.*
Andros, 232, 258 *ff.*, 317, 318, 319
Antietam, 124
Antilles, 305
Antwerp, 286
Apple Tree Point, 360
Appomattox, 154
Arbitration, State Board of, 261
Aristotle, 74
Arlington, 361

Armada, Invincible, 287
Armistice, 94
Armistice Day, 251
Arms Conference, Washington, 96 *ff.*, 145, 351
Army and navy, 86 *ff.*, 348
Art of living, 383
Ashmun, Eli Porter, 332
Athens, 64
Attila, 168
Authority of the State, 197

Babson Institute, 185
Babylon, 81
Baker, Remember, 359, 361, 371
Banking, 78
Banks, 49 *ff.*, 198
Barton, Clara, 262
Batavia, 286
Bates, Isaac Chapman, 332
Beacon Hill, 258 *ff.*
Bell, Alexander Graham, 261
Bennington, 361, 371, 374
Bible, 74, 248, 286, 288, 290
Bogardus, 288
Boston, 260, 315, 361, 398
Boston Gazette, 320
Boston Massacre, 398
Boston Neck, 324
Boston News Letter, 320
Boston Tea Party, 398
Boylston, 261
Bradford, Governor, 14, 320
Bradley, Lemuel, 360
Bradshaw, John, 258
Bradstreet, Anne, 320
Brains, 43
Brattle Church, 318
British Empire, ideal of, 4

411

British Parliament, 200, 396, 397, 399

British Writs of Assistance at Boston, 176

Brooklyn, the, 332

Brooks, Phillips, 262

Bruce, 39

Bulfinch, 262

Bunker Hill, 49, 245, 266, 324, 331, 338

Bureaucracy, 237

Bureaucratic supervision, 390

Burgesses of Virginia, 177

Burgoyne, General, 371

Burlington, Vermont, 357 *ff*.

Burlington Free Press, The, 364

Burlington Sentinel, The, 364

Burns, Robert, 38

Business, 49, 79, 112

Business and government, 20 *ff*.

Byles, Reverend Mather, 320, 323

Cæsar, 74, 141

Calhoun, 271, 340

Cambridge, Mass., 299, 338

Cambridge Platform, 263

Capital, 190, 309

Capital and civilization, 5 *ff*., 9

Carnegie, Andrew, 37 *ff*.

Carnegie Institute, Pittsburgh, 37 *ff*.

Caste, 237

Castleton, 360

Champlain, 357

Channing, 262

Character, 329

Charities, State Board of, 261

Charles I, 252 *ff*., 258, 395

Charles II, 176

Charlestown, 323

Charter of Liberties, 288

Charter Oak, 49

Chatham, Earl of, 401

Chattanooga, 153

Child Labor Law, 261

Chittenden, Noah, 361

Chittenden, Thomas, 359, 369, 373

Choate, 262

Christ Church. *See* Old North Church

Christian church and faith, 60, 74 *ff*., 164, 168

Church of England, 318 *ff*.

Church government, 253 *ff*., 257 *ff*., 263 *ff*.

Citizenship, duties of, 207 *ff*., 279

Civil War, 19 *ff*., 124 *ff*., 152 *ff*., 156

Civilization, 3 *ff*., 14, 38, 71 *ff*., 76, 79 *ff*., 81, 96, 159, 163 *ff*., 169, 205 *ff*., 213 *ff*., 237, 244, 385 *ff*.

Clark, Colonel Isaac, 365

Clark, Reverend Samuel, 363

Classics, 57 *ff*., 61 *ff*., 217 *ff*.

Ciay, Henry, 109, 127, 271, 307

Cleveland, Grover, 304

Colchester, 360, 361, 362

Coleman, Benjamin, 318

Colleges and universities, 9 *ff*.

Commercialism, 55, 58 *ff*., 78, 107

Committee on Ways and Means, 303

Community-Chest Dinner, Springfield, Mass., 1921, 71

Company of Massachusetts Bay, 251 *ff*.

Conant, Colonel, 324

Concord Bridge, 49, 135, 323

Confidence, public, 181

Congress, 199 *ff*., 345 *ff*., 405 *ff*.

Connecticut, Colony of, 231, 255, 289, 318, 320, 336

Conservation, 347

Constitution, American, 31, 33 *ff*., 41, 77, 92, 96, 102, 105, 122 *ff*., 135, 166, 197 *ff*., 200 *ff*., 229, 233, 271, 338, 395, 403, 405 *ff*.

Constitution, the, 326, 366

Continental Congress, 177 *ff*.

Convention to form government, 104 *ff*.

Cook, Rear-Admiral, 332

Cooper Union, 123, 198

Copley, 262

Corporations, 188 *ff*.

Cotton, John, 254, 316

Court of High Commission, 259
Court, World, 351
Cromwell, 75, 135, 141, 166, 230, 241, 254, 294, 400
Crown Point, 361, 371, 374
Cuba, 264
Culture, 57, 59 *ff.*, 377, 386 *ff.*
Curie, Madame, 380
Curtis, Commissioner Edwin U., 29
Cushing, 262
Cutler, Manasseh, 232, 262
Cutler, Dr. Timothy, 318, 320, 321
Cyane, the, 366
Cynics, 169

Dane, Representative, 262
Dark Ages, 75
Darling, Charles H., 367
Davis, Jefferson, 152
Dawes, William, 324
Declaration of Independence, 60, 135, 139 *ff.*, 166, 178 *ff.*, 232, 320, 338, 397
Declaration of Rights, 259 *ff.*
Deflation, 110
Democracy, 64, 66, 75, 183, 185, 187 *ff.*, 231, 255, 289, 343 *ff*, 396
Demosthenes, 73
Dependency Act, 398
Despotism, 287, 344, 348, 395, 396, 397, 399, 401
Disarmament, 145 *ff.*
Discontent of the wealthy, 185 *ff.*
Divine right of the people, 395
Dorchester Heights, 361
Dorset, 360
Douglas, 122 *ff.*
Dudley, Joseph, 252, 319
Dummer, Lieutenant-Governor, 317
Dutch settlers, 285 *ff.*

Eagle, the, 366
Ease and civilization, 236, 239
Economics, 47, 51, 79, 110 *ff.*, 188 *ff.*
Economy, 350
Edison, Thomas A., 388
Edmonds, George F., 367

Education, 3 *ff.*, 8, 10, 43 *ff.*, 58 *ff.*, 61 *ff.*, 66, 77, 137, 163 *ff.*, 169, 209, 211 *ff.*, 240, 243 *ff.*, 256, 260, 272, 283, 363, 369, 379 *ff.*, 387
Edward the Confessor, 395
Edwards, Jonathan, 215, 262, 294, 322, 331
Elizabeth, Queen, 248
Emancipation Proclamation, 124
Emerson, 262
England, 287, 288, 315
English Revolution, 395
English-Japanese Treaty, 146
Episcopal Church, 318 *ff.*
Equality of man, 72, 402
Erasmus, 286
Evanston Sunday Afternoon Club, 229
Everett, 262
Evolution, 61
Expenditures for war veterans, 89 *ff.*

Faneuil Hall, 315
Farragut, 125
Federalist, The, Hamilton, 105, 339
Field, Marshall, 262
Fine arts, 384
Fiske, John, 7
Forbearance, 279
Forbes, Lieutenant-Colonel, 89
Foreign-born population, 239
Foreign relations, 24, 115
Fort Des Moines, 275
Fort Donelson, 153
Fort Frederick, 361
Fort Henry, 153
Four-Power Treaty, 146, 167
France, ideal of, 4 *ff.*
Franchise, 24
Franklin, Benjamin, 245, 262, 266, 321
Franklin, James, 321
Fredericksburg, Va., 173, 179
Freedom, 35, 41, 77 *ff.*, 119 *ff.*, 122, 126 *ff.*, 138, 142, 147, 229 *ff.*, 247 *ff.*, 267, 269 *ff.*, 273, 274, 289 *ff.*, 313, 327, 343 *ff.*, 390, 395, 400, 407

French and Indian War, 317, 397
French Revolution, 135

Gage, General, 325
Gain, desire for, 281, 293
Garfield, 211, 263, 303
Garrison, 262
Gaspée, burning of the, 398
General Council of Churches, 263
George I, 316
George II, 135, 323
George III, 135, 259, 396, 400, 401
Georgia, 245, 266
Germany, 93, 395
Gettysburg, 124, 153
Government, 19 *ff.*, 22 *ff.*, 40 *ff.*, 78,
   104, 136, 138, 183, 197, 199, 205,
   221, 233 *ff.*, 252, 269, 271, 274,
   292, 344, 350, 377, 388 *ff.*, 390, 398
   ff., 400, 407
Government regulation, 327
Grant, Ulysses S., 125, 151 *ff.*, 272,
   300
Great Charter, 288, 395, 398
Great Privilege, The, 286
Great War, 24 *ff.*, 78, 81, 86 *ff.*, 114,
   144, 274, 284, 291, 344, 366
Greatness, 17, 37, 69, 78, 99, 101,
   119, 131, 151, 157, 171, 174, 281
Greece, 4, 64 *ff.*
Greek and Latin, 57 *ff.*, 62 *ff.*
Greeley, Horace, 155
Green, John Richard, 77
Green Mountain, the, 357 *ff.*
Green Mountain Boys, 371, 374
Grenville, Lord, 397 *ff.*
Grey, 262
Grotius, 286
Growler, the, 366
Gutenburg, 286
Gustavus Adolphus, 166

Haarlem, 286
Halfway Covenant, 257, 316
Halifax Explosion, 265
Hamilton, Alexander, 101 *ff.*, 127,
   141, 197, 200, 271, 300, 307, 339

Hamilton Club, Chicago, 1922, 101
Hammurabi, 74
Hampden, John, 176, 372
Hancock, John, 324
Hanna, Marcus A., 304
Harden, Lieutenant Devere, 366
Harding, President, 88 *ff.*, 91, 93,
   96, 113
Harrison, Benjamin, 303
Hartford, Conn., 254 *ff.*
Hartford Convention, 340
Harvard, John, 256
Harvard University, 299, 318, 319,
   320, 337
Hawley, Major Joseph, 331
Hawthorne, 262
Hayes, 155
Hayne, 130
Health, State Board of, 261
"Hell-Fire Club of Boston," 321
Henry, Patrick, 177, 180, 352
Henry VIII, 399
History, 4, 57, 59 *ff.*, 71, 135 *ff.*,
   163, 167, 173, 220 *ff.*
Hitchcock, Loraine Allen, 362
Hitchcock, Samuel, 362
Hoar, 262
Holden, Lieutenant - Commander
   Jonas H., 366
Holmes, 262
Hooker, Thomas, 231, 254, 263, 289
Hopkins, Doctor Mark, 211
Horatius, 64
Hospitals, veterans', 90
House of Representatives, 33
Howe, General, 261, 329
Howe, Julia Ward, 262
Hubbardton, 371
Hudson, Henry, 287, 357
Humility, 381

Ideals, 62, 66, 74, 81, 383, 386
Ideals and civilization, 4 *ff.*, 45, 57
   ff., 61, 131, 165, 220, 232 *ff.*,
   283 *ff.*
Imitation, power of, 216
Impatience in modern life, 212 *ff.*
Imperfections in America, 78 *ff.*

Imperialism, 306
Inaugural address as Vice-President, 33 *ff.*
Independence, American, 179 *ff.*, 402
Individual, development of the, 213 *ff.*, 290 *ff.*, 319, 326 *ff.*, 346 *ff.*, 381 *ff.*, 390
Individualists, Americans as, 40 *ff.*
Industrial Conference, Babson Institute, 1922, 185
Industries and industrialism, 20, 47, 50 *ff.*, 78, 114, 189 *ff.*, 261, 307 *ff.*, 329, 341, 381 *ff.*, 389
Institutions, American, 18 *ff.*, 283 *ff.*, 333 *ff.*, 388 *ff.*
Insurance, State Department of, 261
Insurance, war, 90 *ff.*, 278
Integrity of the people, 99, 103, 111, 115, 181
Intellectual power, 377, 380, 390
Intelligence and civilization, 6 *ff.*
Interest, public, 349
Interstate Commerce Act, 199
Intervale, 360
Invention, 164 *ff.*, 168
Ipswich, 232
Isaiah, 8
Israel, ideal of, 4

Jackson, Andrew, 127, 130, 271, 300, 341
James II, 395
Jamestown House of Burgesses, 175
Jefferson, Thomas, 108, 178 *ff.*, 197, 200, 232, 271, 300, 340
Jeffreys, 259
John, King, 395
Johns Hopkins University, 135
Johnson, Andrew, 154
Johnson, Captain Edward, 256, 321
Judicial power, 201 *ff.*
Justice, 80, 273

Kenmore, 179
Keyes, Stephen, 363
King Philip's War, 331
King's Chapel, 315, 318, 320
Knowledge, 328, 380

Labor, 6 *ff.*, 309
Lafayette, 144
Latin and Greek, 57 *ff.*, 62 *ff.*
Laud, Archbishop, 253, 317, 396
Law, 93, 203 *ff.*, 206 *ff.*
Law and order, 29 *ff.*, 33 *ff.*, 80
Law, Roman, 65
Lawrence, Stephen, 360, 361 *ff.*
Laws, 181 *ff.*, 187 *ff.*, 193, 195 *ff.*, 222, 243, 293, 377, 406 *ff.*
Leadership, 101, 113, 297 *ff.*, 374, 379 *ff.*, 385
League of Nations, 94, 145, 167
Lee, Reverend Chauncey, 363
Lee, Richard Henry, 178 *ff.*
Lee, General Robert E., 156 *ff.*, 272
Legion, American, 85 *ff.*, 88 *ff.*
Legislation, 195 *ff.*
Legislature, 345
Leonidas at Thermopylæ, 64
Levant, the, 366
Leverett, John, 319
Lewis, Colonel Fielding, 179
Lewis, Reverend Stephen Christopher, 324
Lexington, 140, 323, 324, 325
Leyden, 289
Liberal education, 218 *ff.*, 224, 379 *ff.*
Liberty. *See* Freedom
Liberty Bell, 140
Lieber, 244
Lincoln, Abraham, 9, 21, 81, 96, 109, 117, 119 *ff.*, 143 *ff.*, 151, 153 *ff.*, 156 *ff.*, 166, 198, 263, 272 *ff.*, 279, 300
Literature, 57 *ff.*, 71
London Company, 250
Longfellow, 262
Lookout Mountain, Battle of, 153
Low Countries. *See* Netherlands
Lowell, 262
Lucretius, 74
Lyon, Mary, 262

MacDonough, Captain Thomas, 365
Madison, James, 178, 338
Magna Charta. *See* Great Charter

Mahomet, 168
Maine, the, 366
Malcom, Captain Daniel, 323
Man, idealism of, 7 *ff.*, 15, 17 *ff.*
Mann, Horace, 263
Manufacturers, 112 *ff.*
Marcus Aurelius, 74
Marlborough, 135, 315
Marne Day, 250
Marsh, George P., 367
Marshall, John, 109, 127, 178, 197, 271, 300, 338
Maryland, 323
Mason, George, 177 *ff.*
Massachusetts, Commonwealth of, 14, 27, 29 *ff.*, 78, 104, 138, 177 *ff.*, 245, 247–266, 315, 316, 317, 320, 332, 336, 396, 398, 399, 405 *ff.*
Massachusetts Body of Liberties, 263
Massachusetts, Legislature of, 405
Material development and power, 87, 377, 390
Mather family, 316
Mather, Increase, 318, 319, 320
Mayflower, 13, 29, 135, 144, 249 *ff.*, 251, 357
Mayflower Compact, 138, 175, 251, 259, 336
Mayo, Admiral Henry T., 366
McClellan, 153
McKinley, William, 299, 301 *ff.*
McKinley Bill, 303
Mechanics, 5 *ff.*
Memorial Day services at Northampton, Mass., 331
Mental tests, 223
Mexico, 85, 121, 143, 152, 287
Military force, 85 *ff.*
Mills, Elijah Hunt, 332
Milton, 73, 135
Minimum Wage Law, 261
Missionary spirit, 143
Missouri Compromise, 129
Monroe Doctrine, 24
Monroe, James, 178
Moody, 262
Moral force and law, 44 *ff.*, 55, 59,

71 *ff.*, 75 *ff.*, 114 *ff.*, 168, 209, 213 *ff.*, 222, 241, 283, 377, 390
Morris, Robert, 106
Morse, 261
Moses, 74
Moton, President, 276
Mount Holyoke College, 263
Mount Vernon, 179
Moving pictures, 384
Murdock, James, 360

Napoleon, 135, 141, 166
National bank founded, 106
National Geographic Society, 247
National Guard, 331 *ff.*
National Institute of Social Sciences, 29
Nationalism, 141, 144
Navigation, 364
Negro race, 275 *ff.*
Nelson, Admiral, 4
Netherlands, 286 *ff.*
Neutrality, theory of, 113 *ff.*
New England, 49 *ff.*, 53, 77, 127, 214, 247, 289, 290
New England Bankers, dinner of, 49 *ff.*
New England Confederation, 263
New England Courant, 320
New Hampshire, 360
New Haven, 320
New Testament, 64
New York, 286 *ff.*, 357, 360, 373, 388
Newman, Robert, 324
Newspapers, 364
Nicholson, Samuel, 326
Ninety-second Division, 275
Nobility, 83
Northampton, 319, 322, 331 *ff.*
Northwest Territory, 232
Norton, Massachusetts, 379

"Old Ironsides." *See Constitution*
Old North Church, 259, 313 *ff.*
Old South Church, 257, 315, 316, 318
Old Testament, 74

Onion River Company, 360, 369, 373
Open-door doctrine, 111
Opportunity, 281, 293, 345
Oracle of Delphi, 74
Ordinance of 1787, 232
Organization, 40 *ff.*
Otis, James, 176, 190, 258, 372

Paris Conference, 145
Parker, 262
Parker, Peter, 262
Parliamentary Reform Bill, 135
Parsons, 262
Parsons, Colonel Joseph B., 332
Parsons, Ebenezer, 331
Parsons, Joseph, 332
Paternalism, 237
Patriotism, 333, 348 *ff.*
Peace, 115, 145, 279, 305 *ff.*, 351 *ff.*
Peace treaty, 93
Peck, Captain David B., 366
Pendleton, Edmund, 178
Pennsylvania Railroad, 39
Pennsylvania, University of, 57
Pensions, 89
Pepperill, 49
Pershing, General, 276
Peru, 287
Pessimism, 217 *ff.*
Peter the Great, 165
Petition of Right, 395
Pharsalia, 286
Phelps, Edward J., 367
Philadelphia, 140, 338
Philip, 65
Philip, King, War of, 331
Philippines, 305
Phillips, 262
Pilgrims, 13 *ff.*, 29, 49 *ff.*, 81, 137 *ff.*, 230, 241, 247 *ff.*, 289, 315, 336
Pitcairn, Major, 325
Pitt, 138
Pittsburgh Landing, Battle of, 153
Pittsford, Vt., 371
Plattsburg, Battle of, 365 *ff.*
Plymouth Rock, 11, 13 *ff.*, 245, 266, 357

Police powers of law, 204
Pomeroy, General Seth, 331
Powell, Felix, 360, 366, 371
Power, material, 185 *ff.*
Power, spiritual, 287
Preparedness, 348
Primary election, 199 *ff.*
Progress, 4, 73, 76 *ff.*, 80, 137 *ff.*, 142 *ff.*, 163 *ff.*, 167 *ff.*, 173, 206, 213, 218, 220 *ff.*, 227, 235 *ff.*, 240, 253, 269 *ff.*, 284 *ff.*, 292, 313, 355, 385, 390
Prohibition, 405
Prosperity, 47, 51, 69, 78, 91 *ff.*, 185 *ff.*, 283
Protection for national defense, 107; economic, 112
Public Safety Committee of Massachusetts, 265
Public will, 238
Pulling, Captain John, Jr., 324
Puritans, 49 *ff.*, 77, 81, 137, 230, 247 *ff.*, 260, 264 *ff.*, 396, 400
Purpose of America, the, 135 *ff.*
Putnam, General Rufus, 262

Quebec Act, 399
Quincy, 256

Radio, 388
Railroad Commission, 261
Railroads, 52 *ff.*
Randolph, Peyton, 178
Reconstruction and Restoration Service, 277
Red Cross, 262
Reform, legislative, 196 *ff.*, 293, 294
Relief of veterans, 89 *ff.*
Religion, 8 *ff.*, 60, 74, 81, 164, 168 *ff.*, 215 *ff.*, 229 *ff.*, 241, 248, 250, 252, 256 *ff.*, 263 *ff.*, 283, 287, 290, 293 *ff.*, 336, 363, 369, 377, 390
"Report on Manufactures," Hamilton, 106
Representative government, 175 *ff.*,

255, 289 *ff.*, 338 *ff.*, 345 *ff.*, 396 *ff.*, 400, 406 *ff.*
Republic, 19, 66, 142, 230, 338 *ff.*, 346
Republican party, 110 *ff.*, 114
Requirements of the present hour, 63 *ff.*
Resources of America, 37 *ff.*, 49 *ff.*, 343, 349 *ff.*
Responsibility, personal, 292, 294
Revere, Paul, 324
Reverence for great men, 101
Revolution, 19, 85, 102 *ff.*, 140 *ff.*, 178 *ff.*, 181, 241, 257 *ff.*, 264, 288, 294, 300, 331, 365, 393, 395, 396 *ff.*, 400
Reynoldsville, Pa., Teachers' and School Directors' Convention, 211
Righteousness, 292, 295, 327, 333 *ff.*
Rights of the citizen, 35
Rights of the individual, 260, 273
Robinson, John, 249 *ff.*, 263
Roelandsen, 288
Rome, 4, 65 *ff.*, 73 *ff.*, 79
Roosevelt, Theodore, 17 *ff.*, 21 *ff.*, 236 *ff.*, 276
Russia, 73, 81, 165 *ff.*
Rutland County, 360

Sacrifice, 80 *ff.*, 87 *ff.*, 93, 137, 143 *ff.*, 279, 338, 352, 370, 375, 385, 391
Salamis, 65
Salisbury, Conn., 360
Sanatorium, State, 261
Sanders, Reverend Daniel C., 363, 364
San Francisco, 388
Saratoga, Battle of, 140, 371, 374
Sargent, 262
Sawyer, Captain Horace B., 366
Saxton, Frederick, 362
Saybrook, Conn., 360
Schenectady, 388
Science, 43 *ff.*, 55, 58 *ff.*, 72 *ff.*, 164 *ff.*, 168, 328, 388
Sectionalism, 91 *ff.*, 109 *ff.*
Self-confidence, 380 *ff.*
Self-expression, 319, 383

Selfishness as a motive, 165
Senate, United States, 33 *ff.*
Service, spirit of, 137 *ff.*, 144 *ff.*
Sewall, Judge, 318, 320
Shakespeare, 73, 135
Shaw, 262
Shay's Rebellion, 104
Sheffield, 360
Shepard, 264
Sherburne, Brigadier - General, of Massachusetts, 276
Sheridan, 125, 302
Sherman, 125
Shute, Governor, 317, 320
Slavery, 75, 122 *ff.*, 129, 142, 198, 232
Smith, Jonathan, 262
Socrates, 74
Sons of American Revolution prize, 393
South Carolina, 340
Sovereignty, local, 139
Soviet, Russian, 291
Spain, 286
Spanish War, 299, 305 *ff.*, 310
Spanish War Veterans, convention of, 299
Sparta, 64
Spiritual development, 377, 380, 390
Spot Resolutions, 121
Springfield, Ill., 119, 128 *ff.*
Stamp Act, 398
Standards of progress, 163 *ff.*
Stanton, Secretary, 128
Stark, 49
State House, Old, of Boston, 315
Steam-engine, 38
Steel industry, 42
Stoddard, Solomon, 319
Story, 262
Stoughton, William, 256 *ff.*
Strong, Caleb, 332
Stuarts, the, 262, 317, 318, 400
Stuyvesant, 288
Suicide among civilizations, 73
Sumner, 262
Sumter, Fort, 124

Supreme Court, 201 *ff.*, 406
Supreme Judicial Court of Massachusetts, 80

Tacitus, 395
Tariff, 107, 112, 304 *ff.*, 308
Taxes, 135 *ff.*, 177, 199, 255, 351, 389, 399 *ff.*
Teachers, 211, 225, 243
Themistocles, 65
Theocracy, 316, 401
Theory of American government, 19 *ff.*
Ticonderoga, 49, 361, 371, 374
Tilden, 155
Toleration, 243, 248, 289, 313, 316 *ff.*, 336 *ff.*
Townsend's Revenue Act, 398
Traditions, 175, 332
Transportation, 50 *ff.*, 78
Treasury, national, 106
Treaty of peace, 93
Treaty of Utrecht, 315
Tuskegee, Ala., government hospital for colored veterans, 269
Tuskegee, Ala., Institute, 276

Union, 109, 127, 271 *ff.*, 341
Union School, 364
Universal conscience, 148
Universities, 9 *ff.*
Uprightness of character, 80

Vane, Sir Harry, 254
Van Ness, Cornelius P., 367
Van Twiller, 288
Verdun, defenders of, 291
Vermont, 358 *ff.*, 369 *ff.*
Vermont, the, 365
Vermont, University of, 362, 364
Versailles, Treaty of, 93
Veterans' Bureau, 89 *ff.*, 94, 277
Vice-presidency, 31, 33 *ff.*
Vicksburg, 153
Victories of peace and war, 83, 87, 93, 97, 145
"Vindication of the Government of New England Churches, A," 321

Virginia, Old Dominion, 175 *ff.*, 357
Virginia Assembly, 138
Virginia Bill of Rights, 177 *ff.*
Virginia Company, 289
Virginians, great, 173 *ff.*
Virginius affair, 154
Vision of Americans, 174
Vocational education, 58, 62, 218 *ff.*, 277

Wallace, 39
Walpole, Sir Robert, 135, 316
War, 347
War claims, expenditures, and general statistics, 89 *ff.*, 94 *ff.*
War of 1812, 85, 340, 365
War of '61, 198
War Risk Insurance Bureau, 90
Warner, Seth, 359, 361
Warren, Dr. Joseph, 324
Washington, Betty, 179
Washington Conference on Limitation of Armaments, 145, 351
Washington, D. C., 247
Washington, George, 9, 96, 102, 106, 109, 127, 136, 139 *ff.*, 147 *ff.*, 151, 166, 178 *ff.*, 197, 200, 241, 245, 271, 294, 300, 338 *ff.*, 371 *ff.*
Watertown, 255, 259
Webster, Daniel, 125, 127, 130, 245, 262, 266, 271, 300, 340
Wentworth, Governor, 360
West Point, 152
Westminster, Vt., 369
Wheaton College, 379
Whistler, 262
Whitefield, 215, 294
Whitney, 261
Whittier, 262
Willard, Reverend Samuel, 319
William the Conqueror, 75
William III, the Silent, 249, 294, 317
William and Mary, 230, 258, 317, 396, 400
William and Mary College, 337
Williams, Roger, 49
Williams College, 262

Wilson, 262
Windsor, Vt., 369
Winooski, falls of, 367
Winslow, 250
Winthrop, Governor, 231, 252, 254, 289, 320
Wise, Reverend John, 232, 258, 321
Witchcraft, 319
Wolfe, 259
Women, 17 *ff.*, 383 *ff.*

"Wonder-Working Providence," 321
Woodbury, Urban A., 367
World Court, 351
World War. *See* Great War

Y. M. C. A., 283
Yale College, 320, 322
Yale, Elihu, 320
Yates, Governor, 153
Yorktown, 140, 178, 374

Printed in the United States
31635LVS00001B/4-30